ECONOMIC THOUGHT OF THE TWENTIETH CENTURY AND OTHER ESSAYS

Dr. P.R. Dubhashi is a rare combination of an administrator and academician. He had his education in Pune and London School of Economics and holds a Ph.D. and D. Litt. He joined the Indian Administrative Service in the year 1953 on the basis of all India competitive examination. As a member of the IAS, he held senior positions in the State and Central Governments. Besides he headed four national institutions of training and research. He is now the Vice-Chancellor of Goa University. He has authored a number of reports on administration and has several books to his credit.

ECONOMIC THOUGHT OF THE TWENTIETH CENTURY AND OTHER ESSAYS

P.R. DUBHASHI
I.A.S.
Vice-Chancellor
Goa University, Goa

CONCEPT PUBLISHING COMPANY, NEW DELHI 110059

ISBN 81-7022-545-0

First Published 1995

Published and Printed by
Ashok Kumar Mittal
Concept Publishing Company
A/15-16, Commercial Block, Mohan Garden
NEW DELHI 110059 (India)

PREFACE

The papers contained in this book consist of my writings published from time to time during the past few years on the major economic themes and concerns of the twentieth century — namely development, poverty, environment, quality of life, and the choice between the two contending economic ideologies namely, Capitalism and Socialism. The first half of the twentieth century was full of hope regarding what Socialism had to offer particularly to the deprived sections of humanity. The century is ending with the collapse of the socialist system with little hope for its revival.

I joined the Indian Administrative Service in 1953, after completing my post-graduate studies in Economics for Master of Arts in Poona University. In 1962-63, I spent a year for post-graduate studies at the London School of Economics. From the University days till today, economic thinking has been my constant preoccupation—thinking mainly in relation to the economic ideology and the working of the economic system.

Economic ideology is essentially connected with the general choice of the economic system. Every economic system has to work for the fulfilment of human needs. Different economic systems provide alternative ways of fulfilling them. They all have to ask and answer the same questions viz., what to produce, how much to produce, for whom to produce, how to produce, when to produce and where to produce. While these are the universal questions relating to the life of man, it is the solutions to the questions which differ as between the different economic systems. The economic ideologies are essentially connected with the rationale and design of different economic systems.

When I studied the subject of Economics at the middle of the twentieth century, the question of choice of economic ideology, was a subject of paramount importance, particularly in the newly independent developing countries of the world. On one side was the system of industrial capitalism which existed in the western democracies. On the other side, were the socialist economies led by the Union of Soviet Socialist Republic, China and the satellite countries of these two giant powers, namely, the Eastern European countries and North Korea. Indian intellectuals generally felt that while Capitalism was the ideology of the past, Socialism was the ideology of the future. If the Western Countries made progress, it was not because of the economic ideology of Capitalism, but because of Colonialism and the economic exploitation of the colonies by their imperial masters. Capitalism left much to be desired. It suffered from several blemishes, amongst which were inequality, monopoly, unemployment, and neglect of social costs of various sorts. It was universally believed that unbridled Capitalism was not a good economic system anyway, and certainly not for the developing world, unless it was drastically modified.

I was born in the year 1930 when Capitalism had suffered its worst defeat viz., the Great Depression. Some believed that it was the Second World War which proved a blessing in disguise and enabled the Western Countries to get out of the trouble in which their economies had sunk.

When I studied the subject of Economics for my Master of Arts during 1950-52, the Keynesian Economics held an intellectual sway. Keynes had come to the rescue of the capitalist economy under siege and had shown how it could be rescued. While we no doubt studied Micro Economics produced by classical and neoclassical economists, what fascinated us was the "New Economics" of Keynes.

However, later while studying at the London School of Economics in 1962, what attracted me most was Development Economics because that was relevant to India and the other underdeveloped countries. There was no definitive work on Development Economics like Keynes' "General Theory of Employment, Interest and Money" which provided a comprehensive framework of thinking for overcoming the main shortcomings of capitalistic system. Keynesian Economics was not meant for the developing countries. For us from the developing countries, we needed the New Economics of Development.

Socialism as an ideology was always very attractive. The achievements of Soviet Russia were very inspiring. In a few years time, if the USSR could progress from a vast backward semi-feudal society into a modern technologically advanced country, it was felt that it was because of Socialism. Jawaharlal Nehru was greatly impressed by his visit to Soviet Russia in 1927. For us, from the developing countries, an economic ideology was of no use unless it promoted equity. In other words, the fruits of development should reach all-including the masses. We needed an egalitarian, progressive economic ideology and Socialism appeared to be that—a better alternative to Capitalism. Little did we know what was in store for Socialism. Indeed even a few years back, nobody could have imagined that socialism was soon to collapse, and the socialist countries like the USSR and Yugoslavia were to disintegrate.

Thus as we reach the end of the century, we have entered into the era of ideological ambiguity. For the time being, the developing countries seem to have given a go-by to Socialism. In India, Smt. Indira Gandhi as it now turned out quite unwisely, introduced the adjective of 'Socialist' to our Democratic Republic in the Preamble of the Constitution. Even now some people in India pay lip sympathy to Socialism, knowing that even the Nehruvian "socialistic pattern" has now vanished, as the new economic policy of liberalisation is sweeping aside its last vestiges under the continuous proddings of the World Bank and the International Monetary Funds. It is this ideological uncertainty which provides the context for many of the papers compiled in the book.

My preoccupation with economic thinking was never academic. I was an active administrator and always related thinking to management and performance. It was connected with India's economic development, not in isolation, but in relation to other developing countries, and indeed in relation to the World Economic Order. It was connected not just to macro-economic policies but with formulation and implementation of programmes, projects and schemes included in India's Five Year Plans. Though the earlier enthusiasm for planning has diminished with the sweep of marketisation, India has not yet abandoned planning nor has it abolished the Planning Commission.

I am bringing out my 35 papers in the hope that despite tremendous changes in the economic outlook that have taken place in the last few years, they will be of great interest to all those who are concerned with the basic thinking regarding the economic system and economic ideology despite the fear of ideological euthanasia in the atmosphere of today. I have not tried to bring the papers up to date because the original formulations are a part of the flow of a changing economic thinking and is not rendered obsolete by change of facts.

The first part of this book contains five papers, starting with my Dr. Muranjan Memorial Lecture on Economic Thought in the Twenthieth Century, delivered at the Syndenham College of Commerce, Bombay in March 1990. It makes a broad survey in bold strokes of economic thought from the beginning of the twentieth century till today. It sets the stage for all other papers in this book.

The second chapter deals with the most cataclysmic event of our time viz., the collapse of the socialist system and the disintegration of the USSR. It traces the event to the essentially non-functional model of Central Planning on which the socialist system was based.

The third chapter deals with the contribution of the Keynesian economics. On the occasion of the Keynesian centenary while recognising the significance of Keynes, I have made bold to express my assessment that his influence will be of little significance in the long run during which Keynes thought "we are all dead"! Keynes did not deal with development of underdeveloped countries, sustainable development or quality of life because they were not his concerns, though in the long run, they are all significant.

The fourth chapter "Relevance and Irrelevance of Economics" mainly suggests that traditional economics which we have learnt through courses in the Universities is not based on proper view of man and his motivation.

The fifth chapter in the part, a book review article on the economic thought of Indian national leaders in the pre-Independence period, brings out how all of them felt that the capitalist economic system only served to help the imperial powers to exploit the economies of their colonies in Asia and Africa for sustaining their own higher standard of living.

The second part of papers is under the title "Development Planning". They deal with India's approach to development, and my thinking about the more recent five year plans namely the Sixth, Seventh and the Eight Five Year Plans. My paper on Plan Formulation, Implementation and Evaluation attempts a comprehensive survey of the planning system in our country. In the succeeding papers, I have drawn attention to some of the critical areas of planning viz., universal literacy, higher education, social discipline, improvement in productivity and the importance of the maintenance of assets. All these points are of continuing significance. I have also drawn attention to the need for harmonising all the goals of planning, curbing populism, and mobilisation of social energy. In another paper, I have commended the concept of the Rolling Plan. I have also included my review article on Development Planning by Indian economist Chakravorty. Then there are papers on manpower planning and district planning which are all subsidiary but important aspects of planning in our developing country.

The third part deals with Management of Development. This sector begins with my review of the World Bank Report on the subject.

The crucial issues of management are, on one side, connected with the efficacy of the market mechansim, and, on the other hand, sound macro-economic policy framework. The paper deals with how within the macro framework, public sector enterprises could be better managed, and so also the public services provided by the State. The theme is continued in the next paper on "Management of Economic Development—New Horizons", where I have dealt with the importance of productivity of plan programmes as against mere investments and the role of the economist, the politician, the administrator and the technocrat in better management. One of the reasons why Indian economic system has not been able to prove equal to the challenges of the time is our high cost economy, despite its advantages of abundant human resources. Continuous increase in "administered prices" has been one factor responsible for the high cost economy. I have critically analysed these aspects in two papers.

In another paper I have dealt with the role of the Governmental sector in the context of economic development. My paper on liberalisation, privatisation and marketisation was written much before the new policy was introduced in 1991. But it reflects the process which was already started by Indira Gandhi and Rajiv Gandhi during the preceding decade.

The fourth part of papers is on the basic problem of Indian economy namely Poverty. The paper Five Perspectives on Poverty reviews the perspectives of poverty as brought out in some of the major contributions on the subject. Poverty is to be seen not in relation to mere per capita GNP, but in terms of quality of life. The two do not always go together. Developing countries do not have to follow the footsteps of developed countries in a mindless pursuit of material goods and services. They should rather get inspiration from the thinking of Mahatma Gandhi who laid emphasis on the fulfilment of basic needs of the masses and not the fulfilment of greed of the affluent. The entire world today should reflect on the basic philosophical purpose of economic activity.

The fifth part of papers is related to Development and Environment. Poverty on one side and degradation of nature on the other, are the two most important dimensions of development today. Development which destroys the life supporting system of nature can be counter productive. Nor can we neglect the social ecology, and the kind of urban settlements that are emerging in the wake of development. Unless these are immediately attended to, the very purpose of development will be frustrated. We need a system which prevents atomisation of the individual and the loss of traditional skills but indeed strengthens the human society.

Finally, the sixth part deals with the basic thinking that has been developed in relation to the world system. While the Old World Order of colonised and colonial countries has come to an end, the New World Order has yet to emerge. The dream of the New International Economic Order based on equity has received a severe set back in recent years. But this is not the time to give up such an idea. It is rather necessary to steadily pursue the concept of a World Order where no nation is so poor as to be deprived of the minimum wherewithals of living. The world has to go back to the philosophy of Mahatma Gandhi.

P.R. DUBHASHI

CONTENTS

PART I

ECONOMIC THOUGHT

1

ECONOMIC THOUGHT OF THE TWENTIETH CENTURY*

Twentieth Century Transformation

The twentieth century has been a witness to profound changes in the political and economic environment all over the world. The world as it stands today, as we are nearing the end of the 20th century, has changed beyond recognition compared with the world as it existed at the beginning of the century and with this change in environment has come about tremendous change in the outlook and thinking on political and economic affairs. Thinking does not take place in a vacuum; it is a dialogue with environment and develops in relation to time and place.

Hey-day of Capitalism and Imperialism

The beginning of the century was the heyday of Industrial Capitalism which stood triumphant in the western world and so did Imperialism which was the international extension of Capitalism. The British empire was most far-flung extending over a number of countries of Asia and Africa. It was said that sun never set on the British Empire. Close on the heels of England were France with her vast acquisitions in Indo-China, and Holland in Indonesia.

*Dr. S.K. Muranjan memorial lecture, delivered at Sydenham Collage of Commerce and Economics, Bombay in 1990.

Industrial Revolution

British leadership of Capitalism and Imperialism was natural. It was the first country to undergo Industrial Revolution during the period 1760 to 1820. The Industrial Revolution was preceded by transport and commercial revolutions. England became the workshop of the world. In the wake of the Industrial Revolution, factory replaced the household as a unit of production. A series of technological innovations formed the basis of mechanisation of the factory system. Division of labour, and specialisation enabled vast increases in productivity. At the same time, transport revolution led to the widening of the market which replaced old self-sufficient village economy mostly based on barter. Capitalism brought enormous prosperity. Karl Marx who predicted the downfall of Capitalism through inner contradictions, was himself a great admirer of the achievements of Capitalism which, in his words, were more impressive than the Egyptian pyramids, the Roman aqueducts and the Gothic cathedrals.

Classical Economics

The science of Economics, known more appropriately in the earlier days as the Political Economy was born to provide the theoretical under-pinning to the capitalist system.

Adam Smith, David Ricardo and John Stuart Mill laid the foundation of the Classical Economics. The two pillars of the Classical Economics were the concepts of the economic man and the market. The concept of economic man postulated that all economic activities are motivated by the pursuit of self-interest. However, single-minded pursuit of self-interest also redounded to social good, thanks to what Adam Smith called "the invisible hand of providence" working in the market. In a famous sentence, Adam Smith observed that the butcher, brewer and the baker produced and supplied meat, wine, and bread in order to carry out their own livelihood, but while doing so they subserved public good much better than if they were set to do so directly.

The policy implication of this description of the market mechanism was that of *laissez faire*. The role of the State should be limited to the discharge of the "sovereign functions" of maintenance of internal order and defence against external aggression. The State should not enter into the economic activity and the market should be left free to operate in an unhindered manner. The concept of free market extended to international trade as well. Free trade based on the principle of comparative costs across the boundaries of the nations would enable all of them secure maximum gains from the international trade.

Neo-classical Economics

On this foundation of the Classical Economics, the edifice of Neoclassical Economics was erected in the early years of the twentieth century by leading economists like Marshall and Edge worth in England, Knut Wiksell in Sweden, and J.B. Say and Leon Walras in France. The achievement of neo-classical economists was to make the economics of market much more refined and sophisticated. The concept of marginalism was at the core of this economic analysis. The neo-classical economists made a series of formulations regarding the optimisation at the margin by the consumers, the producers and the entrepreneurs and the owners of the factors of production. In a perfectly competitive market, consisting of innumerable buyers and innumerable sellers, an individual firm faced an infinitely elastic demand and the price equalled marginal revenue which in turn equalled the marginal cost and the average cost. Prices of factors of production were also fixed in the same manner as the prices of commodities; wage equalled marginal productivity of labour and interest, marginal efficiency of capital.

Voice of Dissidence

While classical and neo-classical economists constituted the mainstream of Economics, there was a voice of dissidence. Ruskin called Economics a dismal science which was so much dominated by hedonistic values that there was no scope in it for the Christian virtue of compassion. Capitalism gave rise to two distinct classes—capitalist class owned the means of production and the working class had nothing but labour to sell. In an unequal bargaining position in the so-called free market, the workers who were exploited. Karl Marx, the great deviationist thinker of the 19th century, who predicted the downfall of Capitalism, formulated labour theory of value to explain the exploitation of working classes. The value of goods produced by the workers vastly exceeded the value of goods needed to sustain the labour and the surplus was appropriated by the capitalist. But in appropriating the surplus, the capitalist only dug his own grave because the unequal distribution of income led to under-consumption and collapse of Capitalism.

While Marx and other socialist thinkers of different varieties brought out the blemishes of Capitalism, the working classes organised themselves into trade unions to fight against exploitation in the form of long hours of work, low wages and disagreeable working environment. In the face of the trade union movement, the State was compelled to intervene through a series of labour legislation.

Imperialism and Economic Drain

Imperialism was the logical extension of Capitalism. Imperial countries tried to pretend that Imperialism was the White Man's Burden and his mission was to civilise the uncivilised people. It was obvious that the missionary had only followed the flag and the trade. The writings of Marx, Lenin and Hobson had clearly shown that Imperialism was the logical extension of Capitalism in search of new sources of raw material and market for finished products which the colonial countries provided. They also provided the remunerative channels of investment of surplus capital in setting up a network of railways which facilitated the transport of raw materials from the interior to the ports and of imported finished products from the ports to the hinterland.

The economic thinking of the Indian economists like R.C. Dutt, Dadabhai Naoroji and Mahadeo Govind Ranade was to lay bare the process of colonial exploitation by imperial countries. They formulated the doctrine of "economic drain" through high salaries of civil servants, low prices for raw materials and high return on investment and high land revenue.

Aftermath of First World War – Rise of Communism

Germany which was a late-comer to the banquet of Capitalism was not prepared to accept the hegemony of France and England and this inevitably led to the First World War. The aftermath of the First World War saw the dethronement of Czar in 1917, as the Russian

Revolution triumphed under the leadership of Lenin and the establishment of the world's first socialist economy and the system of Central Planning. The establishment of the communist economy and society was heralded as rise of a new civilisation by British Fabian thinkers like Sydney and Beatrice Webb and George Bernard Shaw. The new civilisation was an escape from the evils of Capitalism and its hedonistic value system. On the other hand, economists Ludurg Von Misses and Frederik Von Hayek predicted that the communist system of economy will not work. It will only be a "road to serfdom". The market economy solves innumerable equations of consumption and production of innumerable commodities through the decisions of innumerable producers and consumers. These equations cannot simply be solved by the central planners of the command economy.

Capitalism under Strain – Inequality, Monopoly

At the same time, the years following the First World War saw the capitalist system increasingly coming under strain. With the extension of political franchise to the working classes, the State could no longer allow gross inequalities without taking some positive measures for transfer of income from the haves to have-nots through a system of progressive taxation; nor could the myth of perfectly competitive economy be sustained too long. The presence of monopoly was obvious and could no longer be ignored. Monopoly was the logical outcome of increasing returns to scale from which the economy benefited. At the same time monopoly exploitation could no longer be allowed to hold its sway and the State had to come in with legislation for the regulation of monopoly. The economist also could no longer go on with the formula of optimisation when what the monopolist was interested in was maximisation of profits through limiting production and withholding supply, if necessary, and, therefore, monopoly regulation of prices. A theoretical departure from the perfectly competitive economy was inevitable and that was provided by seminal contributions during the inter-war years viz. Joan Robinson's "Economics of Imperfect Competition" and Chamberlain's "Theory of Monopolistic Competition". As more and more public utilities came to be managed by the State, public utility related Economics also came to be developed.

Modern Corporation

Economists even in later years continued with the theme of the changing profile of Capitalism away from the mythical model of perfectly competitive economy. J.K. Galbraith's contribution "New Industrial State" analyses the modern corporation with its techno structure. The new Corporation far from responding to the forces of an existing market had the strength and the resourcefulness to create its own market. The whole economic sequence was turned topsy-turvy through modern techniques of mass advertisement with the use of monopoly power. Some 200 modern corporations dominated the entire economy. They decided what the consumer would consume, at what prices and in what quantities.

The modern Corporation also saw growing dichotomy between ownership of capital and management. The old concept of capitalist-entrepreneur-manager was no longer valid. While capital was owned by innumerable members of the public, management was in the hands of the professional manager. Professional scientific management came into its own and the science of management became the science of the 20th century. Managerial Economics emerged as a field in its own right. The goal of the manager was seen to be not profit maximisation per se, but the survival of the enterprise and its long-term development.

Depression and Unemployment

But to go back to the inter-war period, apart from inequality and monopoly, another evil afflicting Capitalism was the phenomenon of business or trade cycles and unemployment during periods of depression. The great Wall Street Crash of 1929 sounded, as it were, the death-knell of free Capitalism. The market forces could no longer be relied upon to deal with the phenomenon of unemployment. As depression deepened in the U.S.A. and Europe, President Roosevelt had to come out with his New Deal with a series of measures to provide employment opportunities. The facade of Capitalism crumbled and the new interventionist approach saw the end of *laissez faire*. As in the past, the economists came forward to provide the theoretical under-pinning to the new economic realities and a strategy that was needed to deal with the problems which the realities posed.

Keynsian Economics – End of Laissez Faire

In 1936, John Maynard Keynes came out with his "General Theory of Employment, Interest and Money" which totally revolutionised the economic outlook. Keyesian Economics came to be known as New economics or the Keynesain revolution. Keynes pointed out that the economic equilibrium may be established at a level lower than of full employment. He questioned the conventional wisdom conveyed in the famous saying of J.B. Say, that "Supply creates its own demand". If due to low propensity to consume and low inducement to invest, there is deficiency in demand, then the market forces cannot be relied upon to restore the equilibrium at full employment level. An attempt to increase profitability by lowering wages would come up against the constraint of insufficient demand and the economy would not be able to recover. Keynesian Economics continued to dominate economic thinking for the next several decades and the Keynesian prescriptions regarding the role of the State to intervene through compensatory fiscal policies and programmes of public investment came to be accepted all over the world.

Management of Economy during Second World War

While the state intervention was tackling the problems of unemployment, the emergence of the Second World War in 1939 provided the occasion for the activisation of the economy. Keynsian Economics which provided the theory for the compensation of deficiency in demand was now equally relied upon for curbing excessive aggregate demand to release resources for war production. It proved to be a double-edged weapon. The management of economy during the Second World War provided the western democracies an occasion to experiment with different systems of planning, controlling, regulating and management of the economy and in this the democratic regimes proved even more efficient than the fascist regimes. They could mobilise their resources more effectively. Galbraith has pointed out that while the women labour force remained inactive in Germany, it was fully harnessed in Great Britain. Two or three shifts were uncommon in Germany, while they were frequently resorted to in Great Britain.

Aftermath of Second World War : End of Imperialism

The aftermath of the Second World War was even more extensive than that of the First World War. End of the war was the end of Imperialism. The imperial countries realised that they would no longer be able to keep their hold on countries of Asia and Africa without risking great costs. Freedom of India in 1947 provided the beginning of the process of decolonisation of the countries of Asia and Africa which went apace. Till to-day with the freedom of Namibia the whole process of de-colonisation seems to have been completed.

The second important change was the spread of Socialism to East European countries. These countries became independent States after the First World War. But now after the Second World War, under the influence of the conquering armies of Soviet Russia, the old democratic parties lost power to the communist parties. Mini-Stalins came to rule the East European countries such as Poland, Czechoslovakia, Bulgaria, Romania and Hungary.

Advent of the Welfare State

In Britain itself which was till recently the home of Conservative rule, the Labour Party came into power immediately after the Second World War. Winston Churchill, the great war leader who energised the country to fight against Nazi Germany was rejected by the electorate in favour of Clement Attlee who led his Labour Party which emerged victorious in the first general election after the Second World War. The great achievement of the Labour Party was to usher in the Welfare State. It implemented a comprehensive social security system recommended by Sir William Beveridge in his famous report. It provided protection to the working classes against hazards of capitalism, namely, unemployment and impairment of the working capacity due to death or accident. Beveridge mentioned poverty, unemployment, ignorance, disease and squalor as five great shortcomings of the capitalist system and sought to provide the programme to remedy the same.

World Economic Institutions

The period after Second World War saw the emergence of

international economic institutions. Under the leadership of Keynes at the Bretton Woods Conference, a decision was taken to establish International Monetary Fund (IMF) to regulate currency system frequently threatened by the balance of payments crises and the International Bank for Reconstruction and Development to provide resources needed in the first instance to the war-shattered European countries and later on, to the emerging countries of Asia and Africa. The working of these institutions was to provide a great deal of scope to economic thinking and action on an international scale in the second half of the 20th century.

Development Economics

As the countries of Asia and Africa emerged to freedom they started giving thought as to how to use their freedom to remove the barriers of economic backwardness, to make up for deficiencies of the past and to launch upon programmes of development. This gave rise to new literature in economics which came to be identified as Development Economics. To start with, development was identified with industrialisation. Colin Clerk in his "Conditions of Growth" talked of development in terms of intersectoral transformation. While the economy of the underdeveloped countries mainly consisted of the primary sector, with development, secondary and tertiary sectors underwent rapid growth. While an underdeveloped country was characterised by a dual economy, a developed country saw a growing homogenisation of the economy. First formulations of the economic development theory concentrated on the deficiency of capital and investment and the panacea was to step up capital formation which was considered to be the key for economic development. The famous Harrod-Domer analysis laid down the equation that the rate of growth equalled Investment divided by the Capital Output Ratio. Since capital output ratio at any given point of time was considered to be fixed, development depended upon the size of investment. In the earlier years, great deal of attention was paid to the provision of investible resources to the developing countries on a multi-lateral and bilateral basis. However, it was soon realised that this simplistic formulation of development based on investment was not adequate. Mobilisation of human resources was equally important. Ragnar Nurkse's formulation regarding mobilisation of unemployed manpower as a resource of the developing countries caught the imagination of the developing nations. Several major irrigation projects were carried out in China through mobilisation of manpower. A number of development theories came to be formulated : amongst them, Rostow's Theory of Stages of Growth. He postulated these five stages as follows:

(1) under-development,
(2) transition,
(3) economic take-off,
(4) self-sustained growth, and
(5) high mass consumption economy.

Rostow's formulation was held as an alternative to Marxian stages of economic history. Rostow's theory, however, did not explain what brought about the economic take-off and the search for strategic factors in development continued.

There were comparisons between two alternative strategies to growth – one was export-led growth as exemplified by South Korea and Taiwan, and another import – substitution growth as exemplified by India. The former model was quite often preferred by economists in the West. India's slower economic growth was attributed to its fetish of self-reliant growth and attempting import-substitution all the time. Under the advice of World Bank, India slowly introduced liberalisation, opening the doors for the import of capital and technology. While effective liberalisation and stimulating economic growth were apparent, new problem of debt-trap has proved worrisome.

Another development debate related to the big thrust advocated by Hirschman as against more balanced growth as typified by India. Experience has shown that if the big thrust only meant that some big industrial projects with no links to the economic system were carried out, it will only prove infructuous. In particular, neglect of agriculture can be disastrous.

What brought the development theories in disrepute was the realisation that mere increase in gross national product does not constitute development. The meaning of development has to be sought in terms of Better Living for mass of people. The concept of GNP should be replaced by the Quality of Life Index (QLI) shown by factors such as child mortality, level of literacy, expectation of life and availability of health and educational facilities. Mere increase in luxury sector for the affluent section of the given community would not constitute development. Moreover, development which threatens the ecological balance can be self-defeating. These new realisations have led to the emergence of Gandhian economics and its concept of development. One concept of Gandhian Economics which has received support from Schumacher's "Small is Beautiful" is the concept of appropriate techology—technology which uses available labour resources of the developing countries. Developing countries do not have to follow in the footsteps of the developed countries. They can evolve their own strategies more consistent with the realisation of human welfare.

An issue relevant to development was whether the developing countries should go in for planned economy or rely on the market mechanism. Most developing countries took the view that the development could not be left to the vicissitudes of the market forces and deliberate State intervention would be required, to stimulate investment to provide infrastructure and to modify the institutions through programmes like land reforms. State became the agent of change. But in its wake, the State intervention brought in a series of measures of control over the economy which later on tended to throttle development. The opinion, therefore, has veered to a greater use of the market mechanism and the dismantling of a plethora of controls, which may be fiscal rather than physical.

Privatisation

This debate between planning and market mechanism was not confined to the developing countries only. In developed countries, above all in Britain Thatcherism saw a decisive attempt to depart from the structures, institutions and methods which came into existence as a result of the policies and programmes of the first Labour Government. British economic development was stagnant as compared with more dynamic countries of Europe such as Germany, and France and this was attributed to the British disease of Trade Unionism and the lethargic State Sector. Thatcher fought Cargill, the Trade Union leader and defeated him and launched upon a vigorous programme of privatization including Coal, Railways, Telephones, Airlines and Municipal housing. Here programme of radical privatization brought her great popularity and enabled her to be the longest ruling Prime Minister of Britain in the twentieth century.

Japan and United Europe

Another significant phenomenon of the second half of the 20th century was the spectacular rise of Japan as the leading industrial nation threatening the hegemony even of the U.S.A. In the American market to-day, not Ford, nor Chrysler, but Honda, Toyota and Nissan have become the mark of quality goods. American experts are taking lessons from the Japanese system of management.

Vision of United Europe is another major development which has marked the end of a multi-polar world. United Europe will have a larger population and market than the U.S.A.

Collapse of Socialism

Perhaps the most outstanding development in recent years is the collapse of socialism in the USSR (since disintegrated) and the East European countries. The developments have been so cataclysmic that even a far-seeing leader like Gorbachev (since deposed) was overtaken by events. Communist monopoly of power has ended in Poland, Czechoslovakia, Germany and now in the USSR itself. Recently, Russia has decided to privatise means of production. This is necessary to enable the price mechanism to function. Forty years of socialism have failed to provide the citizen with a standard of living which could be compared to that in the West. The predictions of Misses and Hayek that Communism cannot be mended but be ended seem to have come true.

However, as Galbraith has recently pointed out, Western thinkers need not be too impatient about the fall of Communism. If Communism did not succeed it was because it failed to adapt to changing circumstances, but that holds true of unbridled Capitalism also. Capitalism cannot function with total reliance on the market and complete elimination of the role of the State. Like Communism, Capitalism also should adapt to changing circumstances. Recently, Prof. Amartya Sen in his address on the occasion of the award of Senator Giovannie prize has warned against the limitations of the market mechanism in the context of the current euphoria for it. Market mechanism cannot provide health care and education. Some of the countries have failed badly in making provision for public health and epidemiological environment. It would be unwise to talk of market-decision without recognising that some aspects of economy are not handled well by the market. In particular, health and education require a collective organisation. One can hope that economists such as Milton Friedman and Bauer and others in World Bank would pay some heed to this kind of thinking.

Concern for Environment

As we approach the end of the 20th century, there is a growing concern with environment and the threat which development poses to it. It was Prof. Pigou whose Economics of Welfare sowed the seeds of this thinking. He brought attention to the divergence between the private product and the social product, and the private costs and the social costs. Pollution and congestion are economic costs which are not paid for by the private enterprise. Prof. J.K. Galbraith in his "Affluent Society" drew attention to the contrast between private affluence and public squalor. Pure air and water have become scarce in the wake of development. Acid rains have threatened agriculture. This accounts for the rise of the Green Movement in Europe and economists will have to pay growing attention to the ecological impact of development.

End of Ideology?

Where do we stand as we approach the end of the 20th century? Neither Capitalism nor Communism can any longer provide the panacea either to the developed or to the developing countries of the world. The world is seeing an end to the confrontation between the capitalist and the communist countries. At the same time, we are also witness to the phenomenon of convergence between the two systems. Thus no economic ideology can command any longer our unquestioned commitment. But this does not mean the end of the ideology itself. It rather means that mechanical adherence to ideology can no longer provide solutions to the practical problems of humanity and a more eclectic and inter-disciplinary approach would be needed to usher in a new International Economic Order which is to-day merely a dream. Willy Brandt Report on North-South Co-operation has proved to be a cry in the wilderness since developing countries were unwilling to pay adequate attention to it. South-South Co-operation has yet to make a good start. The New Economics is, therefore, faced with new challenges to get the best out of the two worlds to promote private enterprise, freedom and democracy and at the same time promote commitment to social justice, equality and preservation of the environment.

2

DEMISE OF THE SOVIET UNION AND THE SOCIALIST SYSTEM

Events have been taking place, in what once was Soviet Union, which is no more, at such breath-taking and mind-boggling speed that the full implications of these changes and their consequences have not yet been fully grasped, much less clearly analysed, even by thinking observers of the scene. What we have witnessed is not just the fall of an outstanding statesman of world stature, nor even the disintegration and disappearance of a superstate, or collapse of an entire economic system or the final and decisive defeat of an ideology but indeed a basic transformation in the very context and structure of our thinking and our outlook on the course of history.

Fall of Gorbachev

That Gorbachev with all his initiative and leadership and his vision of *glasnost* and *perestroika* was faltering, because he had no clue for translating his vision into concrete reality had been evident for quite sometime past. *Glasnost* was running ahead of *perestroika* and mere invocation of *perestroika* could not make up for a miserable failure to ensure availability of supplies of essential consumer goods in the shops which became scenes of empty shelves and long queues. As Yeltsin, who usurped his place without undue ceremony, observed, Gorbachev tried a half way house between Communism and Capitalism, the public sector and the private sector, free market and planning, centralization and decentralization and utterly failed in his attempt to harmonise the incompatibles. A country like India has worked precisely with such a system of "mixed economy" and has been, with all its defects, able to get along with it, because unlike the USSR, India never abolished the market or the private enterprise; therefore, the system of mixed economy could function.

Disintegration of a Superstate

The disintegration of one of the two Superstates could have been expected to lead to a situation where the sole surviving Superstate could appear to have the whole world left to itself to dominate and to command, but ironically enough already it would appear that the Superstate has been left without a role. With the threat of a competitive Superstate having vanished, it is appearing with all its faults naked and visible to the entire world. The threat of the competitive Superstate is no longer available as a red herring to condone its lapses. It has helplessly to watch the emergence of an alternative power, even sounder and stronger than itself, though not necessarily hostile to it, that is the new United Europe. Nor can it continue to find fault with the emergence of Japan as a super economic power when the fault lies with the lack of competitiveness of its own economy.

Collapse of Communism

Less than three decades ago Khruschev proclaimed from the podium of the United Nations that "we communists would bury capitalism". He was articulating the arrogant self assurance and confidence of the communists the world over, that the capitalist system was bound to collapse under the weight of its inner contradictions and give way to the superior socialist economic system. This confidence was based on the law of dialectic materialism of the so called "Science of Marxism". The Marxists confidently asserted that the capitalistic system could not be mended, it had to end. However, the theoretical formulations on which this conclusion was based were suspect from very beginning. Marxian critique of Capitalism as an exploitative economic system was derived from the Marxism theory of value which stated that the value of a good was equivalent to the socially relevant labour embodied in it, whereas the labour itself, the basic factor of production, got no more than what was necessary to sustain it. The latter was much less than the labour value of goods and services that labour produced. This was the origin of the surplus value which was grabbed by the capitalists. Thus Capitalism flourished on the exploitation of labour. But Capitalism could not indefinitely flourish based as it was on such exploitation because it inevitably led to under consumption, to depression and the collapse of the capitalistic economic system.

All such Marxist progonistications regarding the collapse of Capitalism proved to be utterly wrong. John Maynard Keynes was able to provide the theoretical basis for the understanding of the phenomenon of depression and to suggest a set of measures to sustain the capitalistic economy such as a compensatory fiscal policy and a public investment programme. The welfare economists suggested measures for social insurance, for re-distribution of income and regulation and control of monopoly. A capitalistic system need not be ended because it can be very well be mended.

Western capitalistic economies were also able to show that despite their democratic political organisation, they could muster and mobilise resources during the war period much better than the totalitarian regimes.

The Marxian formulation of dialectic materialism was based on the economic interpretation of history. While Marxian formulation was quite right in underlining the significance of economic factors in the historical evolution of the human society, it was quite flawed in turning this into sort of inflexible economic determinism which deprived it of a proper understanding of human factors and values in human affairs.

On the other hand, economists like Fredrick Von Hayek had shown long back that the socialist system was not workable. The coordination of transactions of hundreds of producers and consumers of hundred of goods and services can be done only by the market and not by the planners. Any attempt on the part of the planners to assume omniscience and omnicompetence in solving the simultaneous equations relating to hundreds of goods and services was doomed to failure. The plan of decentralized management of the socialist system proposed by Oscar Lange remained only on paper. The innovative management of Socialism attempted in socialistic countries like Yugoslavia and Hungary had only a limited success. The predictions of Hayek relating to unworkability of the socialistic system of management of economy have been fully vindicated. In retrospect it is obvious that whatever success the socialistic economy was said to have accomplished in areas of industrialisation and high technology was only at the cost of an unacceptable level of oppression. As Hayek had pointed out, concentration of economic power in a planned socialist economy was a road to serfdom. Those who concentrated economic power in their own hands had also the levers of political power through a monolithic party and intelligence services mechanism which they mercilessly used for exploitation of the society. This has been shown in all its nakedness by Alexander Solzhenitsyn in his famous book *Gulag Archipelago*.

Socialism could not even achieve equity and social justice its apparent strong point in comparison with Capitalism. On the other hand Acton's dictum – "power corrupts and absolute power corrupts absolutely" came true and the sluggish Breznev era saw the worst forms of corruption and misuse of power for personal aggrandisement.

It is obvious that defeat of Socialism as an ideology is not temporary; it is complete and final and irreversible. There will be no second chance for the establishment of a socialistic economy. It is gone once and for all. It is to be seen how much time surviving socialistic economies like Cuba and China would take before they also follow the Russian and Eastern European way.

However, it is obvious that the task of going from socialistic economy to capitalistic economy is going to be much difficult than that of going from capitalistic (feudalistic) economy to socialistic economy. It will take years before the problems attendant to this transformation could be sorted out. In the meantime, these economies would be faced with severe economic problems in providing even the basic necessities of life to their citizens.

However, the very existence of socialist economies had served a much bigger purpose of focusing attention on the importance of social justice and equity. It is this which inspired the newly independent developing countries not to go for a unbridled Capitalism or *laissez faire* but for planned socially oriented economic system. Even the Western capitalist countries could not overlook these considerations and had within them parties, groups and intellectuals who stood for policies aimed at these goals. The decisive defeat of Socialism might well be detrimental to the very values of equity and social justice.

These values are of great importance even in the capitalistic economies. It is reported that even in the affluent countries like Germany, hundreds of people are houseless and are staying in open parks and abandoned public buildings. Can they be left to the market forces? Perhaps in the market euphoria generated by the eclipse of Socialism, this may well happen.

The eclipse of Socialism and the triumph of the market has led to the strident and unqualified assertion that only the market can provide the clue to poverty alleviation and "sustainable" development because the market alone can provide for efficient allocation of resources. Poverty alleviation and environmental preservation can only be the by-product of efficient allocation of resources. All resources invested now on various kinds of public programmes or welfare measures are being interpreted as less than an efficient allocation of resources. The uncompromising admirers of the market like Margaret Thacher would like public services like housing and education and even basic state functions like tax collection to be privatised. At a time when the U.S.A. had a fiscal deficit of $250 billions it is seriously contemplating that it could get out of recession by providing further tax concessions to the affluent classes. It would be great pity if the removal of Socialism from the face of the earth were to mean the triumph of crass materialism, total rejection of all human and spiritual values and the denial all together of the moral basis of the economic order.

The eclipse of Socialism is bound to lead to an ideological vacuum. Capitalism with its emphasis on pursuit of private profit as the sole motivation of economic activity is unlikely to satisfy humanity. The founding father of Economics, Adam Smith, argued that the pursuit of private profit would ultimately redound to social good, thanks to the "invisible hand of providence" in the market. The proponents of private enterprise and Capitalism have always relied to this day basically on this very argument to vindicate their ideological conviction. But this has never carried full conviction because it has been found to fly against facts – facts of exploitation of and injustice to the weaker sections of the society. Nor is it clear why humanity should always rely on a serendipitous route for the attainment of social good rather than a direct resort to orgainsed social action. The ideological vacuum left by the eclipse of Socialism is bound to lead for search or reassertion of alternative ideological formulations such as those of Gandhism which would assume new relevance in the context of the pressing problems and challenges faced by humanity today, problems of economic disparity, poverty in developing as well as developed countries and the threat of erosion of nature's life supporting system.

3

KEYNESIAN REVOLUTION IN RETROSPECT

To commemorate Keynes Centenary, articles on the life and work of John Maynard Keynes have appeared in different newspapers and journals all over the world. The influential British Weekly *The Economist* invited four Nobel Prize winner economists Milton Friedman, Frederick Von Hayek, John Hicks and Paul Samuelson to write essays on Keynes, assessing his contribution to the economics and the way his ideas have influenced policies. In India also a number of articles have appeared, notable amongst them, Prof. Sukhmoy Chakravarty's article "The House that Keynes Built" which appeared in the Sunday Edition of *Times of India* of July 31, 1983 and L.K. Jha's article "Relevance of Keynes" which appeared in *Economic Times* of August 1, 1983.

On reading these articles, the reader cannot but feel bewildered. He perhaps cannot help comparing these authors of essays on Keynes to blind men, feeling the elephant in different aspects and describing him in their own ways, despite the fact that the authority and perception of Nobel Prize winning authors cannot be questioned.

Of the four Nobel Prize winning authors, Friedman has focused his attention on the *A Tract of Monetary Reform* published in 1923, describing it as Keynes' best book and totally neglecting the 'General Theory of Interest, Employment, Interest and Money' on which as Prof. Sukhmoy Chakravarty has rightly said, Keynes' claim on immortality rests. Undoubtedly, the *Tract on Monetary Reform* was brilliant, the *Treatise on Money* was erudite, but only the "General Theory" was truly path breaking. Milton's essay on Keynes which totally neglects General Theory should be compared to Hamlet without the Prince of Denmark.

The essay by John Hicks on Keynes is also out of focus but for another reason. Hicks no doubt concentrates on the General Theory but he begins with the observation that "Keynes was essentially a monetary economist and his writings are an intellectual counterpart to the monetary revolution of our time". This hardly does justice to the General Theory. The General Theory is by no means a Tract on Monetary Reform. It deals with the worst challenge that capitalistic system ever faced, namely, the Depression of 1929 and it provides a theory on employment which was not only comprehensive but was also fruit bearing in that it opened out clearly the path to a fiscal policy thorough which the State could intervene to meet the challenge of depression and unemployment. Having thus made a false start, John Hicks has gone on to pin-point labour standard as the major weakness of the Keynes' theory and of the policies that have been based on it. This is ignoring the main pillars of the Keynes' theory and attacking the obiter dictum. Surely, the General Theory itself does not mention "labour standard". This is a concept coined by Hicks. The main achievement of the General Theory has been to point out that equilibrium for an economy as a whole exists at various levels of employment and the main goal of policy should be to establish it at the full employment level; that the equilibrium is at the point of intersection between aggregate supply and aggregate demand; that supply does not create its own demand; that the two basic components of aggregate demand are investment and consumption and that by stimulating investment and consumption the aggregate demand could be boosted to jackup the economic activity to the full employment level. The theoretical concepts like the propensity to consume, the multiplier, the liquidity preference and the marginal efficiency of capital were so many convenient analytical tools which Keynes devised to build up the structure of his theory which at once came to be looked upon as the new "macro economics". Keynes' reference to wages was only to bring out the "money illusions" which prevents wage as the price of labour from playing its equilibrating role. Because the trade unions suffer from many illusions, they resist any reduction in money wages despite the fall in prices and rise in the real wage and this prevents the economic recovery which may be expected to take place with the reduction of money wages and the consequent reduction in the cost of production. Though sticky wages may be one of the factors which comes in the way of recovery, there is no doubt that in the Keynesian theory what emerges as the main instruments of recovery, are not wage adjustment but increase in investment and consumption. Indeed reduction in money wages could well impede recovery because of reduced consumption and hence aggregate demand. If this is so, Hicks' criticism of Keynesian theory cannot but be considered to be out of focus.

Hayek has blamed Keynes and held his theoretical work largely responsible for the longest period of general inflation and the widespread and severe depression that has followed. Hayek who has taken extreme postures regarding any intervention of the State in the economic activity can be expected to put Keynes in the dock but others who have no such allergy to State intervention are bound to recongise that Keyesian theory was a double edged sword. Keynes' theoretical framework could as much support the case for public investment to stimulate the economy as it could support strict monetary and fiscal discipline to curb expenditure and reduce and eliminate the inflationary spiral. That is why Keynes' 'How to pay for War' was a legitimate extension of the application of his theory in a period of inflation. As Hayek has pointed out Keynes' theory in some aspects was a revival of under consumption approach but Keynes' theoretical analysis of under consumption and the prescriptions that followed from his theory were far more advanced and sophisticated than under consumption formulations of the past.

What I have said above in defence of Keynes against the attack of Nobel laureates such as Friedman, Hicks and Hayek does not mean that his General Theory cannot be found fault with in any way. But for the deficiencies in Keynesian economics, one has to look into different directions all together. These deficiencies are two-fold. Firstly, his theory is of little help in its application, to what are called the 'developing economies' and secondly it is essentially concerned with the short-term rather than long-term. The two points are really correlated because it is the long-run development which is more relevant to the developing economics.

Keynes' theory concentrated entirely on the factors at the back of aggregate demand. As for aggregate supply, Keynes' theory seems to assume that supply is bound to grow in response to demand. This assumption could be postulated only in a resilient productive economy. Where resources are inelastic, where productive system suffers from attitudinal and institutional constraints as well as from infrastructural deficiencies, the level of economic activity cannot be raised merely by manipulating aggregate demand. What is required are a series of measures to build up the productive capacity of the economy and on this his General Theory has very little to say. Of course Keynes cannot be found fault with for this deficiency because he hardly addressed himself to the situation of the sort that exists in the developing countries of the world. It is no wonder that in Development Economics that has grown over the last three decades, little inspiration is drawn from Keynesian formulations. In fact, there are two types of Macro Economics today—the Macro Economics which is the legacy of Keynes and the Macro Economics of Development which is still an inchoate bundle of various formulations rather than one comprehensive integrated theoretical framework.

To the Macro Economics of Development, it is the earlier classical economists rather than Keynes who could be said to have provided several leads. Thus Adam Smith's concept of market expansion as a spur to development could still be considered to be one of the important elements of Macro Economics of Development. So is the analysis of division of labour and specialisation as an important means of building productive capacity. Ricardo's theory of rent can still be illuminating in understanding the inelasticity of resources in constraining development as well as in giving birth to unearned incomes in the process of development. As regards Malthus, 'the prophet of woe', the ghost of population is still there, not to be easily exorcised in many developing economies of the world. Marx, the great deviant from the orthodox classical line, still continues to be the perennial source of inspiration in many aspects to those who think about the developing countries of the world.

They rather than Keynes are relevant to the developing countries because they all have, in one context or the other, dealt with the long run while Keynes, as Hayek, has pointed out, adopted the haughty approach that 'in the long run, we are all dead'! The productive capacity of the developing countries can only be built in the long-run and not by any miracle like digging holes and filling them up.

Jha has tried to argue that global application of Keynesian analysis would make it more relevant to the developing countries. Jha argues that Keynes' remedies do not work in developed countries because of technological advance and the change in character of consumer demand. He, therefore, postulates that if the purchasing power were to be transferred from the developed to the developing countries through transfer of resources (grants or loans) it would generate demand from the developing countries for the products of the developed countries and would thus help the developed countries to deal with recession and unemployment. He, therefore, seems to advocate Keynesian theory as the basis of inter-dependence between developed and developing countries. But his analysis seems questionable on many points. First, with the transfer of resources through grant or loan from the developed to the developing countries being nowhere near one per cent of the GNP of developed countries, stimulating effect of such transfer on the economies of the developing countries would almost be insignificant. Secondly, if the so-called transfer of resources from developed to developing countries is intended only to generate demand for the products of the developed countries, its effect on the development of the productive capacity of the underdeveloped countries would to that extent greatly diminish. If the developing countries aim at self-reliant economic development, its process of development must be based on the indigenous appropriate technology and the use of local manpower resources and skills. Such self-reliant process of development would be based on minimum imports of the products and skills from the developed countries.

If Keynesian remedies are not relevant to the developing countries, they also seem to be not relevant to the current conditions of stagflation in the developed countries.

At the back of stagflation are the growing constraints appearing in the productive system in the shape of excessive consumerism and wage push inflation where opportunities for growth seem to be swallowed by uncontrolled tendencies of inflation. There are deeper factors at work at the back of these tendencies. In recent years it has become clear that natural resources including hydro carbon resources on whose extravagant consumption the affluence and extravagance of the living standards of people of West are based are reaching the point of exhaustion and hence western style of living must come to terms with the inexorable fact that nature's resources though bountiful are finite and affluence cannot be at the cost of a permanent damage to the life supporting system which nature provides. With those ecological factors basic to long-term economic growth, Keynes has no occasion to be concerned.

Paul Samuelson has bestowed scientific immortality on Keynes of the kind that Newton, Maxwell, Planck and Einstein possessed. However, if in the years to come, relevance to problems of development and ecology is going to be the touchstone of greatness, then I am afraid, that despite the great contribution that Keynes made at the moment of the crisis of Capitalism, his importance and relevance are bound to recede and not grow and if this happens, Kaynes may well miss the crown of immortality which Samuelson has offered to his memory and work!

4

THE RELEVANCE AND IRRELEVANCE OF ECONOMICS

I THE IRRELEVANCE OF ECONOMICS

In his Dharma Narain Memorial Lecture entitled "Carrots, Sticks and Economics", Prof. Amartya Sen has questioned the validity of the very basic assumption on which the edifice of Economics is based namely the assumption of *homo economicus* which says that human behaviour is entirely motivated by pecuniary considerations. It is this motivation which is supposed to govern the behaviour of man as a consumer, as an owner of the factors of production (whether land, labour or capital) or as a producer employing these factors of production in an enterprise to produce goods and services.

The economists had no apologies to offer for taking such a view of economic behaviour in terms of an unmitigated pursuit of purely self-interest, because the very founder of the science of Economics, Adam Smith had pointed out that even though the butcher, the brewer and the baker set out to supply meat, wine and bread to the consumer only in order to make the maximum profits for themselves, they ended up by serving the society by providing the where-withals of life. Thus, pursuit of self-interest ultimately redounds to social benefit, thanks to the "invisible hand of providence".

In his lecture Prof. Amartya Sen has made a subtle distinction between two aspects of this assumption of individual behaviour. First, the economic entities, whether individual or firm, try to seek the fulfilment of their goals and secondly that these goals correspond with the individual gains to themselves. He has further asserted that this view of the economic behviour is not convincing at all. Does it mean that the entire economic theory based on this assumption is invalid? Prof. Amartya Sen has not gone to the extent of saying so but he has drawn attention to two outstanding contemporary examples of the economies where the pecuniary motivation does not prevail namely the Japanese economy based on the ethos of individual obligation to the society and Maoist China where payment is made according to the needs rather than according to the contribution to work.

He has also pointed out that even in the capitalistic economy, in a moden industrial enterprise the relationships between the worker and management are not based on the calculus of profit and loss but on variety of considerations including trust, application and sense of duty. This, of course, is not a new point at all. Prof. John Kenneth Galbraith in his "New Industrial State" had drawn attention to the motivations of the members of the techo-structures of modern corporations. These motivations are of survival and growth of the organisation rather than profit maximisation.

Writers on organisational behaviour have also pointed out that each organisation has its own objectives and the principal function of management is to make the organisational objectives meaningful in terms of the goals of individuals working within the organisation. The success of management lies in harmonising the individual goals with the organisational goals. The role of work environment, recognition, appreciation and the quality of work in providing motivation have been extensively analysed in management literature.

Economic motivation of persons working in large organisations apart, recently George Gilder in his book *Wealth and Poverty* has also questioned the very basis of the assumption of pecuniary motivation as a force driving the capitalist economy. He has asserted "capitalists are motivated not chiefly by the desire to consume wealth or indulge their appetites but by the freedom and power to consumate their entrepreneurial ideas . . . . they are movers, shakers, doers and givers; their main urge to understand and act, to figure out a part of nature and society and to turn it to the common good. It is the "giving impulse" which is as much important to modern capitalism as a traditional society. Capitalism transforms the gift impulses of the people into a disciplined process of creative investment based on a continuing analysis of the needs of others."

If economists have not so far taken note of the diverse psychological and socio-psychological aspects of human motivation and behaviour and have not modified their formulations, it is mainly because of their infatuation with increasingly complex models and sophisticated jargons which gave economic laws a resemblance of natural laws and created an illusion that Economics is the most advanced amongst the social sciences and is indeed the "king of social sciences". This makes economists forget that "the king has no clothes", that their sophisticated formulations are based on wrong assumptions!

Economists always try to qualify their formulation of economic laws with the ceteris paribus clause. But the economic motivation is not covered by this clause. Economic motivation is not a variabale but the fundamental assumption of economic analysis. This makes "economic laws" all the more questionable.

From this discomfiture, Economics can be rescued only if it liberates itself from the trap of its own make-believe, its ivory tower of mathematical abstractions, and joins the main stream of social sciences and starts analysing human behaviour in the ordinary business of life on the basis of a multiplicity of motivations and circumstances which govern human behaviour. Man has to be looked upon as a whole and cannot be segmented into economic man, family man, social man or political man.

There has always been a dichotomy between the state of Economics per se and the study of Indian Economy in our universities and academic institutions. While the study of Economics was based on precise formulations under strict assumptions, the study of Indian Economy was allowed to go into historical and institutional aspects of economic and social life. However, this was greatly coloured by the view of the Western writers. For example, Indian social institutions and religion were always considered to be a stumbling block in economic progress. The joint family was supposed to be a disadvantage to the effort of an individual and Hindu religion was held accountable for the other worldly outlook of the people which was a hinderance to economic growth. Now that same Hindu religion is chastised for the corruption in our society! That a joint family provides social security and that Hindu religion has other positive aspects which have a beneficial effect on motivation was clearly forgotten. Even in a monumental work like *The Asian Drama*, a liberal thinker like Gunnar Myrdal finds fault with the Hindu religion. An Indian economist like Amartya Sen (Indian though based at Oxford) readily remembers the individual's sense of obligations of the Japanese and the Cultural Revolution of the Chinese but does not think of the need to analyse the positive elements in Indian culture, religion and social institutions, which if proparly handled can provide a big motivation for change and development. For example, the greatest scripture of the Hindus, the *Bhagvatgita* enjoins every Hindu to do his work out of a sense of duty rather than with an eye on the returns. Another Sanskrit verse talks of the need for the individuals to sacrifice himself for the family, the family to sacrifice itself for the community and the community for the nation and the world. In many ways, these idealist forms of behaviour are deeply rooted in the psyche of the common people of India. It is this which explains the durability of our culture and civilization, though they are under the threat of being overwhelmed by the growing forces of hedonism. It is a matter of regret that the leaders, thinkers and academicians in India have not given adequate recognition to these factors nor mobilised them for the progress of the nation.

II RELEVANCE OF ECONOMICS

I Dont's fully agree with many of the views expressed by Mr. P.R. Dubhashi (The Irrelevance of Economics, FE dated 4th May) nor of his extensive elaboration analysis on what Prof. A. Sen had spoken in his lecture questioning the validity of certain basic assumptions on which the science of Economics is based. The article (otherwise thought provoking) treats quite harshly the so-called views of economists on the "economic man" as one who necessarily and incorrigibly is motivated by pecuniary considerations.

But this contention is no longer relevant, because the modern economists have effectively re-interpreted the old views which had understandably caused some misgivings in the minds of very many non-economists, behavioural scientists.

Perhaps, Adam Smith was partly responsible for perpetuating some myths on the subject. He did expound the monetary myopia through his book *The Wealth of Nations*. But, then subsequently he was severely criticised by classical, neo-classical contemporay economists who have reinterpreted the fundamental assumptions of this branch of social science. They have effectively laid to rest the myth of the "economic man" as a pure mercenary under all circumstances. This is not to say that Adam Smith and his ideas have been superceded. They still are strikingly relevant particularly to third world countries.

Economic Man

But going back to the "Economic Man" the great Victorian economist Alfred Marshal has said that Economics was about the study of man in the ordinary business of life. To which Cairncross adds -- not about all aspects of human behaviour but about man as buyer and seller, producer and consumer, saver and invester, employer and worker. This definition has the advantage of stressing that economic is a social science concerned with social problems. It studies that part played by money or money's worth in human affairs. It is about the getting and spending of money or resources, how men earn a living and what sort of living they earn, how money affects their way of life and their outlook on life.

Pursuing this Economics is really not so much about money as about some things which are implied in the use of money -- three of these -- exchange, scarcity and choice. Having said this, he gives a compact definition as -- "Economics is a social science studying how people attempt to accommodate scarcity to their wants and how these attempts interact through exchange". Further requirements stress on the capacity for alternative uses of these scarce resources referred to above.

According to modern concepts, Economics assumes that all human beings wish to economise resources whatever their views and philosophies and whatever the objectives they wish to attain. By this we mean that they prefer to achieve more, rather than less, with any given set of resouces or -- which is the same thing achieve any given objective with fewer, rather than more resources, since thereby more resources are left for other purchases. We should recognise the indispensable roles, the money plays in all strata of societies, be it business or religion charity or benevolence or philanthropy. Gone are the days, when one can influence his fellow humans without cash. In point of fact, religion and their symbols viz., temples, churches, mosques and godmen themselves have all become centres of a lucrative industry. Massive deployment of black money in these areas cannot be denied. What makes God and godmen thrive is money.

It is clear that resource economization is applicable to churchmen building cathedrals, philosophers preaching wisdom, religious men erecting temples (from donations), philanthropists indulging in charity, scientists spreading knowledge, dictators waging wars, managers running business or politicians ruling states.

Even, when we normally speak of achieving a given result in two different ways, one of which will consume less time—so in turn less value than the other—we regard the former as the more economical. It is impracticable in Economics, as in other fields, to insist on working to very close margins of error at all times; it is often desirable having regard to the cost and trouble of precision, to accept quite rough approximations. Nevertheless, it is essential to bear in mind that the power to purchase goods and services is what economic measurement is ultimately concerned with.

In business when one speaks of target profit costs, it does not mean that the manager would not prefer, other things being equal, to achieve a higher level of profits (income). We believe, however, that actual business behaviour is, in fact, best described as an attempt to achieve a number of objectives, of which one relates to a minimum required level of profit (or in some situations, a maximum permissible level of loss). The early econoimists' misleading concept of the business man as one who maximizes profit has now been modified to mean maximizing profit (or minimizing loss) in the context of a given set of circumstances, including one's views about business aims, duty to customers and employees, and so on.

Business operations tend to resemble, not so much the steady pursuit of a single well-defined objective, as a number of parallel skirmishes and campaigns conducted within the framework of a general overall strategy. In war some operations may in themselves be unsuccessful, while yet contribute through diversion of enemy strength and in other ways, to the success of the campaign. Similarly in business, it does not follow that all opertions are expected to be profitable in themselves. It is also true of many of the individual activities of a business taken seperately. What the management or entrepreneur has to decide is whether the net advantage of any given activity to the business as a whole justifies the continuance of the acticity at some given level of cost. There is also interdependence over time. If, as often happens, the effects of a proposed activity will not be limited to the present, an attempt has to be made to assess the future effects positive (+) or negative (–). The net advantage to the business must be considered over time, as well as over the complex of business activities.

Making Laws

Mr. Dubhashi sounds needlessly critical of establishing *ceteris paribus* "other things remaining equal" clause while advancing economic laws. He fails to realise that it is impossible to make satisfactory judgement in coming to reasonable conclusions about a given set of data propositions, without the aid of such standard assumptions. This is not peculiar to economic data, it is a problem that will arise in the interpretation of information in any field of knowledge. It is never possible to make satisfactory use of information unless some kind of theoretical pattern is present or is built up during the examination, in the mind of the person who is using it. Unless action is to be purely intuitive it must be considered in relation to some kind of hypothetical constrict. It is the ability to build hypothesis and to act upon them, indeed, that distinguishes, among other things, human being from animals.

Coming to Mr. Dubhashi's point on segmental analysis of MAN in economics into 'economic man', family man, social man or political man etc. what is meant is that these are all agreed ways of viewing the different roles played by people, the multiple aspects of the individual behaviour being depicted in a society. These are all mere convenient ways of analysing human behaviour under different circumstances.

The retardation of Indian economy needs special emphasis mainly because of the unique state of affairs in our country where non-economic factors greatly influence economic issues. Our society is afflicted with inconsistencies not seen conspicuously operative in other countries. The Hindu religion lays down lots of do's and dont's, yet it is all being practised quite upside down. Scientists surrender to cheap, illiterate godman charlatans in our country.

III TOWARDS NEW ECONOMICS

The rejoinder *article* by J. Prakash entitled "Relevance of Economics" (F.E. dated 25-5-83) would have been slightly different, if the question-mark after the title Irrelevance of Economics, which was included in my original text sent to the *Financial Express*, had not been left out from the article as published in the *Financial Express* of 4th May. As a result of the omission, what was a questionable proposition appeared as a categorical assertion.

However, the main point of criticism of the traditional text-book Economics still remains, namely, the assumption of the economic man's exclusively pecuniary motivation and maximization of profit as the sole aim of economic activity has led to wrong formulations which do not always correspond to reality. Even leading economists like John Kennneth Galbraith, who dared to question the traditional assumption of Economics, have exposed themselves to be categorised as lesser economists from purely technical point of view, if not actually consigned to the category of sociologists rather than economists.' The grudging concession to the possibility of non-pecuniary motivations has not led the economists to reformulate the economic theory. They are mostly satisfied with some obiter dicta. The Basic Economics is still confined to the formulation of propositions of profit maximization in various branches of economic activities.

What I said in my article of 4th May is that the assumption of "Economic man" is not covered by the assumption ceteris paribus but is the fundamental assumption of Economics.

But there are several other ceteris paribus cluses which further whittle down the relevance of Economics in understanding the actual conditions. For example the assumptions of a perfectly competitive market are perfect mobility, perfect knowledge and communication, and inability of any single economic unit to influence the conditions of the market, whereas in underdeveloped countries like India, prefect mobility or communication never exists. Monopolies or Oligopolies are predominant and bargaining strength of various parties are strikingly unequal. The perfect market propositions relating to optimum benefit or optimum utilisation of resources, no matter how nicely chiseled by the classical or neo-classical economists, are not simply applicable or relevant to actual conditions in the underdeveloped countries. However, the dominance of the traditional economic formulations on the assumptions of the beneficial effect of the market is still reflected in the policy prescriptions of international financial institutions while extending their benevolence to the under-developed countries. We still do not have a comprehensive economic theory to challenge or rebut the propositions of the traditional Economics however irrelevant they are to reality.

On the other hand, we seem to be in a bizarre situation where pecuniary motivation has degenerated into naked hedonism and the market economy into a black market economy thus having few of the benefits of the pecunairy motivation and spur to the market for greater production as against greater manipulation for easy money-making.

The Macro-Economics Theroy which came to be formulated and accepted as New Economics following the publication of the *Ganeral Theory of Employment, Interest and Money* by J.M. Keynes is also equally irrelevant to the conditions of the under-developed countries. Keynesian theory pointed out to the deficiencies in agraian demand as the real culprit whereas in the under-developed countries the real problem is that of under-production. The flippant prescription of Keynes to provide full employment viz. "dig holes in the earth and fill them up", might have had some bearing to the conditions of the thirties in Europe and America but it has hardly any relevance to the conditions in the underdeveloped countries which cannot afford to squander away scarce resources on digging holes. Keynes could say that "in the long run, we are all dead", but the real goal of the developing countries namely building of the productive capacity of the economy is something which could be reached only in the long-run.

To what extent does Economics help in the real task of the developing countries, namely, the building up of the productive capacity of the economy and the people? It is to this question that the economists, particularly of the developing countries, have to devote their theoretical attention and practical labour. What the under-developed countries require is a new text book on Economics based on valid assumptions, aimed at helping solve the real problem of the under-developed countries. In such an effort, much of the traditional Economics might have to be rejected and much inspiration will have to be drawn from indigenous philosopy and experience. The New Economics may not be entirely pure. It might have much interface with organization and technology.

5

ECONOMIC THOUGHT OF LEADERS OF INDIAN NATIONAL MOVEMENT

An active debate is currently going on in the country about the economic philosophy relevant to our conditions. It is being stated that our approach should be oriented towards labour intensive rural development with emphasis on agriculture and cottage industries making amends for the wrong emphasis placed on heavy capital intensive modern industries. It is seldom realised that the debate and discussion on economic philosophy relevant to Indian conditions is not of contemporary origin. It has its roots in the past and it is indeed the heritage left to us by all those important national leaders who heralded the resurgence of modern India even before the achievement of freedom. They included such gallaxy of outstanding individuals as Raja Rammohun Roy, Dadabhai Nauroji, Mahadev Govind Ranade, Gopal Krishna Gokhale, Romesh Chandra Dutt, Rabindranath Tagore, Mahatma Gandhi and Jawaharlal Nehru. They were not academic economists but they were great patriots for whom service to the motherland was an overhelming passion and who wanted to create for their fellowmen a richer, better and fuller life. They were utterly absorbed in the thought of their country and its welfare. Their economic ideas were not borrowed from the western economists but were derived from their own analysis of the exploitative economy brought into existence by the British imperialism and their own constructive thinking about the lines on which India or rather free India ought to organise and plan its economic development. In their writings Indian economic analysis and speculation reached a high water mark of excellence. Contemporary claims to original economic thinking will vanish into thin air if only those who claim to originality could learn from the economic thought of those great leaders of the 19th century and early part of the 20th century. We are grateful to Dr. Ganguli for having produced an excellent book on Indian economic thought which contains the quint essence of the economic thoughts and ideas of those great masters. Their basic preoccupation was with the progressional impoverishment of the Indian masses under British imperialism.

They attributed this to two causes; first what Dadabhai Nouraji called the "economic drain" and second deindustrialisation leading to lop-sided occupational structure.

As regards the first, Dadabhai Nouraji as well as G.V. Joshi, Romesh Chandra Dutt and Mahadev Gobind Ranade, among others pointed out how the extravagant expenditure on top heavy colonial administration and military establishment, reckless expenditure on railways development, accumulation of sterling debt incurred to meet this investment, high level of taxation on the low level economy to extract resources needed for extravagant expenditure and finally adverse and unfavourable terms of trade for agricultural commodities led to continuous economic drain through which economic surplus was extracted out of a poor colonial economy. The colonial rulers indulged in economic parasitism of the worst sort. Gandhiji broadened Dadabhai's thesis on internal-cum-external economic drain by pointing out that the most important aspect of economic drain was India being made a nation of idlers. Thus his idea of economic drain covered the other major reason for the impoverishment of the masses viz. the deindustrialisation of the Indian economy which led to its unbalanced character. Before the British conquest, India was a great manufacturing and agricultural country but the British discouraged Indian manufacturers in every way in the early years of the British rule in order to encourage manufacturers in England. While they talked of free trade based on the doctrine of Adam Smith and Bentham, when it suited them, they did not hesitate to put on tariff walls to protect their own textile industries or to impose excise duties to discourage textile production in India.

The economic drain combined with deindustrialisation led to the fact that poverty in India had no parallel to that found in any other civilised country. Romesh Chandra Dutt pointed out that the successive famines of 1877, 1892, 1897 and 1900, which took a toll of

15 million people were the worst manifestation of the impoverishment of India brought about by the colonial rulers.

These great patriots not only analysed the causes of the impoverishment of the Indian people but also suggested a long-term national strategy of dealing with these problems of poverty. In this they drew their inspiration from the historical school of economic analysis led by Muller and List in Germany rather than the classical English economists. The only English economists, whom the Indian thinkers respected was John Stewart Mill and that was because of his deep humanism.

The economic agenda of these thinkers could be broadly described by the term *Swadeshi* or economic nationalism. This stood for the industrialisation, diversification of the economy, revival of agriculture and the traditional arts and crafts and revitalisation of the village institutions like the Panchayats and the cooperatives. From Raja Rammohun Roy to Jawaharlal Nehru, all shared this national programme of India's economic resurgence.

There was, of course, some difference of emphasis; broadly speaking, Raja Rammohun Roy, Mahadev Govind Ranade and Pandit Jawaharlal Nehru could be described as the representation of the modernist school of thought. Rabindranath Tagore and Mahatma Gandhi and certain other less known writers like Satish Chandra Mukherjee represented the school of rural communitarianism i.e. a decentralised economic system based on the village economy. The position of Gopal Krishna Gokhale was midway between the two – eclectic and pragmatic.

Raja Rammohun Roy stood for agricultural and industrial development with aid of Western technique, capital and enterprise. He even suggested selective colonialisation of the British citizens to initiate in India a process of economic modernisation. Ranade felt that industrialisation and diversification of economic activity was the key to India's economic development. He pointed out that growth was many-sided and depended on non-economic factors like aptitude for mechanical skill, love of science and research, of daring and adventurous discoveries which he wanted to be fostered among the Indian people. Jawaharlal Nehru believed that without industrialisation the problems of poverty, unemployment, national defence and economic regeneration could not be solved. He, therefore, felt that a national industrial plan was necessary. According to Nehru, the three fundamental requirements of modern economic development were heavy engineering and mining machinery, industrial and scientific research and electricity.

Gokhale attached importance to irrigation, scientific agriculture, rural credit, handloom sector, social services, mass education and rural self-government. Gokhale thought of a national plan of action broken up into annual plans with great care and foresight. Thus he heralded the era of planned national development which actually started only after independence. Gokhale's concept of national plan was brought to the realm of reality by Nehru. He believed in planning. He was the chairman of National Planning Committee even before independence. To him socialism in practice meant construction of a planned economy and it was under his inspiration that India launched on the successive Five Year Plans.

Mahatma Gandhi and Rabindranath Tagore, on the other hand laid greater emphasis on rural reconstruction. Tagore developed his positive and constructive ideas of Swadeshi in relation to community development in Indian villages. All villages must be organised to satisfy local needs with local efforts. He thought of an association of villages called *Mandali* – an intermediate unit of rural organisation. His Swadeshi also comprehended cooperative farming, cattle rearing, weaving and dairy. Gandhiji's Interpretation of *Swadeshi* was based on the *Charkha*, and other village industries organised through rural cooperatives. He wanted both production and consumption to become localised. This was the key point in his economic philosophy which could be described as that of communitarian socialism. Gandhiji described the State as a soul-less machine while Ranade, Gokhale and Nehru expected the State to take the lead in the plans and programmes of economic development.

It would not however be correct to describe these two approaches of schools of thought as irreconciliable opposites. Even Gandhiji believed that some key industries were necessary. He was not opposed to machinery as such or electricity as such but he was not in favour of any machinery which deprived masses of men of the opportunity of employment and livelihood. He wanted the mechines to add efficiency to the individual. Similarly, Jawaharlal Nehru did not rule out labour intensive industries; on the other hand he thought that they could provide employment and adequate supply of consumer goods. He was also a great enthusiast for Panchayat Raj and cooperative commonwealth.

Problems of Indian poverty are by no means a thing of the past, even forty years after the attainment of Independence. Even today we are still groping for the right approach to economic development and social change. In this effort we should be greatly benefited by the economic thoughts of these great masters, who are a tremendous link between Indian's glorious past and glorious future that we want to build up. The economic thoughts and ideas of our national leaders from Raja Rammohun Roy to Jawaharlal Nehru, through Gandhi and Tagore are indeed our precious heritage which is so lovingly treasured in Dr. Ganguli's book.

PART II

DEVELOPMENT PLANNING

6

INDIA'S APPROACH TO DEVELOPMENT PLANNING

India embarked on the process of planned economic development in the year 1951. The National Planning Commission headed by Prime Minister Jawaharlal Nehru was set up to comprehensively assess the natural and manpower resources of the country and to prepare plans for the mobilisation of these resources for economic development aimed at raising the level of living of masses of people. Jawaharlal Nehru was committed to planning ever since the year 1927 when he visited Soviet Russia and saw how the plans brought about economic transformation in that country. Even before independence, he was appointed by the Indian National Congress as the Chairman, National Planning Committee which produced valuable development plans for different sectors of the economy. However, after Independence, when Nehru broached the idea of planning, he was opposed by his Finance Minister, John Mathai who raised many objections to the introduction of planning. As a result of the difference of opinion, John Mathai resigned. It was not that Jawaharlal Nehru alone was amongst the public men who accepted the idea of planned approach to economic development. As far back as 1934, Sir M. Viswesurariah, the engineer stateman, advocated planning for India's economic development. Even private businessmen had produced a Bombay Plan before Independence. Hence adoption of planning as the instrument of development was but a logical culmination of ideas that had gathered momentum in years before Independence.

India has now completed more than four decades of planning. Except for the three Annual Plans during the years 1966 to 1969, which came to be described as Plan holiday, India has been following the system of preparing Five Year Plans in the context of long-term perspective plans. Within the framework of the Five Year Plans, annual plans are also prepared and are integrated with the budgetary process. Every Five Year Plan has a mid-term appraisal.

Indian plans are comprehensive in the sense that they cover both public investment and private investment and also all sectors of economy. Secondly, Indian approach to planning has been described as that of democratic planning as distinguished from totalitarian planning as is in Soviet Russia. It gives an important place to popular participation. While it envisages that public sector would be in charge of commanding heights of economy, it gives considerable scope to private enterprise also as well as the cooperative sector which is expected to provide a sense of value and direction to the economy. Thirdly, India's approach to planning is for balanced development, in the sense that all sectors including agriculture, industry, infrastructure as well as the service sector have been accorded their own place. The Second Five Year Plan followed the Mahalanobis model and put greater stress on heavy industry. However, the importance of agriculture and rural development was always recongnised and the plan strategy was based on inter-dependent and mutually enforcing growth of different sectors of the economy.

Fourthly, India's approach to planning was aimed at the establishment of the socialist pattern of society. In other words, equitable distribution of income and provision of full employment opportunities had been the objectives along with that of increasing the rate of growth of the Gross National Product (GNP). Latterly the objective has been defined in terms of the anti-poverty approach. Planning for development has not always succeeded in reconciling the different goals. Indian approach to planning for development aims at evolving the "third way", – steering clear of unbridled capitalism on one side and unmitigated totalitarianism on the other side.

Finally, India's approach to development has tried to combine economic, technological, human and institutional aspects of development. Within the field of technology the concept of "intermediate technology" has also found its place. It is the assumption of India's plans for development that science and technology provide the basis for development. India has established a Central Ministry for Science and Technology and has also enunciated a science policy. One of the assumptions of Indian approach to development is that of self-reliant economy and society. In order to have self-reliance in the field of science and technology, India has introduced a chain of scientific laboratories. However, so rapid has been the technological advancement in some of the developed countries that India has also found it necessary to import high technology in various fields of development. At the same time attention has been bestowed to the improvement and upgradation of more traditional technology adopted by village and cottage industries and handicrafts. India's approach to planning is therefore, eclectic in every sense of the term. It tries to reconcile planning with democracy, increased production with equitable distribution, establishment of large industry with promotion of cottage industry, introduction of high technology with upgradation of traditional technology and upholding human values with the pursuit of material values.

7

PLAN FORMULATION, IMPLEMENTATION AND EVALUATION

The process of Plan formulation, implementation and evaluation has not undergone any fundamental change since India launched upon the First Five Year Plan in the year 1951.

Advent of Planning in India

After the attainment of Independence, India took a conscious decision in 1951 to embark on a planned process of economic development, rather than leaving development to the vicissitudes of market forces. The task of planning was entrusted to the Planning Commission which was set up in March 1950 by a resolution of Government of India which defined the scope of its working. The resolution recalled the ideals and objectives enshrined in the Directive Principles of the Constitutions viz. a social order in which justive, social, economic and political shall inform all institutions of national life; adequate means of livelihood to all citizens; a pattern of ownership and control of material resources as to subserve common good and the operation of economic system as to prevent concentration of means of production to the common detriment. Plans were intended to realise these objectives. The Planning Commission was entrusted with the responsibility to formulate plans for the most effective and balanced utilisation of country's resources for realising these objectives. This task of planing would include a number of functions including (a) assessment of material, capital and human *resources* (b) determination of *priorities*, (c) *allocation of resources* to meet the priority needs (d) setting up *machinery for successful* execution of plans, (e) formulate *policies* and measures and (f) *appraise* progress in the implementation of plans.

Organisation and Machinery of Planning at the Centre

The Planning Commission consists at present of Prime Minister, Dy. Chairman, six full time Members and the Ministers of Human Resource, Finance and Agriculture as mambers. The day-to-day work of the Commission is looked after by the Dy. Chairman. Each Member is given a group of subjects though the Commission has a collective responsibility for planning.

The Secretariat of the Planning Commission has three types of divisions:

(a) *General Divisions* connected with certain aspects of certain economy e.g. perspective planning, general economic matters, international economic matters, financial resources, plan coordination, State plans, labour, employment and manpower, statistics and surveys, science and technology, project appraisal, monitoring and information and plan information and publicity;

(b) *Subject Divisions* connected with specific fields of development such as Agriculture, Cooperation, Rural Development and Village and Small Scale Industries, Irrigation and Command Area Development, Power and Energy including Rural Energy, Industry and Minerals, Transport, Communications, Information and Broadcasting, Education, Health and Family Welfare, Housing, Urban Development and Water Supply, Social Welfare and Nutrition, Backward Classes and 20-point programme;

(c) *Service Branches* connected with administration, accounts and general services. These Divisions maintain contacts with Central ministries concerned, State Governments and various non-official agencies for dealing programmes and policies of the respective divisions. Five senior officers known as Advisers (State-Plans) help the Commission to keep in touch with progress of planning and its implementation in the States and dealing with difficulties faced in the implementation of the plans.

The Commission on Centre-State relations has dealt with the criticism of the Planning Commission that it has functioned more as a limb of the Union Government rather than as a truly federal institution. The Commission has not agreed with the suggestion that the role of the Planning Commission should be limited to the Central sector of the economy and preparation of State plans should be exclusively left to the State Planning Boards. The National Plan comprises of both the Central and State plans and close coordination between the Union and the States in the planning process is essential. The Planning Commission should be an expert body commanding the confidence of both the Centre and the States. At the same time it cannot be a purely technical or statutory body with an autonomous status divorced from the political executive of the Union. It is the association of the highest political executive which is the motive force behind the planning process.

National Development Council

This was set-up in August 1952, on the suggestion of the Planning Commission itself. It was the assigned four important functions namely: (1) *Reviewing* the working of the national plan from time to time; (2) recommend *measures* for the achievement of *aims and targets of national* plan; (3) consider important questions of social and economic *policy* affecting national development; and (4) prescribing guidelines for the formulation of National Plan. The NDC includes all Ministers of Union Cabinet, Chief Ministers of States, Lt. Governor and Chief Executive Councillor of Delhi, and Administrators of Union Territories.

The Commission on Centre-State relations has recommended that the NDC, re-named as National Economic and Development Council (NEDC) should be reconstituted under Article 263 to give it a constitutional status and authority. A convention should be developed that the advice given and decisions taken in this forum should be respected. The frequency and duration of its meetings should be adequate. The Planning Commission should place before it alternative perspectives. It should deliberate on policy questions affecting national development. The summing up of its deliberations should reflect a variety of views expressed. Its working should be characterised not by formalism but systematic and effective participation. It should be the focal point of national debate on planning.

Planning Machinery in the States

For improving planning capabilities in the States, a Central scheme for strengthening planning machinery has been introduced under which 2/3 of expenditure on strengthening States level machinery is reimbursed by the Centre. Recently the scheme has been extended on the district level. The expenditure on strengthening the district level machinery meeting would be shared equally between the Centre and the States. State Governments have been advised to set up the following units in the State Planning Board viz. (1) perspective planning unit (2) Monitoring, Plan Formulation and Evaluation Unit (3) Project Formulation Unit (4) Regional/District Planning Unit and (5) Plan Coordination Unit. The Sarkaria Commission has observed that though the Planning Boards have been created in all States except Sikkim, they have not been drawn in real planning work. The Planning machinery has not been sufficiently strengthened in many States. In most of the States, the members of the State Planning Boards are only Part-time. The Sarkaria Commission has recommended that the State Planning Boards should perform functions for the State Government, as the Planning Commission does at the national level.

Long term, Medium-term and Annual Planning

Planning in India has been essentially for the medium term of five years. The plans were designed as follows :

1.	First Five Year Plan	1951-52 to 1956-57	Perspective simple projection of economic growth 1951-81.
2.	Second Five Year Plan	1956-57 to 1961-62	Perspective up to 1976.
3.	Third Five Year Plan	1961-62 to 1966-67	First phase of 15 years plan 1961-76
4.	Three Annual Plans	1966-67, 1967-68, 1968-69	Poor Harvest 1965-66, 66-67 and suspension

5.	Fourth Five Year Plan	1969-70-Mar.74	Perspective up to1980-81
6.	Draft Fifth Five Year Plan	1974-79	Profile of growth till 1985-86
7.	Sixth Five Year Plan	1979-80; 1980-85	
8.	Seventh Five Year Plan	1985-90	

Project Formulation

There is another aspect of plan formulatin which is relevant in this connection. The plan consists of projects and project costs under the existing system are based on figures available before the inception of the plan. These soon get out of date due to the rising prices, leading to cost over runs. The cost over run of project is considered objectionable but cost over run may be result of factors for which the project authority may not be responsible, such as general inflationary trends or increase in the cost of imported components due to appreciation in the value of foreign currency and not due to delay in the construction of the project. In such cases, resources must be provided commensurate with the cost escalation. However, since the resources stipulation is on the basis of stationary cost, the project suffer because of lack of adequate allocation of resources leading to time over run leading to further cost over run.

State Plans

Another aspects of plan formulation is in relation to *State plans. The National plan consists of the Central Sector and the State sector.* Discussions are, therefore, held with the State Governments for the formulation of the size of the State Plans. However, since the requirements of every State are very high, every State tries for a bigger plan but since the resources are limited, the plan is ultimately to be fitted on the basis of the allocation of available resources to the States rather than commensurate with requirements as advocated by the representatives of the State Governments. An element of horse trading is bound to enter into the process which may not be consistent with objective of formulation of a plan.

However these medium term or quinquennial plans are conceived against a long-term perspective, generally for 15 years.

The links between perspective plan and the Five Year Plans are established with a view to (a) promotion of long-term policies involving structural changes and (b) planning investments spreading over more than five years to yield investment. Planning Commission has undertaken expert study of selected sector like Energy and Transport to work out long-term strategy for those sectors.

Five Year Plans

The Five Year Plan sets out –

(a) More *immediate objectives* regarding *rate of growth* having regard to various constraints and possibilities;
(b) size of *investment* within the limits of estimated resources;
(c) *sectoral break down of investment* and *growth rate*;
(d) pattern of consumption;
(e) *policy framework* for successful implementation of plans.

In formulating the Five Year Plan, the Planning Commission coordinates the development programmes of the Central Ministries and the State Governments.

Annual Plans : These are prepared for each year within the broad framework of the Five Year Plan. In other words, the Five Year Plan is implemented through the mechanism of Annual Plans. The Annual Plans set out in detail the programmes of development to be implemented each years. The Annual Plan is adapted to changing conditions and emerging situations and in particular the likely availability of resources. The annual planning exercise is closely related to the budgetary exercise. Since the Annual Plans are within the frame work of Five Year Plans, the process of formulation of Annual Plans is simpler than that of the Five Year Plan and lays emphasise of reviewing the progress of implementation and inter-sectoral balances.

Process of Plan Formulation

Approach Paper

This is the first step in the process of formulating the Five Year Plan. The approach paper is prepared on the basis of background studies and preliminary exercises undertaken by the Planning Commission in regard to major parameters of growth – both over the long-term perspective and in relation to the Five Year Plan period – and the likely availability of resources. Objectives, strategies, policies broad magnitudes of growth in major sector and programme thrusts are enunciated in this paper. In preparing this paper consultations are held with Central Ministires, State Governments, Consultative Committee of Members of Parliament, panel of economists, industry and labour representatives and cross-section of the public. It is considered by the Cabinet and thereafter by NDC. After approval by NDC it is placed before Parliament. Based on the approved paper, guidelines are issued by the Planning Commission both to Union Ministries/Departments and to State Governments for preparation of detailed plans.

Draft Five Year Plan

After the approval of approach paper by NDC, the Planning Commission takes on hand, the task of formulating the draft Five Year Plan. This entails the following :

(a) Macro Plan laying down *overall physical targets* based on assessment of likely *availability of resources* – done on the basis of study of the working group on financial resources which recommends measures for mobilisation of resources;

(b) *Sectoral and Subsectoral plans* : These are based on the deliberations of working groups which are constituted 1-1/2 years to 2 years before the start of the Five Year Plan period. Members of the working groups are drawn from officials of the Planning Commission, Central Ministries/ Departments, State Governments, other institutions and experts in the field. As many as 126 working groups were set up in connection with the Seventh Plan. State Governments are also advised to set up working groups wherever considered necessary. The Working Groups take stock of process and problems and future requirement and make detailed schemewise recommendations for the new plan including inclusion of continuing and new schemes. The Estimates Committee in their April 1987 report have recommended that the number of working groups may be reduced by remitting subjects of allied nature to one working group. Also they should be given at least some idea of availability of resources since a large number of their recommendations are outright rejected for lack of resources since eventually size of the plan has to be pruned in accordance with availability of resources;

(c) *Formulation of State Plans* : The recommendations of all the Working Groups on the proposals of a State are considered by the State Plan Adviser concernced. On the basis of his report, discussioins are held between Planning Commission and State Government for finalising the Plan of the State concerned i.e. size of the State Plan and its programme content, and resources to support the plan including State's own resouces, additional resource mobilisation, Central assistance and maket borrowing;

(d) *Formulation of the Central Plan* : Development programmes of each Ministry are discussed between the Planning Commission and Secretary of the Ministry concerned on the basis of status paper prepared by the Division concerned of the Planning Commission after taking into account recommendations of the working group concerned;

(e) *Assessment and Allocation of Resouces* : The State/Central Plans prepared in the manner indicated above are based on needs and feasibility of the programme rather than on a clear idea of availability of resources. They are suitably pruned after precise assessment of resources becomes available on the basis of examination of the Working Group on Resources which thoroughly examines all aspects – taxation (both Centre and States), internal resources of public sector units and department undertakings, market borrowings, draft on public sector financial institutions etc. Thereafter through an iterative process, in the light of resource availability, sectoral outlays are determined, and lists of programmes/ schemes/projects to be included in the Plan are finalised.

Final Five Year Plan

The Central and State Plans after finally approved by the Planning Commission are incorporated in the National Plan which is brought up for consideration and approval by the Union Cabinet, National Development Council and ultimately the Parliament.

Plan Formulation

As stated above, the process of plan formulation consists of the preparation of the *approach paper*, its approval by the NDC followed by the preparation of the *Draft Five Year Plan*, approval of the draft by the NDC leading to the final version of the five year plan. The plans have always been for five years, except during the period of plan holiday when annual plans were prepared. During the Janata period, a methodological innovation was thought of in the shape of the concept of the *rolling plan*. The concept implied that every year the five-year plan would be reformulated deleting the year passed by the adding one more year. The rationale for the concept of the rolling plan was that it would always keep the plan *up to date and consistent* with the changing economic scenario. However, the concept of the rolling plan was not seriously pursued because Janata Government fell and the succeeding Government gave a go by to the concept and came out with the formulation of a new five-year plan. However, the point remains that the Five Year Plans should have *built-in flexibility* to deal with unforeseen developments like vagaries of weather, uncertainties in international economic environment which affects flows of aid, terms and trade etc.

The concept of updating the plan to take note of the changing requirements is important from the point of view of ensuring that the plans continue to be realistic. A number of assumptions lie behind the plan. For example, seasonal condition may be worse than expected because of the on-set of drought in large parts of the country or because of the emergence of inflationary trends or change in the value of foreign currency *vis-a-vis* Indian currency. At present there is procedure of preparing *mid-term appraisal* but this is only once in five years and the opportunity may not always be taken for correcting the design of plan. Another device for mid-term corrections and introduction of an element of flexibility is that of the Annual Plans.

Commission on Centre-State Relationship (Sarkaria Commission) have in their report dealt with the criticism that States are not involved sufficiently in national planning. There is too detailed a scrutiny by the Planning Commission and Central Organisations of the States' Plan proposals. Secondly, the Centrally-sponsored schemes have made deep inroads into States' sphere of activity and have affected their initiative and priorities. Thirdly, States' crucial earmarking of outlays has restricted their manoeuverability to allocatae resources among development heads. Fourthly, the State level Planning Boards and Substate level planning have not been effective so far.

The Commission has rigthly observed that taking an overall view from conceptual, functional and institutional aspects, planning at both formulation and execution stages has to be a cooperative process of shared action between the Union and the States. It has recommended more active involvement of States in evolving plan objectives, priorities and strategies, better representation of the States in various working groups, also coordinated action between the Central and State working groups. It has recommended that the Planning Commission should convene a meeting of Dy. Chairman/Secretaries of State Planning Boards two weeks before NDC meeting to consider the Approach paper and draft Five Year Plan. The Commission has recommended that the present practice of States submitting plan proposals whose financial implications are far higher than estimated resources should be discouraged. State Plans should be based on a realistic view of resources. Planning Commission should not try to scrutinise in detail individual sectoral schemes in the States' plan but concentrate on key ones – involving large outlays, foreign exchange component or inter-sectoral aspects.

Financing State Plans

During the first three Five Year Plans, Central assistance to State Plans was in the form of assistance to specific projects and programmes. Since the Fourth Five Year Plan in place of different schematic patterns, Central assistance is given in the form of block grants (30%) and block loans (70%) except for special category States such as Arunachal Pradesh, Himachal Pradesh, Manipur, Meghalaya, Mizoram, Nagaland, Sikkim and Tripura where a more liberal pattern of 90 per cent grant and 10 per cent loan is followed.

Central assistance constitutes about 37 per cent of States' Plan finance in the Seventh Plan. The total quantum of Central assistance is determined by the Planning Commission in consultation with the Ministry of Finance, keeping in view the overall availability of resources. Out of the total amount available, the provisions for externally aided projects, special assistance for sub-plans and special category States are first set aside and the balance is distributed on the basis of formula called Gadgil formula which became operational since 1980 after approval by NDC. The modified Gadgil formula consists of following citeria and weights for allocation of the overall amount – (a) Population 60 per cent, (b) per capita State domestic product below the national average 20 per cent, (c) per capita for effort of the State (10 %) and (d) special problems 10 per cent. About 55 per cent of total Central assistance is passed on to the States under the modified Gadgil formula.

District Plan

The State Plans are expected to reflect the district plans. However, the concept of *planning from the bottom*, that is, district plan leading to State Plan and the State Plan leading to National Plan has not worked partly because of the limitation of available resources in relation to requirements and partly because of the weaknesses of the planning machinery at the State and more so at the district level. Expert Committees have gone into the methodology of district (Hanumantha Rao Working Group, 1982), and block level (Dantwala Committee, 1977) plans. The CAARD Committee (Committee to review existing administrative arrangements for Rural Development and Poverty Alleviation Programmes) also made recommedations for comprehensive and integrated District administration and District Budget for formulation and implementation of District Development Plans and Programmes. But despite these, plans in India continue to be top down rather than bottom up.

However, a number of steps taken for decentralisation of planning may be mentioned. The concept of decentralised planning goes back to 1953 when Community Development Programme was launched for promoting decentralised economic development. As a part of this exercise, State Governments were requested in 1954 to prepare District and Village Plans. Following the recommendations of Balwant Rai Mehta Study Team in 1959, Panchayati Raj institutions came into being at district and lower level to provide an institutional base for people's active participation and involvement in development. There are now 2.17 lakh Village Panchayats in the country covering 96 per cent of about 5.8 lakh inhabited villages and 92 per cent of rural population.

An important step towards decentralisation of the planning process was taken in the Fourth Five Year Plan (1969-74). Certain important departures were introduced both in the planning process and content of planning. A new formula known as Gadgil formula was introduced for devolution of plan funds to the State level. At the same time, State Governments have been gradually building up their own machinery of planning at the State level and improving their planning machinery down to the grass-root level of villages.

Popular Participation

Planning Commission has been impressing upon the States that various development programmes will be meaningful only if people's representatives are actively involved and associated in the local level planning and implementation of various rural development and poverty alleviation programmes and employment programmes such as IRDP, NREP, RLEGP – specially in selection of beneficiaries. One of the aspects of improvement of plan implementation is strengthening the delivery system.

Public Sector Enterprises

Another aspect of decentralisation relates to planning and management of the activities of public sector enterprises.The latter have to go to Public Investment Board for getting sanctioned projects above Rs. 20 crores while those beyond Rs.5 crores go to the Expenditure Finance Committee. Only projects below this amount can be sanctioned by the Project authorities. In August 1986, Government delegated power to public sector enterprises to sanction expenditure up to Rs.5 crores without prior approval of Government in respect of investment with gross block of less than Rs.100 crores, Rs.10 crores in respect of those between Rs.100 to 200 crores and Rs. 20 crores in respect of those above Rs. 200 crores.

Spatial Planning

Plans in India are sectorally formulated. This leads generally to the weakness of *spatial planning* in India's planning process. One important spatial division in India is between the urban areas and the rural areas. The urban areas consist of the metropolitan cities, other cities and small and medium towns. Each of the metropolitan city is bursting with population growth with tremendous pressure on infrastructure facilities such as transport, water supply or sanitation. These cities require physical development plans but it should not be over looked that physical growth is connected with economic development and physical development plans should take into account the operation of the economic factors. If cities are the focal points of growth, they are bound to be a magnetic attraction to a continuous inflow of population from rural areas in search of employment facilities. The city planning is not just isolated exercise of providing physical infrastructure. It is an integral part of the configuration of the national development process. In rural areas, there is problem of over population, under employment and disguised unemployment, because of ever growing pressure on land.

From a spatial point of view, there may be an advantage in finding a via-media between metropolitan cities teaming with millions and suffering from intolerable pressure on infrastructure facilities on the one side and villages with insignificant population of 200 to 500 people and lacking minimum wherewithal of facilities such as approach road or supply of potable drinking water. The via-media may consist of promoting small and medium towns with a population of a lakh dotted all over the country with congenial environment for living. A scheme for promotion of small medium towns was introduced some years ago but could not be a conspicuous success because of limited perspective and resorces. Small and medium towns are not promoted just by providing a shopping complex or similar other projects.

The Ministry of Urban Development has come into existence in place of the erstwhile Ministry of Works and Housing. This could have provided the beginning for the process of urban planning in the country. However, the reorientation has yet to come about in full measure. Meanwhile, urbanisation is going apace and by the end of the century 35 to 40 per cent of the population will be in the urban areas. Without planning the urban scenario may be chaotic with abominable conditions of living for millions of people without proper shelter or supply of drinking water or electricity.

Sectoral Plans

In the absence of proper approach of spatial planning our plans have remained in the *main sectoral* in character. For each sector there is a separate Ministry (or sometimes more than one Ministry) and at the beginning of plan formulation, a number of working groups are set up to deal with the different aspects of the sectoral plan. These working groups prepare the *sectoral plans* which together constitute the national plan. As in the case of each State asking for a bigger plan, the Ministry on behalf of each sector also claims a larger chunk of plan funds. The whole exercise of plan formulation then becomes one of making a bigger claim on the resources bigger than even what could be justified by objective considerations in the hope that the eventual allocation after the scaling down process, could still be quite large. Ultimately, it is for the Planning Commission to reconcile the claims of various Ministries and to ensure that the sum total of outlays of the Centre and the States is consistent with resources available to the public economy. Indeed this exercise of matching outlay with resources has to go beyond the public economy and has to cover both public and private sectors.

Maintenance of Assets

Furthermore, in the name of priority to plan schemes, the *non-plan sector* is subjected to greater cuts. Thus resources for even essential maintenance functions are hard to come by. It is now getting increasingly recognised that without adequate provisions for the maintenance of assets creating out of past plan, there is no point in creating new assets out of the new plans. We have yet to fully reflect this realisation in our process of plan formulation.

Project Appraisal

Even though a project may be included in a plan, inclusion in the plan is not an investment decision; it has to undergo its own process of examination and scrutiny by Project Appraisal Division of the Planning Commission (PAD) and the Public Investment Board

(PIB). A recent innovation for the clearance of the project is the introduction of two stages—the first stage for clearing the project in concept so that DPR could be prepared and the second giving approval on the basis of DPR (Detailed Project Report).

The PAD undertakes appraisal of Central Government project costing more than Rs. 2 crores. In approving the project, PAD examines the need for the project, its linkage with the plan, technical and organisational aspects, as well as economic and financial viability of the project. As a result of this appraisal, projects are either dropped, deferred, modified or revised wherever necessary.

The Estimates Committee in their report of April 1987 noted that the time lag between inclusion of a scheme or a project in the plan and decision about financial investment was too large and recommended improvement in the quality of feasibility studies and expeditious clearance to them in order to reduce the time lag. It also recommended that while sanctioning schemes, *inter se* priority should be determined with reference to availability of funds so that projects taken on hand get completed in time and undue loss to public exchequer on account of delay and cost escalation avoided.

Inclusion of Schemes in Plan

Schemes are included in the Plan on the basis of criteria like their consistency with plan priorities, objectives and strategies possibility of accommodating them within tentative sectoral outlay ceiling after providing for essential on going schemes, programmes and projects. A system is sought to be developed whereby a shelf of projects is always available. There is a tendency to take up a large number of new schemes in every Five Year Plan with the result that the limited resources are distributed very thinly over a large number of schemes leading to time and cost overrun. It was, therefore, thought desirable to give priority to continuing schemes and consolidate the benefit by completing these schemes.

Inter-se priority : On-going and continuing schemes get precedence over new schemes. In respect of projects of economic returns, gestation period, location etc. are taken into account. Projects for replacement and renewal, modernisation, removing bottle-necks for better capacity utilisation are criteria for according higher priority.

The sectoral plans consist of the *Central schemes, States schemes* and *Centrally-sponsored schemes*. The Central schemes normally relate to those items which lie entirely within the jurisdiction of the Central Ministry such as for example railway and air transport, information and broadcasting or major industries in the central sector such as steel, coal and aluminium. The State sector schemes are for items which are within the jurisdiction of the States such as agricultrue, small scale industry and primary education. However, such has been the concern of the Central Government with items in the State list, that from time to time Centrally-sponsored schemes have been introduced to promote development relating to those items; for example – community development in earlier days and later on schemes such as small and marginal farmers' development (SFDA and MFAL), Integrated Rural Development (IRDP) and National Rural Employment Schemes (NREP) which are predominantly in the State sector but are supported by the Centre with resources as well guidelines for the implementation of these programmes. Central resources for such schemes are conditional on the provisions of resources by the States on shared basis. From time to time, the existence of the Centrally-sponsored schemes has come under attack. They are criticised as needless centralisation through involvement of the Centre in areas which essentially lie in the State Sector. But there is a persistent tendency for the new centrally schemes to crop up even while some other such schemes have been terminated; there are reasons why there is a tendency for the centrally sponsored schemes to recur. There are rural areas without potable drinking water and centre wants to intervene, or the production of oilseeds is far short of requirements and the Centre is perforce required to introduce its own schemes. Recently, some technology missions have been started by the Centre relating to removal of illiteracy, supply of drinking water, increasing production of oilseeds and immunisation of children from communicable diseases. These areas of activity are very much in the State Sector. The Commission on Centre-State relations has recommended that the number of centrally sponsored schemes should be kept to the minimum. It has endorsed the criteria laid down by Ramamurti Committee that all centrally sponsored schemes should satisfy one of the following criteria namely:

(1) pace setters with definite time frame within which

objectives would be realised;

(2) demonstration ard pilot projects;
(3) aiming at building up infrastructure for the country as a whole; and
(4) regional or interstate in character.

The Commission also recommended that an overall review of the Centrally-sponsored schemes should be made periodically.

Once the sectoral plans are prepared, the separate chapters on sector plans which go into plan document are formulated, but the various sectoral plans should form a consistent whole of the national plan. There are certain aggregate targets for national growth and employment on which there are separate chapters in the plan documents but problem may still remain of ensuring consistency between various sectoral plans and harmonising them for realising certian overall objectives of the Plan.

Policy Formulation

An important part of plan formulation is exploration of development policy alternatives and feasible options relating to major areas such as poverty, employment, income distribution, urbanisation, regional imbalances, finances, balance of payments, industrial development, agricultural price policy, human resource development, etc.

Plan Implementation

Once the plan is prepared and issued as a document, the effort of the Planning Commission is to ensure adequate funding of projects included in the Plan so that these are implemented in an optimum manner, but the Plan and the programmes and the projects included in it have to be implemented either by the central agencies or by the State agencies. The Central agencies or ministries are concerned with the implementation of the Central schemes/projects and centrally sponsored schemes. The Central ministries are divided into various functional divisions each concerned with the relevant plan schemes. Ministry of Agriculture may have divisions for seeds, fertilisers and implements and would respectively be concerned with schemes related to promotion of improved varieties of seeds, fertilizers and implements. Plans are divided into programmes and projects and each ministry would have to plan the implementation of these programmes and projects. This involves allocation of adequate budgetary resources, formulation of plan schemes and getting them cleared by the authorities concerned and setting up organisations or machinery for implementing the plan schemes. The procedure for these may sometime lead to delay in the implementation of plans. Improvement of plan implementation, therefore, requires improvement of procedures both in the stage formulation and at the stage implementation of the schemes.

Very often it is stated that the financial and physical plans do not always go together. There are plan outlays but there are no plan outputs. This is a matter of serious concern in relation to implementation of plans.

In respect of centrally sponsored schemes as well as the State Schemes, it is the State administration which has to provide the machinery of implementation. Almost all the schemes in the rural sector are to be implemented through the district machinery of administration. At the State level, the machinery of plan implementation consists of the Secretariat Organisations, Heads of Departments such as Director of Industry or Director Agriculture and the district administration headed by Collector with District Officers incharge of various sectors such as agriculture, cooperation or irrigation. Unless funds are allocated in time to implementing agencies at the district levels and competent officers posted to implement schemes in various departments, there is bound to be delay in the implementation of the plan schemes or there may be unsatisfactory implementation.

An important aspect of plan implementation is popular participation. In our scheme of planning, a lot of importance has been attached to people's participation in various programmes. For example strong Panchayati Raj institutions are considered *sine qua non* for effective implementation of the anti-poverty programmes at the grass-root level. The plans have emphasized the need for strengthening and associating Panchayati Raj institutions in identifying and implementing projects for the benefit of the local people. In addition, cooperation and non-governmental or voluntary organisations in various sectors including agriculture, industry, trade, social services and labour are also associated with the formulation and implementation of plans.

Monitoring

The officers of the Central ministries as well as advisers of the Planning Commission often visit the States to review the progress of the plan schemes. It is the job of every ministry and its executive agencies to keep close watch on the implementation of various schemes. Each Ministry as well as the Planning Commission have also their monitoring mechanism, but often the information is not received in time from the states on plan progress and the monitoring of the progress of the plan may not be entirely satisfactory. The Commission on Centre-State relations has recommended that the Planning Commission should pay special attention to the efficacy of the monitoring system of Government by advising on techniques and formats. It has further recommended that under the general reviews contained in the Annual Plan and the Mid-term Appraisal, a comprehensive quinquennial review should be brought out by the Planning Commission which should be taken advantage of in formulating the next plan. It has also recommended that the Advisers should visit the States more frequently and be permanent invitees to the meetings of the State Planning Board.

Central Sector

For central public sector undertakings, MIS was introduced in the year 1975 by BPE in consultation with the Planning Commission through monthly and quarterly reports. In February 1985, a Flash Monitoring System was introduced under which information was directly collected from Central projects under implementation costing more than Rs.100 crores.

State Sector

State Governments have developed monitoring system under which copies are sent by State Governments to Central Ministires and Planning Commission. In case of power and selected major irrigation projects, periodical reports are received by the Central Electricity and Central Water Commission. The administrative ministries hold quarterly review meetings. In the case of industry and infrastructure, Members of Planning Commission also hold quarterly review meetings. In spite of this, the Estimates Committee (1987) observed that no fool-proof monitoring system has so far emerged and deficiencies continue to persist. As a result, the execution of most of the projects has gone aray and projects have been inordinately delayed resulting in huge cost escalation.

The Ministry of Programme Implementation was created in September 1985 to (a) monitor performance of infrastructure sector, (b) Central projects costing Rs. 20 crores or above and (c) implementation of 20-point programme. There is a plan for computerisation at various levels to facilitate monitoring. The Minister has to keep PM, Cabinet and Ministries abreast of progress and identify slippages. The Estimates Committee (1987) drew attention to the need of avoiding overlaping and duplication of effort.

Plan Evaluation

The Programme Evaluation Organisation was set up in the year 1952 as an independent organisation under the general guidance of the Planning Commission. However, the Programme Evaluation Organisation does not deal with all the plan schemes. It only takes up selected programmes. These studies of the plan evaluation bring out the progress and short-comings, if any, in the implementation of plan schemes. For carrying out field surveys and investigation for evaluation of studies, the Programme Evaluation Organisation has seven Regional Evaluation Offices located in different regions of the country. Twenty-seven Project Evaluation Offices are attached to Regional Evaluation Offices. The work of the Programme Evaluation Offices was reviewed by the Dubhashi Committee in 1978. The Estimates Committee (1987) was unhappy that recommendations of the Committee have yet not been fully implemented.

There is also the mid-term appraisal. However, the appraisal and evaluation have not had so far any major impact on the process of plan formulation and implementation.

Summary of Points

(i) After the attainment of Independence, India embarked on the process of planned economic development;

(ii) The process of plan formulation, implementation and evaluation has not undergone any fundamental change since that time;

(iii) Machinery of planning at the Centre consists of the Planning Commission and the National Development Council;

(iv) The Planning Commission should be an expert body commanding the confidence of both the Centre and the States;

(v) The National Development Council should be the focal point of national debate and planning;

(vi) The Planning machinery at the States and district levels should be strengthened;

(vii) The plans in India include the perspective plans, the medium-term five-year plans and the annual plans;

(viii) The process of planning consists of the preparation of the approach paper, the draft five-year plans, sectoral and sub-sectoral plans, formulation of States' plans and assessment of allocation of resources;

(ix) The plans should have built-in flexibility to take note of the changing requirements;

(x) The project formulation should be improved to avoid time and cost escalation;

(xi) States should be given adequate idea about the financial resources so as to lead to realistic planning;

(xii) The district plans have not yet become a success;

(xiii) There should be greater scope for popular participation in the planning process;

(xiv) One of the important aspects of improvement of plan implementation is strengthening the delivery system;

(xv) Public sector enterprises should have adequate delegation of financial powers to formulate and implement plan projects;

(xvi) Spatial planning should receive greater attention. In the name of the planning, rural areas should not be neglected;

(xvii) There should be a limit on the centrally sponsored schemes and a proper criteria established for the choice of schemes;

(xviii) Policy formulation is an important part of the plan formulation;

(xix) Plan implementation should be improved so that the financial and physical planning go together;

(xx) The monitoring procedure should be streamlined both at the Centre and at the States;

(xxi) The work of Programme Evaluation Organisation should be strengthened by implementing the recommendations of the Dubhashi Committee.

REFERENCES

Planning Process, Government of India, Planning Commission.

44th Report of Estimates Committee 1986-87 on Planning Commission and System and Procedure for Appraisal of Plan Schemes.

Chapter XI—Economic and Social Planning Report of the Commission for Centre-State relations.

8

PURPOSEFULNESS OF THE ROLLING PLAN

It was announced that the Sixth Five Year Plan would mark the beginning of the new system of Rolling Plan which was being introduced as a distinct innovation in the methodology and process of planning in our country. In the new system of Rolling Plan, Five Year Plans would be formulated every year. Every Five Year Plan would have a four-year period overlapping with the last four years of the previous Five Year Plan as the first four years of the succeeding Five Year Plan. There would thus be a continuous cycle of the Five Year Plans.

The purpose and rationale of the new system had been explained in the authentic statements emanating from the Planning Commission. The new system was intended to deal with some of the short-comings in the process of planning which had come to notice since the advent of planning in our country in the year 1951. The major shortcoming of planning in our country had been the persistent divergence between aim and achievement. All our Five Year Plans had aimed at a growth rate of 5 per cent. None of them had been able to exceed an actual growth rate of 3.5 per cent. There had thus been a persistent shortfall in our plan performance which has called into question the very credibility of planning in our country.

Planning would not serve its purpose if its goals are not realised. It is true that attempts had been made in the past to explain the gap between the aims and achievements of the previous Five Year Plans. But a mere *post-mortem* evaluation to explain the gap would be of academic rather than of operational significance unless some mechanism is devised which would enable the planner to identify the reasons for the divergence and take timely steps to see that the factors which are responsible for the divergence are taken into account and timely steps taken to influence those factors in such a way that the divergence between aim and achievements is eliminated.

It has been seen in the past that some of the major factors which lead to such a divergence between aim and achievement are the seasonal factors which in our predominantly agricultural economy are of decisive significance and which upset all the calculations of the planners and all the programmes of the administrators. Moreover, these seasonal conditions differ from place to place with excellent seasonal conditions in some part of the country and very adverse seasonal conditions in other parts. Plans which do not include a flexible response to the seasonal vagaries are deemed to frustration. Unfortunately one of the defects of the system of fixed Five Year Plans of the past was that the total five year target was somewhat mechanically allocated over the five years, and got into difficulties when such mechanical allocations did not square with the changing realities of the economic situation as it emerged at the beginning of every new year.

A fixed Five Year Plan neither takes advantage of the opportunities offered by a good agricultural season nor does it contain an adequate safety margin to deal with the adverse seasonal conditions. As a result the apple cart of the Five Year Plans of the past was continuously upset by the fluctuations of the seasonal conditions. All the assumptions about the material balances, sectorial balances, price level and relative prices with considerable significance for real value of plan outlay were all upset and the fixed Five Year Plans did not have the adaptability to adjust to these situations.

The fixed Five Year Plans were also upset by the sudden changes in the global conditions. It is true that the Indian economy is predominantly based on domestic market but it is not a closed economy, it is an open economy. Though imports and exports constitute a small sector of our economy, they can sometimes be of a decisive importance. Nothing brought this out more strongly than the sudden hike in the petroleum prices by the Organisation of Petroleum Exporting Countries. When in 1973 they suddenly decided to jack up the petroleum prices, thus escalating, by one move, the petroleum products import bill several fold, they gave a severe jolt to the resources position and planning in our country.

It is the purpose of the Rolling Plan system that planning is not thrown overboard or turned topsy turvy by internal or external disturbances which materially affect the economy. This it does by taking a fresh look at the economy as a whole at the beginning of every year, taking note of all changes in the economic situation caused by seasonal factors etc., and on the basis of such assessment introducing the necessary corrections in the plan including its investment patterns, schemes, programmes and policies. Such corrections would bring about appropriate adjustments in the mechanism of planning.

It would be easy to exaggerate the extent of adjustment which the Rolling Plan system can introduce. The plans may well contain a number of large projects, which once undertaken would have to be concluded more or less according to schedule as demanded by the technological considerations governing the project. Thus major factories or irrigation and power projects, once taken in hand have to be constructed according to the schedule. These are in the nature of indivisible investments which would start earning only on completion. If the work schedule is unduly changed, it would not only mean locking up resources in an idle manner but jeopardising the progress of the projects as well. These major projects constitute the bulk of plan investment; they would very much limit the degree of re-adjustment which the Rolling Plan system is intended to allow.

That is why, in any of the two successive Five Year Plans, the investment for the overlapping period of four years may not greatly differ. The two successive Five Year Plans would , therefore, be very much like each other except that a Plan for any five year period would contain outlay for one more year not belonging to the past Five Year Plan and would delete the initial year of the previous Five Year Plan. It would also introduce necessary corrections or adjustments in the over lapping Four year period. The manoeuverability for adjustment or corrections is however, necessarily limited.

This does not mean that the limited manoeuverability is of no significance whatsoever. Indeed it could well be an effective method of dealing in a timely manner with the changing factors in the economic kaleidoscope and of bridging the gap between aims and achievements of planning.

It has been alleged in the criticism of the Rolling Plan system, that in such a system the targets of the Five Year Plans would lose all their sanctity, since every year a new Five Year Plan would be initiated. The above analysis would show that such fears are groundless. Many of the targets for the common four-year period adopted for the previous plan would hold good. Indeed if the economic situation is favourable and the correctional mechanism of the Rolling Plan really succeeds, it could bring about progressive improvement in the targets with every successive Five Year Plan. On the other hand, if the previous Plan had unrealistic targets, then scaling down of these targets in the light of the exercise of preparing a new Five Year Plan should not be regretted at all. It is much better to fix up realistic targets and fulfil them rather than fix up unrealistic targets and keep on shifting the blame through a post-mortem evaluation of the failure of planning. One of the aims of the Rolling Plan system should, therefore, be to restore the credibility of the planning itself.

Nor should the Rolling Plan system mean the abandoning of the Perspective Plans which are prepared for a longer period for 15, 20 or 25 years. The perspective plans provide the long-term goal and direction of the economy, having regard to the availability of the natural resources, the progress of science and technology and the rising expectations and aspirations of people. But in the Rolling Plan system, every Five Year Plan also would give a new direction to planning where necessary and the planners would have continuously to engage themselves in the task of reconciling the new direction provided by the Five Year Plan and the long-term directions envisaged by the perspective plan.

It would, therefore, be obvious from the above analysis that it is entirely an unjustified exaggeration and indeed a travesty of facts to say that the Rolling Plan system amounts to abandonment of planning itself. Indeed though Rolling Plan is an innovation in the methodology of planning, it is not as though it has not been discussed in the past in India nor that it has not been a part of the planning system of other countries. The pros and cons of the system of Rolling Plan had been considered in the past and the rolling plan also characterises planning in some other countries of the world.

Indeed rolling plan is bound to be a much more intensive exercise of planning than the fixed Five Year Plan period of the past. In the past, there used to be only one exercise in a block period of five years to make an appraisal of progress of the plan. It used to be called a mid-term appraisal. In the new system of the rolling plan, the appraisal will be an annual feature and what is more important it would not be an appraisal just for its own sake. The appraisal exercise will be directly connected with the exercise of the formulation of a new Five Year Plan.

Such an appraisal and formulation process every year are bound to make the discipline of planning much more intensive than in the past. In the past, it has happened that there is a lot of activity at the beginning of the formulation of the Five Year Plan, but later the planning impulse becomes more or less dormant and annual planning exercises turn out to be mere mechanical exercise. Such periodicity of hectic activity at the time of the formulation of the Five Year Plan and subsequent somnambulism in the remaining years of the plan will not be permissible in the rolling system of planning which would demand every year a fresh effort towards appraisal and planning. The Planning Commission as well as other organisations in administration will have to be much more alert and alive to the process of planning in the system of Rolling Plans. The statistical capabilities would have to be much more strengthened in order to enable such annual exercises envisaged in the Rolling system of Planning to be made. If eternal vigilance is the price of liberty, eternal planning is the price of success and this is where really lies the purposefulness of the Rolling Plan.

9

THINKING FOR THE SEVENTH FIVE-YEAR PLAN

The Seventh Five-Year Plan is on the anvil. The Planning Commission has already embarked upon the exercise for the formulation of the approach to the Seventh Five-Year Plan. In conducting this exercise it is of utmost importance that "more of the same" is not just all that we have by way of grist to the mill. Rather, we must go all out to make a thorough introspection, critically examine every single aspect of the past performance, and on that basis, not hesitate to introduce innovations and to take bold initiatives even though they may imply a sharp break from the past.

In his recent key-note address at the Seventh Economic Development Conference, Mr. L. K. Jha, Chairman, Economic Administration Reforms Commission put forward the suggestion that the Seventh Five-Year Plan should be productivity-oriented rather than investment-oriented. It has been noted with concern in recent years that the capital-output ratio has gone up alarmingly. That is why, in spite of the increase in the rate of savings in the economy, the rate of growth has not gone up to any material extent. We should, therefore, go deeper to find out the roots of productivity.

In the ultimate analysis, the productivity of the economy depends on the quality of the people and the most single important factor which influences the quality of the people as participant in the productive process is their level of education and training. The historical experience of all the developed countries of the world conclusively shows that no country can make the transition from an underdeveloped to a developed country without a very high level of literacy which is the most important prerequisite for the progress of any society. This was brought home dramatically to my mind during my recent visit to South Korea. In course of two decades from 1960 to 1980, covering a span of four Five-Year Plans, that country has completed its economic take-off through a sustained process of economic growth at the rate of more then 10 per cent per year. Its average standard of living has gone up from US $ 82 to US $ 1700. How has this Korean miracle been accomplished? When I asked this question, one most important explanation was the fact that the rate of literacy in South Korea is 95 per cent. This near cent per cent literacy has made it possible for the government in South Korea to ensure the participation of the people in all programmes and projects of modernisation and economic development. Literacy has made the Korean people highly conscious and this accounts for the speedy success of its development programme.

On the contrary, in spite of three decades of planning, the literacy rate in India, as 1981 Census dramatically brought out, has been no more than 36 per cent. The 1991 census showed that it has gone up to 50 per cent. The female literacy has lagged much behind male literacy and the proportion of female literate population is much less. Indian literacy rates are much lower than even those of neighbouring countries of Asia, whether it is Thailand, Malaysia, not to talk of Sri Lanka, where literacy had always been higher. With such vast illiteracy India cannot make speedy progress, no matter how much we invest in plant and machinery. The primary goal of the Seventh Five-Year Plan should be to attain near cent per cent literacy in India. Is this impossible? It does not take much reflections to realise that attainment of cent per cent literacy is a labour intensive rather than a capital intensive task. If our vast educated but unemployed population is harnessed to the task of attaining universal literacy, we might be solving simultaneously the problems of literacy as well as the problem of unemployment amongst the educated youth. Unorthodox methods may have to be employed in this task for pushing up rate of literacy from 50 per cent to nearly 100 per cent. The school rooms will have to be used in the morning and late evening hours for conducting literacy classes but the task is certainly not insurmountable or beyond our capacity. On the other hand, it is overwhelmingly important and brooks no delay. The achievement of cent per cent literacy is bound to be reflected in better success of our development programmes and projects and a quicker pace of development.

While attainment of cent per cent literacy is a quantitative task, development requires qualitative improvement, specially in two specific fields namely higher education and public administration. It has been complained that standards of university education have pathetically declined, even in well established universities of the past who were standard bearers of high quality. Standards have fallen even in technological institutions like engineering and medical colleges. This has been attributed to indiscriminate expansion which has diluted quality. We often boast of India being third in the world in respect of the scientific and technical manpower but the relevant question is, "of what quality"? Students coming out of the portals of educational institutions which are impoverished in the essential assets like libraries and laboratories can hardly be reckoned as qualified scientific and technical manpower. For higher education, what is required is quality and not quantity. More important than laboratories and libraries are the quality of teachers and their devotion to their profession. Complaints have often voiced that university professors go with impunity even though they do not deliver their assigned lectures.

What applies to higher education also applies to public administration. The strength of people employed in public administration in India is more than 15 million. For a population of 700 million we have the ratio of 23 persons in public service for a thousand population as compared with 17 to 1000 in Japan. With a continuously expanding scope of public administration and the enlargement of function, there has set in a proliferation of organisation and increase in the number of personnel with noticeable lower productivity in performance.

The national performance in both these fields of higher education and public administration will vastly improve if we make a shift from increase in numbers to improvement of quality.

There is another aspect of expansion which deserves notice. With increase in numbers has come decline in discipline. Because of the "demonstration effect" of elite behaviour, the decline in discipline, both in higher education and public administration has spread to other layers of society. The consequences of falling standard of social discipline have been serious. Just as an illiterate society cannot make rapid progress so also a society without discipline cannot achieve results. It is not necessary to have an authoritarian order to ensure social discipline. In a country like

India, it would be true to say that elite behaviour can do much to engender social discipline. But, if the elite behaviour is itself characterised by cynicism or lack of social concern, it sets a bad example and permeates throughout the society.

Here again, we have a lesson to learn from South Korea. It is the critical combination of enlightened political leadership, dedicated bureaucracy, disciplined military leadership, enterprising business leadership and conscious public that has brought about such a miraculous progress and such a rapid transformation in South Korea. Social discipline is not a matter of plan outlay but it is the basic prerequisite for successful planning.

Preoccupation of our planning has indeed to shift from plan outlay to the impact of planning. At present, our whole plan review and monitoring system gives excessive attention to progress of plan expenditure and next to that to realisation of the physical targets. Very little attention is paid to the impact of planning, though what matters is really the impact. Expenditure which does not create the necessary impact is indeed counter productive. Examples could be given of several projects and programmes which have resulted in expenditure but not the desired impact. The most notable example of inadequate return to massive investment is, of course, that of irrigation. Large industrial projects with underutilised capacity also fall in the same category. The whole of administrative machinery is itself a case where it is possible to have better utilisation of capacity to produce a greater effect in terms of socio-economic progress. The phenomenal gap between outlay and impact can be described as that of "the implementation gap". Many reasons account for the implementation gap. One of them is the lack of necessary linkages between various programmes, which in turn, arises because of our failure to think through programmes from the starting point of concept and design to that of implementation and results. The planners must so design plans and programmes as to eliminate the implementation gap. They must take care of "instrumental targets" to ensure the fulfilment of the ultimate targets. To make plan allocations without taking care of constraints whether in the form of lack of materials or lack of infrastructure including marketing arrangements, delivery system etc. is to plan for failure. In the ultimate analysis this failure is not of the agency incharge of implementation but of the planners themselves. If there is under-production because of lack of power, it is the failure of planning because it provides for production targets without providing for overcoming the constraints.

Another important reason for plan shortcoming is the mismatch between plan schemes with an All-India design and location specific needs and requirements. The only way to bridge this is greater measure of effective decentralisation of our planning process. It is astonishing that after four decades of planning we do not yet have successful operational district plans. It is of paramount importance that at least during the Seventh Five-Year Plan we do have operational district plans.

Finally, the view which has indeed become conventional that resources should not be spent on non-plan but should be diverted to planning also needs to be questioned. It is no use allocating investment for new plan projects if the projects already established and assets created are not well maintained. What is the use of adding to more dispensaries and hospitals if the existing ones are without essential medicines and equipments? The so-called non-plan items and maintenance items are often crucial to the performance of the economy and should not be overlooked in our enthusiasm for planning for new assets.

10

ISSUES BEFORE THE EIGHTH FIVE YEAR PLAN : Consensus needed on Plan Objectives*

The newly reconstitued Planning Commission has prepared its own approach paper to the Eighth Five-Year Plan. The paper prepared by the previous Commission was set aside on the ground that it is necessary to reflect the ideas of the new National Front Government.

This brings out the essential contradiction between planning as part of a long-term perspective and democratic elections which give rise to new governments every five years. When the same political party and even the same person as Prime Minister continued over long periods, this contradiction did not come out sharply. But now, and as when the Janata Government was formed in 1977, the whole concept of planning as a long-term exercise has come under strain.

If governments with different complexions throw out of the window the plans of previous governments, the whole concept of continuous long-term planning is likely to be put into jeopardy. Planning should be a matter of national consensus and supraparty endeavour. Can we distinguish between the essential or core part of Plan and the peripheral part which can change with a change of government? In this context, it is significant that as committed an ideologue as Mr. E.M.S. Namboodiripad has recently given a call for an all-party consensus on development.

There should be a national consensus on the objectives of the planning, viz. increasing gross national product, equitable distribution of the gains of planning, provision of gainful employment

---

* *Times of India*, dated 23rd March, 1990.

opportunities, raising people above the poverty line and sustained but sustainable development. However, even when there is a consensus on the broad goals of planning, there could be basic differences of approach regarding the manner in which the goals are to be accomplished.

Multiple Goals

Moreover, the goals enumerated above are multiple goals and may be mutually contradictory. There ought to be a full-fledged debate on these issues in the National Development Council as well as other national fora. These issues can no longer be put under the carpet. In a way, they were raised at the vary inception of planning when Dr. John Mathai resigned disagreeing with Jawaharlal Nahru's decision to set up a Planning Commission and adopt planning as an instrument of development.

While planning is for people, it does not mean that it is an exercise in populism. Yet on account of political compulsions well-thought planning has been superseded in recent years by abrupt introduction of populist schemes and programmes. The most outstanding example of populism intruding into the orderly process of planning was the introduction of the 20-Point Progamme by Indira Gandhi. Prof. D.R. Gadgil, the then Deputy Chairman of the Planning Commission who felt uneasy about it, had to go.

It is another manifestation of populism that the greater the size of plan, the better. There has been relentless increase in the size of successive plans but it is an illusion to believe that the larger the size of the plan, the greater is welfare or even the rate of growth. Mere size of the Plan cannot achieve the objectives unless it is buttressed by sound policies, competent network of institutions and organisations, efficient administration and a social climate conducive to growth. All these have been pushed to the back because of the overwhelming preoccupation with the size of the plan.

Populism also comes in the way of less than requisite attention being paid to the several essential tasks. Of these the most important is that of population control. One of the essential targets of planning ought to be the attainment of a zero rate of population growth.

Another unwelcome task which everyone, including the planners, seems to avoid is the inculcation of social discipline and spread of work ethic so necessary for raising productivity. The revolution of rising expectations is engulfing progressively larger sections of the poulation stimulating the long supressed urge to possess ever-widening range of material goods. Unfortunately it is accompanied by a social climate in which everybody wishes to make his claim on the good things of life but none feels an obligation to contribute to the collective effort which can produce them.

Rural Development

Unfortunately, the emergence of a vast black economy, supported by corruption in public life, specially corruption in high places, has put an end to any incentive to hard, honest work in factories, banks or government offices. Populist schemes like writing off of agricultural loans threaten to destroy the discipline of the credit system and consequently endanger its viability.

Finally, there is the question of inter-sectoral priority. India's approach to the plan in the past has been of balanced development in which all sectors are supposed to have their due place and importance. The heavy industry bias introduced in the Second Plan consequent on the adoption of Mahalanobis model was corrected in the later Plans when the importance of the agricultural and the wage goods sectors was recognised. The sectoral inter-relationships make simplistic approach to sectoral allocation somewhat inappropriate. Under the new dispensation agriculture and rural development are to be given at least 50 per cent of planned allocation. But should it include investment in rural areas in creating social and economic infrastructure?

Above all, systematic attention is needed to be paid to the mobilisation of "social energy", that is the productive capacity of the people. It is unfortunate that we are still far away from one essential factor in economic and social development, viz. universal literacy. To accomplish this by the end of the century should be the most important task of the next two Plans.

Little attention has been paid to spatial aspects of planning. Spatial policy should aim at curtailing further growth of Indian metropolitan cities and the dispersal of economic activity. Above all, government planning should pay attention to ecological aspects. Development will prove self-defeating if it destroys nature's life supporting system. These are the issues which need to be cleared before India embarks on the Eighth Plan.

11

PLANNING IN THE CONTEXT OF THE NEW ECONOMIC POLICY

The new economic policy calls for an agonising reappraisal of the system of planning that was ushered in India soon after independence when it embarked upon the planned process of economic development. Since then Eighth Five Year plans have been formulated.

The rationale of planning was clear in the mind of Jawaharlal Nehru who was at the helm of affairs as the first Prime Minister of free India. He strongly felt that the economic fortunes of the country could not be left to the vicissitudes of the market forces but should be the result of solemn and deliberate process of planning directed towards mobilisation of natural and man power resources for the realisation of predetermined objectives such as quickening the rate of growth, abolition of poverty, expansion of gainful employment opportunities and economic self-reliance.

From this position, the new economic policy appears like a complete U-turn. The new economic policy would like the economy to be shaped by the market rather than by the plan. That would mean the inevitable process of market superseding planning.

That planning was the very antithesis of the market mechanism and therefore if the market was to be relied upon, planning could not be ushered in, was a point raised by Dr. John Mathai, the Finance Minister in Nehru's Cabinet. It became the point of conflict between the Prime Minister and the Finance Minister when planning was introduced in the country. Jawaharlal Nehru as Prime Minister of free India was commited to planning. He had visited Soviet Russia way back in 1927 with his father Motilal Nehru. He saw how through planning the USSR had transformed a backward economy into a very strong self-reliant industrial economy, overcoming the usual shortcomings of the capitalistic economies, viz. monopoly, inequality and unemployment. Even in pre-independence days, he had set up, in his capacity as the Congress President, a National Planning Committee under his chairmanship and when he became the first Prime Minister of free India, he lost no time in forming the Planning Commission responsible for the process of planning. His Finance Minister John Mathai could not be persuaded to accept Planning and Planning Commission and resigned on this issue. He thought that after planning was introduced and Planning Commission set up, it would superseded the Finance Ministry and the relevance of his Ministry would be reduced.

The issue has once again come to the forefront. Can planning in the present form continue in the context of marketisation? Old controversies regarding planning and Planning Commission have again become relevant. What is the place of the Planning Commission in a federal setup, when it is entirely a central agency with no representatives of the States? Is not Planning Commission with all its functional or subject matter divisions something like a parallel Government? Can it do planning for the State as well? Can the Planning Commission override the State government as well as the Central ministries? Moreover the Planning Commission has been brought into existence through the administrative fiat of the Central Government. No legislation has brought it into existence. What then is its sanctity? Can it claim to do planning for the entire country? No doubt Planning Commission is guided by the deliberations of the National Development Council of which the Chief Ministers of the States are members but since the Planning Commission provides the secretariat for the NDC, its decisions are very much influenced by the Centrally-appointed Planning Commission. These and other questions could no longer be pushed under the carpet and will have to be faced.

Planning as it has been practised for the past several years in India may be described as comprehensive planning which covers the entire economy i.e. all sectors of the economy including public, private and cooperative sectors as well as various subject matter sectors of the economy such as agriculture, industry, transport, health and education. It determines public investment as well as private investment and lays down targets of increased production in all sectors of the economy. In the context of economic reforms, private investment would be determined by the market – by signals of demand and supply, by prices, costs and profits. With continuing process of deregulation, the State would not have at its disposal various levers which will enable the State to regulate the performance of the private sector. If this is so, planning could no longer be comprehensive. It could only be partial – confined in the main, to public sector investments and targets. As for the private sector, planning could only be indicative. It could, as in the system of Japanese planning, be strong on forecasting – forecasting trends and policies which would facilitate reliable planning by private enterprise.

Marketization and dismantling of the command economy would require great interface between the Planning Commission and the private enterprise. Planning Commission would have to evolve a new mechanism for much a continuous interface with the private sector – such as the industrywise Planning and Development Councils in the French mechanism for indicative planning.

In the context of the new concept of planning, the composition and methods and procedures of the Planning Commission will have also to undergo a change. Because of the concept of comprehensive planning, the Planning Commission virtually evolved into machinery of parallel Government with the whole panoply of divisions related to each sector and sub-sector. Planning now should return to the original concept of the Planning Commission as an agency incharge of mobilisation of natural and manpower resources of the country. The terms of reference of the Planning Commission as originally formulated were as follows:

(1) It shall make an assessment of the material, *capital and human resources* of the country;
(2) It shall formulate a plan for the most effective and balanced utilisation of the country's resources;
(3) It shall determine priorities, decide stages of plan and *allocate resources* for completion of each stage; and
(4) It shall indiacte factors responsible for successful implementation of the plan.

The emphasis in these terms of reference is on resources and not on investment and outlays which over years have become the main preoccupation of our planners. This lop sided approach of the Planning Commission would change if the structure of the Planning Commission is related to various types of resources – natural, human and technological, and their optimum mobilisation. The advice of the Planning Commission would be in terms of a strategy for development and mobilisation of resources. Planning Commission could also pay attention to the heitherto neglected aspect of development viz. regional planning. It could divide the country into homogeneous agro-climatic and socio-economic regions and evolve strategies for development of different regions which may go across various State boundaries. Nature is not delimited by political boundaries. Mountain ranges, valleys, watersheds and rivers cross state boundaries. For optimum development, natural regions are more relevant than political boundaries. If planning in the new context could lead to the new approach of regional planning, it would be a wholesome departure from the old approach of stereotype centrally sponsored schemes uniformally applicable to all the States.

12

DEVELOPMENT PLANNING: The Indian Experiencne*

With the Eighth Five-Year Plan on the anvil, it is but appropriate to review this succinct but comprehensive appraisal of India's development planning by one of India's leading economists who has been a member of the Planning Commission for about six years.

In the first chapter, dealing with basic features and analysis, Prof. Chakravarty has explained the rationale of planning in terms of the limitations of the market mechanism. While the market is capable of efficient allocation of existing resources, it cannot expand and modify the resource base, which requires far-sighted action beyond the horizon of the private sector. Hence the need for 'planning' !

But this is precisely the point. The protagonists of the market would not accept that the planners are necessarily more farsighted than private entrepreneurs. On the other hand, not being affected by profits and losses, they are likely to fritter away scarce resources in overambitious investments which, because of inadequate returns, are likely to lead to erosion rather than expansion of resources available for development. Chakravarty has not found it necessary to go into this and thus, has not taken us beyond our traditional ideological predisposition in favour of planning. The issue is still open-whether we could do with less planning and more play of market forces.

In the second chapter (on the foundation of India's development strategy), Chakravarty discusses the "the Nehru-Mahalanobis

---

*Review of the book "Development Planning : The Indian Experience" Prof. Sukhmoy Chakravarty.

approach", giving pride of place to the capital-intensive industrial sector side-by-side with agriculture and the private industrial sector confined to relatively labour-intensive light consumer goods. While the former would lead to diversification of the economy, the latter would provide consumer goods and employment.

The large investments in the public sector were expected to generate large profits which would be reinvested. This approach did not succeed to the expected extent. While on the one side, the needed increase in consumer goods did not materialise, the development of the heavy capital goods industry did not lead to sufficient diversification of the export basket, generate sufficient surplus resources.

While noting that the results "fell short of expectations", instead of admitting that the approach failed, Chakravarty rather euphemistically describes this as "the failure to consider the full set of logical implications of what accelerated growth implies in the context of a mixed economy". In retrospect, he feels that there could have been a greater emphasis on the cotton textile sector (or perhaps, a whole range of consumer goods) and intermediate product industries and agriculture, though he does not specifically say so. This would have happened, the market protagonist would argue, if the consumer choice rather than the planners' choice had prevailed. However, Chakravarty gives credit to the Mahalanobian model for the diversification of the industrial structure, and the upgrading of the skill base of the population.

Corrections to the Mahalanobian approach were introduced in the Third Plan which put greater emphases on agriculture and the consumer goods industries. However, rising defence expenditure following the Chinese aggression and the successive monsoon failures during 1965-67 proved a setback for development planning. The formulation of the Fourth Plan was deferred and the *interregnum* was filled with three annual plans. But it was during the period of the so-called 'Plan holiday' that the Green Revolution took shape.

In two other aspects, the Plan approach failed. First, in ensuring that the fruits of development go to weaker sections of the community and, second in generating adequate returns from resources invested in public sector enterprises. As regards the first, the response was to base the Five Year Plan on the strategy of "redistribution with growth". With the specific objective of poverty alleviation/eradication, a number of programmes were initiated for small and marginal farmers and landless workers. The Fifth Five Year Plan was also more specific regarding self-reliance – it aimed at the elimination of net aid. Food and fuel consequently emerged as the leading sectors in the Fifth Plan.

In the fourth chapter on the problems of implementation, Chakravarty takes up the common observation that "though Indian plans may be good on paper, they are rarely good in implementation". He rightly questions the validity of the dichotomy between planning and implementation because a good plan must also be feasible. However, a plan may not work if there is no desired co-ordination of activities among different agencies in the absence of relevant information, delayed response or simply because of lack of capacity and motivation and goal-adequate behaviour. These deficiencies are manifested in lagging infrastructure, failure in technology transfer and low productivity of investment. Chakravarty's discussion of the problems of implementation is somewhat theoretical. He does not come to grips with the problems of converting goals and objectives into targets, ultimate targets into penultimate and instrumental targets, targets into tasks, tasks into allocation of responsibilities to agencies, providing the agencies with appropriate organisation and personnel with requisite capacity and motivation, monitoring of tasks and evaluation of results. He does not enter into an assessment of development administration nor does he look at the problem of time and cost overruns in project implementation or sloven implementation of programmes.

Prof. Chakravary looks at the spatial implications of development strategy important for a large country like India with considerable agroclimatic variations. He draws attention to the disparity of development manifested by the fact that the average per capita domestic product in the richer State is nearly three times as high as in the poorest one. The problem of poverty is emerging as an inter-regional one. Chakravarty links this to the relationship between planning at the Central, State and local levels.

States complain about inadequate funding of sectors like health and education and predominance of Centrally-sponsored schemes. But they are unwilling to tap the agricultural sector to raise resources.

Chakravarty suggests preparation of perspective plans for the development of different agro-climatic regions. Market forces tend towards polarisation of development which does not trickle down. If the state is to counter this tendency, it should undertake a major attemp at resource mobilisation on the national scale. This includes raising the efficiency of public corporations.

Chakravarty also emphasises the development of human capital, restraining population growth and better use of locally available resources. He does not go into structure methodology of the operational strategy of State and district plans and the reasons why they have not met with adequate success so far.

In the fifth chapter, Chakravarty deals with some current issues of economic policy. First, the rising capital-output ratio in the economy (from 3.5 for the period 1951-52 to 1959-60 to 5.50 for the period 1970-71 to 1979-80). This is attributed to rising infrastructure capital costs and the energy-intensive nature of modern agriculture. Besides, Chakravarty believes that Indian industry has not benefited from increasing returns to scale in the absence of a competitive market in a sheltered economy. Delay in the completion of projects in the absence of adequate monitoring is another reason. An erratic pattern of investment with excess capacity in one sector and supply bottlenecks in others is a third reason. Budgetary procedures do not allow sufficient funds necessary for quick completion of projects.

In the field of agriculture he feels that with greater attention to land relations, water management and credit in the eastern and central parts of the country, agricultural production will show significant result. With an increase in the marketed surplus of foodgrains, greater efficiency of the industrial sector and technological improvement, agriculture and industry could grow in tandem.

The main reason for industrial inefficiency is outdated technology, the lag being of the order of ten to fifteen years. The Indian capital goods sector is outdated. Without modern technology and productive use of labour, domestic costs of production are unlikely to come down. Chakravarty underlines the need for a breakthrough in utilisation of solar energy, application of biotechnology in agriculture and energy saving. He fears that the liberalised import policy regarding capital goods will largely be continued. In the case of the sector design capabilities for sectors like chemicals and fertilisiers, it would not be possible to avoid repetitive import of technology. Chakravarty, however, makes no mention of "appropriate technology" as relevant to socio-economic priorities in India.

As regards foreign trade, he raises the question as to why India's export performance has been unsatisfactory and why it cannot repeat the performance of South Korea. He gives the plus points of South Korea (an authoritarian regime, significant flow of foreign funds, sharp increase in the saving rate to 31 per cent, Korean goods displacing high-wage Japanese items) and the minus points of India (open democratic regime, weak infrastructure, aid tied to old technologies, and the size and heterogeneity of the country).

But the so-called minus points like size or democracy can be big and plus points provided we overcome the characteristics of the soft state and society. The soft society cannot realise higher levels of porductivity of capital and labour.

Chakravarty suggests a higher funding for health, education and nutrition. But this by itself is not enough. Greater social discipline and a work ethic are needed. Chakravarty does not deal with this, though he identifies power, transport, steel and fertilisers as specific areas where inefficiency is widespread.

In conclusion, he has laid stress on population growth, a qualitative upgrading of labour, innovations in agriculture and large-scale creation of productive assests through work programmes in rural areas. He does not advocate a move towards a free market. Rather, he wants appropriate planning, giving greater scope to market signals but taking countervailing measures with a redistributive policy to ensure growth with equity. All these suggestions deserve to be taken into account while planning for the future.

13

DISTRICT AND LOCAL PLANNING

District and local planning is an area where precept has run ahead of practice. Successive Five Year Plan documents have dealt with the subject and provided prescriptions but in practice. District Planning has not been very successful. The appointment of a working group on the subject under the Chairmanship of Dr. C.H. Hanumantharao, Member, Planning Commission provided the occasion to look once again at the subject of District and local planning. One question naturally arises. How is it then that even after three decades of planning in this country, we do not yet seem to have an adequate horizontal planning at the local levels, i.e. the district, the tehsil and village levels—the levels which are close to the people of the country? We talk of democratic planning in India. Democratic planning means participation of people in the process of planning. How is it then that planning seems to be advanced and sophisticated at the levels which are farthest from the people; but at the level or areas which are closest to the people, planning seems to be still far from reality? Why is it that the economists and administrators feel that there seems to be as yet no satisfactory theory and techniques of district planning and why are we groping in the dark at the level where planning touches the people? What are the deficiencies in the horizontal planning in the country? What should be the content of horizontal planning? What should be the machinery of horizontal planning at the local level? How do we go about it? These are some of the vital questions that need to be raised.

On these and other subjects thinking has been indeed going on from the very inception of planning. An attemp has been made here to review this thinking and offer some suggestions which may arise out of the analysis.

The basic reason for the weaknesses of horizontal planning in the planning process of our country is rooted in the very nature of the planning process adopted from the inception. In spite of three decades of planning in India, planning at District and local levels still seems to be very weak. In spite of the lip service paid to decentralised planning, our planning has been essentially centralised and vertical rather than decentralised and horizontal. The centralised plan begins with certain predetermined objectives as regards rate of growth of the aggregate national economy. The growth rate is further related to the sactoral growth rates i.e. rates of growth in agriculture, industry, transport etc. To bring about the predetermined growth rate is adumbrated a certain size of plan investment on the basis of certain data regarding capital-output ratio. Thereafter, total investment or outlay is allocated sectorally for the nation as a whole. These sectoral investments are then divided into the Central Plan and the State Plan. The detailed sectoral plans for the State are then prepared in detail by various departments who in turn propose the break-up for the districts. The planning at the district level therefore, amounts to nothing more than the allocations of sectoral or departmental investments. A plan consisting of such departmental allocation and schemes is not found satisfactory since it does not satisfactorily assess and reflect the possibilities and opportunities arising out of local resources or the ambitions and aspirations of the local community. Only a horizontal local plan can achieve this.

Such integrated horizontal planning for rural areas or decentralised planning or planning from the below was certainly envisaged from the very inception of the planning process in India.

Thus explaining the rationale of coordinated approach, the First Five Year Plan Review document observes :

> "When different departments of the Goverment approach the villagers, each from the aspects of its own work, the effect on the villager is apt to be confusing and no permanent impression is created. The peasant's life is not cut into segments in the way the Government's activities are apt to be; the approach to the villager has, therefore, to be a co ordinated one and has to comprehend his whole life. Such an approach has to be made, not through a multiplicity of departmental officials, but through an agent common at least to the principal departments

engaged in rural work."

But it is in the Second Five Year Plan that the concept of a local horizontal plan was discussed in greater detail:

> "A State plan has to be presented in two different ways, namely, according to different sectors of development represented in it and according to regions and districts. Programme for different sectors include those which are to be executed directly by departments at State level and others which are to be executed through districts but are coordinated at the State level. Thus, a district plan would include programmes prepared on a territorial basis for villages, groups of villages, talukas, extension blocks, municipal areas, etc. and also programmes to be executed within the district which are derived from departmental plans formulated at the State level. That part of the district plan which is prepared within the district is important both for the range of activities which it embodies and for the fact of association with the people at every level and the opportunity afforded to them to determine their needs and to contribute towards their fulfilment. Just as in drawing up State plans, the preparation of district plans is an important stage, so also in the implementation of the State plan its break up into district plans is an essential step. In particular, in different sectors in the State plan programmes or schemes in which local participation and community action have a special contribution to make are to be separated out and shown as constituents in the plans of districts. These items of work become part of the district plan in which, in the main, the resources provided by Government are in the nature of a nucleus to be augmented through popular support and participation. The value of district plans as a method of approach in planning is enhanced by the ambitious scale on which national extension and community projects are proposed to be undertaken. The district plan has, therefore, to take into account the requirements and activities of areas under the extension programme as well as of these outside, it. This makes the district plan an important influence in educating public opinion, in bringing together various programmes in the district within a common frame and in developing community

participation, co-operative self-help and local initiative and leadership. The people of each district are thus enabled to assess their needs and resources, judge for themselves the tasks to be undertaken with the active support of the administration, and put forth the requisite effort. Moreover, as a partnership in effort between the administration and the people a district plan will specify obligations to be met by both."

The main constituents of a district plan are :

(i) the community development and national extension programme;
(ii) social welfare extension projects;
(iii) agricultural production programme and allied activities in the field of rural development such as animal husbandry, soil conservation etc.;
(iv) development of co-operatives;
(v) village panchayats;
(vi) village and small industries;
(vii) schemes for utilising effectively resources developed through State projects for irrigation, electricity, communications, industrial development and extension of training facilities;
(viii) housing and urban development;
(ix) the programme of small savings;
(x) aiding construction projects through labour co-operatives and shramdan;
(xi) programmes for the welfare of backward classes;
(xii) programmes in rural-urban areas relating to social services, especially expansion of education at primary and secondary levels, health units, health education, sanitation, malaria control, family planning etc.;
(xiii) utilising and assisting voluntary organisations engaged in constructive social work;
(xiv) land reform;
(xv) prohibition work; and
(xvi) dissemination of information about programmes of national, state, regional and local development.

These programmes are undertaken through several official and non-official agencies, and in a number of them there has to be coordination between more than one agency. Thus, in addition to administrative officials and the officials of the various development departments, each district will generally have a rural local board, a large number of village panchayats, and a number of municipal bodies in rural areas. The importance of towns as focal points in economic growth is likely to increase, and urban and rural areas have to be viewed together in terms of planned regional development".

The methodology of preparing state plan for rural development on the basis of the District and Block plans was explained by the Third Five Year Plan in the following words –

> "Along with the district, the block should serve as a unit of planning and development. It was suggested that in the following fields proposals for the Third Plan should be drawn up by States on the basis of district and block plans:
>
> (i) agriculture, including, minor irrigation, soil conservation, village forests, animal husbandry, dairying etc.;
> (ii) development of co-operatives;
> (iii) village industries;
> (iv) elementary education, specially provision of school building for local communities;
> (v) rural water supply and the programme of minimum rural amenities, including construction of approach roads linking each village to the nearest road or rail-head; and
> (vi) works programmes for the fuller utilisation of manpower resources in rural areas.
>
> Although efforts were made in several States to prepare block plans specially in agriculture, in the main, the plans to States have been prepared independently of local plans. The inference to be drawn from this is that much more effort will be needed before local plans can become a distinctive stage in the initial preparation of a Five Year Plan. In the present context of the Third Plan as formulated, what is important is the local plans should be worked out as a means for the more effective implementation of the State plan."

Within the general framework of the district plan, the block plan, is intended to include all social and economic activities undertaken within the block which call for (a) planning initiated locally at the block of village levels, and (b) coordination with the plans of various departments which are implemented within the block. The following are the principal types of activities which will fall within the block plan:

(i) items in the schematic budget of the community development block according to the stage reached;
(ii) items included in the budgets of different departments which can be executed through the block organisation;
(iii) works undertaken by the local community or beneficiaries in accordance with the obligations laid down by law;
(iv) works involving unskilled and semi-skilled labour undertaken in the block; and
(v) other activities undertaken in the block or by the block organisation with a view to securing greater contribution from local communities in respect of development schemes in different fields."

Since the ideas regarding local plans and planning from below contemplated in the Second and Third Five Years Plans did not meet with practical success, the *Fourth Five Year Plan* underlined the need for strengthening the planning machinery in the District.

It is expected that the planning apparatus at the State and the district level will be strengthened. This can most appropriately be done at the district level through Panchayati Raj organisations. Such a development should lead to formulation of plans closely related to the preference of the people and to the physical conditions of the area, and better coordinated and synchronised implementation. Also, with more active popular participation resources raising for local plans should prove easier and a proper appreciation of national objectives and policies can be induced among local communities.

In September 1969, the Planning Commission under the leadership of the late Prof. D.R. Gadgil developed a set of detailed guidelines for the formulation of District Plans which it issued to various States.

The Fifth Five Year Plan reflects the feeling that the expectations from the Panchayati Raj institutions as planning agencies were not fulfilled and a need was felt for setting u specialised planning organisations.

"It is generally desirable that the agriculture, animal husbandr and fisheries hierarchies in the State are controlled from th field to the State level by the department. At the same time, suitable coordination machinery will have to be built up at th district and block to liaise with the sister departments and th local bodies for coordinated action in the field. Where Zill Parishads have taken intensive interest in agriculture, it i desirable to utilize this powerful weapon to control th agricultural hierarchy in the district with technical supervisio from the technical expertise at the State level.

What is needed is an organisation which, whilst having th hierarchical frame for the technical and service disciplines i the structure, provides for the close working together of th disciplines at various levels upto the shop floor in multi-disciplined programme. Such a structure can b developed and maintained only by a single authority in contro of the whole orgainsation who has got the administrative an the financial power to order, to delegate authority. It is therefore, proposed that in the area development schemes o the nature of Command Area Development, an Drought-Prone Area Schemes and any such similar scheme which may be worked in the tribal or backward areas, an Are Development Authority is constituted by the Governmen which has got administrative and financial powers dul seconded to it by Government and which controls the staff o all the disciplines which are important for the fiel programmes. This authority must also be enabled to liaise a their level with the credit institutions and seek commitment and undertake risks. The authority must also be able to emplo agencies to perform the custom services required in the area o undertake such services themselves. Such an Authority can b invested with a corporate character. In the command area o the 55 major irrigation projects taken for special developmen during the Fifth Plan, and the drought prone area district included in the Fifth Plan, the authority must be constitute before the programme is launched in the area.

> The District Planning organisation is too general to meet the detailed needs of the varied and complex agricultural programmes. It is, therefore, proposed that there should be a separate Planning, Monitoring and Evaluation Cell in each district for the Agricultural Plan alone and the Cell should be suitably staffed with not only technical specialists but also economists and statisticians. This Unit will be linked to a Planning, Monitoring and Evaluation Cell at the State headquarters."

At the same time, apart from setting up specialised agencies for planning and development, the Fifth Five Year Plan also contemplated the strengthening of Panchayati Raj Institutions. Integrated Rural Development (IRD) would be possible only through cooperation and participation of the people. This could be secured by strengthening the Panchayti Raj institutions at various levels. It would be necessary on this context to review the size and viability of Gram Panchayats, whether the Panchayat Samiti or Zilla Parishad could be the best agencies for carrying out these programmes and what specific programmes the Panchayat Samiti or Zilla Parishad could and should administer. It would be desirable that the panchayats are entrusted with the implementation of specific programmes. Efforts will have to be made to attract institutional finance for augmenting the resouces of Panchayatti Raj bodies. In any scheme of strengthening the panchayats, it is essential to lay down norms and criteria of viable panchayats. Such criteria for viable panchayats in terms of area, population etc. would be considered and laid down.

The *Sixth Five Year Plan* (1980-85) has underlined the necessity of making arrangements for horizontal linkages at the block level. It states that at the District level the task of planning and implementation of development programmes is acquiring greater complexity. It suggests that the District administration should be strengthened by the appointment of District Development Officers who should have complete responsibility with respect to development work and should enjoy the same rank and status as the District Magistrate/Collector. The DDO must have professional competence and his continuity should not be disturbed during the plan period if found effective and dedicated. The process of democratic decentralisation will be strengthened and Panchayati Raj institutions will be involved in planning and extension of Integrated Rural Development Programme (IRDP) and National Rural Employment Programme (NREP) and will play a prominent role in district and Block level planning and planning of Minimum Needs Programme in their area of operation.

In spite of the importance accorded to the local planning, decentralised planning or for planning from below in successive plan documents in India the actual performance in respect of preparation of local plans has not been satisfactory. During the Second Five Year Plan an attempt was made to prepare village plans first and then out of the village plans to prepare taluka or block plans and out of the taluka or block plans to evolve a district plan which in turn would be the basis of State plan and the national plan as a whole. This approach, however, never succeeded and indeed was hardly given even a proper trial. What came out of the exercise were long lists of requirements at the village level without any possibility of getting any adequate financial resources to meet these requirements.

The reasons for the failure of this exercise are apparent. The village *per se*, as an individual unit is hardly able unit for planning and development. Prof. John P. Lewis, the American economist described this preoccupation with village planning as mere 'villagism' which must be considered to be inconsistent with any rational or viable planning. Planning cannot attempt to provide self-sufficiency for every village. Planning must have a broader perspective and cannot be contained within the narrow confines of the single village economy. Planning has to be a general and comprehensive process for a much larger area if not the nation at least the state or the region. Village, therefore, must find a place in the overall process of economic developement of the region. In this process some small villages may even disappear. There can, therefore, be no successful micro-planning at the village level at all. The economic fortune of the village is linked with a much bigger macro plan.

If the village could not be the unit of horizontal planning then what other area could be? After the advent of community Development Programme in 1953 it was advocated that the block consisting of about a hundred villages should be the unit of planning and development. The block budget consisting in the initial year of the Community Development Programme of some Rs. 15 lakhs with allocation for various sectors such as agriculture, animal husbandry, irrigation, social education, youth development, rural industries, co-operative developement etc. provided nucleus for planning at the block level. It was expected that these resources would be supplemented by the dapartmental funds and public contributions. So much for the resources side. As regards the requirements, the block development programme began with a surveys a block plan of requirements was to be chalked out. This exercise of horizontal planning at the block level was carried out during the first ten years of Community Development Programme. This experience, however, showed that the idea of block as a unit for planning and developement had not completely materialised. The developement activity of the block level was confined, in the main, to the block budget. Even the plans for other departments were not supplemented with it. After the expiry of ten years of the period of community development programme even the block budget disappeared. The Panchayat Samitis and the elected rural local self-government institutions at the block level were not able to raise any material rosources to substantially augment the development plans at the block level, and thus after the expiry to block period, the block organisation was left with limited number of schemes implemented by Government at the block level.

The concept of block as the unit of planning and development was also related to the structure of the Panchayati Raj institutions. In the beginning when the block was chosen as a unit of planning and develpment, the idea was that of the three tier local self-government institutions or Panchayati Raj institutions, at the district, block and village levels. Panchayat Samitis at the Block Level should be the most crucial agency for local planning. However, later on when in the States of Maharashtra and Gujarat, District was chosen as a more viable unit for planning and development, the Zilla Parishad emerged as the most important local development agency. The development plans at the district level were, therefore, attempted in all those States where Zilla Parished was the most effective unit. Zilla Parished had more resources, more competent technical staff and therefore had greater strength to attempt planning for development. However, the nature of planning attempted at the district level by the Zilla Parishad was on the same lines as that attempted by the Panchayat Samitis at the block level. It is true that the local sector at the Zilla Parishad level attempted to cover a much larger spectrum of schemes of developement but even then mere combination of schemes within the budget of the Zilla Parishad and the allocations of the State Government at the district level could not be considered to be an adequato concept of horizontal planning at the district level.

The unsatisfactory nature of the district planning has been recognised and thought has been given by economists, planners and administrators to this subject.

One of India's leading economists, the late Prof. D.R. Gadgil gave a good deal of thought to this subject and delivered a lecture under R.R. Kale Memorial Lectures on the subject of District Planning. Under his guidance a District Development Plan was being prepared for Wardha District. In evolving this plan, Prof. D.R. Gadgil worked out certain concepts regarding the framework of the district plan. He identified four principal components which must be part of the district plan viz.,

(i) Development of natural resources of the district;
(ii) Development of infrastructure facilities;
(iii) Development of productive employment in the field of agriculture and industry; and
(iv) Development of the growth centres in the economy.

However, formulation of a horizontal district plan on such a basis would require adequate collection of data, interpretation of this data and formulation of concrete and feasible plans, programmes and schemes for the various components of the plan.

The district plan is a horizontal plan. It is, therefore, one form of 'Spatial Planning'. District plan formulated as a by product of vartical plan is not the same thing as the 'Spatial Plan'. The 'Spatial Plan' concentrates on the analysis of the local resources and works out measures for the maximum utilisation of these resouces, for the production of needed goods and services. 'Spatial planning' combines geographical, demographical and economic approach to the subject of planning.

In working out the spatial plan, the economists divide the aggregate economy into regions which are homogeneous in characteristics – natural, physical, sociological, economic etc. Thus river valley areas, or urban rural areas under the influence of a city centre or a tribal area are examples of the earmarking of special areas from the point of view of spatial planning. The working of Tennesy Valley Authority under David Lilienthal has provided a pioneering example of spatial planning. In India also, in the Fifth

Five Year Plan, 55 areas under the major irrigation projects have been selected for command area development. The major irrigation projects in this country create substantial irrigation potential but its utilisation was somewhat tardy in the absence of integrated irrigation development plans. The concept is, therefore, now accepted that an integrated area development plan must be prepared for the command area. Such integrated command area irrigation development plans will include a series of inter-connected items like the construction of canals, distributories, water courses and field channels and drops, levelling and reshaping of land, drainage facilities, agriculture extension, training of farmers in irrigation development, prescription of an appropriate cropping pattern, supply of agricultural inputs, rural communication, marketing, storage, processing and town and country planning in the developing area. The irrigation development plan has necessarily to be evolved with the cooperative and conjoint efforts of the various departments such as PWD, Agriculture, Cooperation, Revenue, Development etc.

Another example of such a regional planning is the Drought Prone Area Programme (DPAP). Some 70 districts in India are in the rain-shadow area and are prone to scarcity and famine. The old approach of extension and remission of land revenue, grant of *tagai* or *takavi* and supply of foodgrains at concessional rates is no longer found adequate from the point of view of the objective of providing permanent insurance to these areas from the effect of drought. A programme has, therefore, been contemplated to restore ecological balance in these drought prone areas by the development of soil and water resources in such a manner as to provide permanent insurance to these areas from the onset of drought.

A programme of this sort would include the identification of drought prone area, identification of water shed areas within this dry zone, an intensive attempt in these watershed areas to conserve water and moisture and protect soil through minor irrigation, afforestation including planting wind breakers, soil conservation, pasture development etc. and developing subsidiary occupations which are suitable for such dry zone like animal husbandry, sheep rearing, sericulture, fishery, horticulture, etc. The drought prone areas may run accross several districts.

A third example of horizontal planning is special programmes for areas along the western ghats which not only extend to several districts within the State but also over several States of Maharashtra,

Karnataka and Kerala. Such horizontal plans for natural regions would be receiving increasing attention in the years to come and would form part of local planning.

Horizontal planning could exist not only for special areas with special physical characteristics like agro-climatic conditions and homogeneity of soil and water resources but would also exist for special groups of population who need special attention because of their neglect in the past.

The leading example of such planning is the project for small farmers and marginal farmers and agricultural labourers. Special development agencies in the shape of registered societies have been established for formulation and execution of such projects in selected districts. These agencies prepare horizontal plans of an integrated sort for dealing with special problems of small and marginal farmers. The programme for the small farmers include their enrolment as members of cooperative societies, giving them short-term, medium-term and long-term loans, subsidising 25 per cent of the loan, providing common projects like a common irrigation well, common fencing or custom service centre and providing supplementary occupations like horticulture and dairy.

The concept of spatial planning is also linked with another approach evolved by the demographers viz., that of identification of growth centres. The basic idea behind this is that development does not take place without some pattern and the pattern is that of a series of linked centres of growth, each growth centre providing a stimulus to the surrounding areas. An approach to planning which does not take into account the growth centres is bound to lose sight of the dynamics of economic development. The concept of growth centre has received a great deal of attention from the regional scientists and considerable literature has grown. An attempt has also been made to apply these concepts of regional and district planning and to evolve concrete plans which make these growth centres the nodal points in the framework of planning. This approach envisages a planning hierarchy of growth centres. Four hierarchies of centres have been distinguished:

(i) Central Village providing minimum facilities to a cluster of villages like primary school or a health dispensary etc.;

(ii) A service centre providing all basic facilities like a market centre;

(iii) A growth point providing market-cum-service centre to 5-10 service centres of category. Such a growth point can provide scope for industrial growth;

(iv) A growth centre serving 5-10 growth points with a number of secondary and tertiary activities and specialised facilities. These growth centres provide consumer products both finished and semi-finished of the lower hierarchy. They have a large number of processing activities. Planning for such growth centres would ensure best use of investment in a region since –

(a) it concentrates resources in growth centres in such a manner as to have the maximum spread effect.

(b) they take into account linkages as between the growth centres.

A pilot research project in growth centres was implemented as a centrally-sponsored scheme during Fourth Plan period. The scheme envisaged the setting up of a total of 20 research and investigation cells to evolve techniques and the methodology for the development of emerging and potential growth centres by providing social and economic overheads in delineated areas in terms of a carefully prepared inventory of local needs.

A major development in recent years has been the increasing role that the banks have been called to play in the socio-economic development in our country, particularly, after the nationalisation of the major banks. Before the introduction of social control and nationalisation, the banks were mostly concentrating in the urban or metropolitan centres and their involvement in the planning was somewhat limited. Now the concept of planning includes a combination of budgetory resources with banking resources. Banks are expected to provide institutional finance for economic development, even in the rural areas. The responsibility for such planning for area development through banking resources has been entrusted to the 'lead bank' which is expected to survey the area and identify the opportunities for economic development. Such credit plans by the banking institutions have to be inextricably and intimately related to the economic plan.

The credit plan would provide extension of available banking funds to priority projects and needy individuals – be they small and marginal farmers or artisans. Such a credit plan must consist of economically viable projects since all banking funds have to be used on a commercial basis and have to be repaid with interest by the beneficiaries. There is a provision for lending by commercial banks at concessional rate of interest under the DIR (Differential Interest Rate) scheme. Opportunities for use of banking funds would depend to a great extent on the facility made available by the general development plan in terms of technical assistance, organisational support and infrastructure facilities made available by the departmental and other agencies.

Even before the entry of the commercial banks in rural development, the cooperatve banks were actively engaged in rural development. While the Primary Cooperative Credit Societies supported by the District Cooperative Central Banks provided short term credit for seasonal agricultural operations, the Primary Land Development Banks supported by the Apex Bank and the Agricultural Refinance and Development Corporation (ARDC) provided long-term credit needed for investment in land in forms such as Soil Conservation, Land Reclamation, Land levelling, Well digging, Horticulture etc. The ARDC and the International Development Association of the World Bank which supported these projects insisted on P.L.D. Banks adopting the area development approach.

The District Plans will have to integrate all these different approaches and components within an overall framework. The following components will, therefore, have to find a place in an integrated district plan:

(i) Identification and full utilisation of natural resources;
(ii) Full utilisation of the man-power resources;
(iii) Building institutions and organisations and using them for maximum productive effort;
(iv) Mobilisation of efforts of financial institutions for mapping up savings and their productive investment;
(v) Building up of infrastructure facilities;
(vi) Identification and development of growth centres;
(vii) Provision of minimum needs of social consumption; and
(viii) Plan for technological development in rural areas.

Each of these elements would have to be incorporated in the

area or horizontal development planning for a District.

Identification and Utilisation of Natural Resources

The natural resources of an area consist of the soil, water, minerals, forests and marine products. In the words of Dr. Swaminathan "Of the highest priority is more intensive work on the preparation of an integrated inventory of land, water, mineral and other natural resources, area by area, and the development of scientific plans for land and water use". A district can conveniently be divided into planning units in accordance with the prepondant characteristics of the natural resources available and for each of such units plans could be devised. Apart from the extent and degree of certainty of rainfall, the water resources available through the rivers and underground water resources will have to be taken into account.

The soils also differ in their characteristics making it possible for different crops to be grown. The black soils are useful for cotton and perhaps wheat and sunflower while the red and light soils are good enough for millets and groundnut specially if the land is somewhat sandy. Thanks to the discovery of new varieties of short duration seeds, it has been possible to grow more than one crop in a season. It is possible also to scientifically analyse the soils by taking soil samples. Cropping pattern and planning will have therefore to be made on the basis of a comprehensive understanding of soil, water and climatic conditions.

Just as an understanding of the soil resources is possible through soil survey and soil testing, the availability of groundwater resources can also be assessed by groundwater survey which is now being carried out comprehensively throughout the districts. The district plan, therefore, must take into account the groundwater resources and programme the number of wells-dug or bore—that could be attempted on the basis of this water potential. In areas under major irrigation projects conjunctive use of water resources can be attempted.

Planning for agriculture will have to be supplemented by planning for dairy, horticulture, sericulture, fishery and other supplementary occupation.

In all coastal areas and with large rivers and ponds, fishery development planning has to be attempted.

Development planning whether for agriculture, animal

husbandry or fishery has far reaching backward and forward effects. Thus, for planning for agriculture development, it is necessary to plan for a series of inputs like seeds, fertilisers, pesticides, implements etc. Planning for animal husbandry also requires supply of pedigree animals, artificial insemination centres, forage and feed for animals, veterinary services etc. Similarly, planning for production must be accompanied by planning for marketing, storage and processing or else planning for production may face frustration.

It has been recently realised that planning for agriculture must be planning for different groups who participate in farming viz., large farmers, small farmers, marginal farmers, tenants and agricultural labourers. It is first of all necessary to identify the farmers belonging to the various groups and pay special attention to the small and marginal farmers and agricultural labourers. To the latter, both for supply of inputs and sale of output as well as for productive operations special facilities on a group basis have to be provided. They have to be brought into the main stream of production.

The above analysis will show that though agriculture falls within the primary sector of the economy, planning for agriculture and allied productive occupations involves planning for secondary and tertiary sectors in addition to planning for the primary sector. Agriculture development necessarily involves development of marketing and agro-processing industries, development of industry and supplying of agricultural inputs and development of social enterprises like marketing and distribution, banking and insurance.

Full Utilisation of the Man-power Resources

If land is the first factor of production, labour is the second. Labour, i.e. manpower resources need to be developed and utilised in a planned manner so as to get the maximum productive benefit from the skills and talents of the manpower. All the strength, the skill and the capacities of the manpower have to be fully utilised. It is true that most of the manpower is engaged in agriculture and possesses only traditional skills. But different agriculturists do specialise in different types of operations, there are some groups who specialise in horticulture, others, in sheep and dairy development etc. All these traditional skills have to be identified and will have to be further developed through a number of short duration training courses in modern technology, educational tours of the farmers and agriculturists.

At the same time skills of artisans will have also to be identified so as to make use of them for modernising agriculture. Agriculture requires new implements. These are not available but could be locally manufactured. The traditional artisans should be trained, organised and financed for production and supply of such agricultural implements like improved bullock-cart, or seed and fertiliser drill, or the various implements required for re-shaping of land in irrigation command areas.

The technology of the future will demand collective action by farmers in a village or a watershed for efficient adoption of modern techniques of collective management so as to make the maximum use of man-power and natural resources.

Education has been spread in rural areas and more and more educated man-power is now being available in the countryside. Educated man seems out of place in rural surrounding. However, if properly motivated and re-oriented, he could be an asset in the rural areas. If the farmers' sons are educated in agriculture or veterinary services they could be direct agents of change. Development plans may make use of the services of such educated men and after giving them necessary training put them into use in implementing the programmes of rural development. Unfortunately, there is less of advanced agriculture education, and more of general higher education which is being availed of by the farmers' sons. But even here, the farmers' sons though qualified with general degrees may work to build up rural institutions such as agricultural workshops, co-operative societies, tractor and distribution centres etc. rather than jostle for clerical posts in the cities. We must make full use of the knowledge of the available talents of the rural people. It has to be borne in mind that the industrial revolution was ushered in Great Britain not through the efforts of modern scientists but through the innovation of machinists and artisans.

Building Institutions and Organisations and Using them for Maximum Productive Effort

The entire development process may be looked upon as the end product of the efforts of individuals and institutions. A network of institutions is needed to initiate support to the development process. In the process of local planning the institutions which are to play a prominent role are the following:

(a) At the village level, the village Panchayat, Primary Co-operative Society or the newly set up Farmers' Service Society and auxiliary institutions like the Youth and Womens Clubs etc.;
(b) At the tehsil/block level, the tehsil/block development board, land-development bank, branches of commercial banks, taluka agricultural produce marketing society, the Agricultural Produce marketing Society (ADMS) etc; and
(c) At the district level, the Zilla Parishad, or District Development Council, District/Central Cooperative Bank, Commercial Banks etc.

Each of these institutions has a definite role to play and must prepare a development plan for its own area of its activity. Thus the Village Panchayat, the Tehsil Development Board and the Zilla Parishad or the District Development Council have to produce general development plan while the co-operative and the commercial banks have to prepare credit plans. The marketing society and the Agricultural Produce Marketing Committees have to produce marketing plans. Finally, Youth and Womens institutions and similar other institutions may prepare their plans limited to their purposes.

In addition for the city and town areas the corporations or the municipal councils have to produce plans for their areas and where there is the linkage effect, an integrated town and country plan must also be prepared.

Mobilisation of Efforts of Financial Institutions for Mopping up Savings and their Productive Investment

The role of credit plans as complementary to the economic plan and the planning to be undertaken by the co-operative and banking institutions has been mentioned earlier. The co-operative credit institutions sometimes look upon themselves as mere lending institutions, channellising the credit reimbursed by the higher credit institutions reaching right up to the level of the RBI and the ARC. The commercial banks work only in limited area around their centre. As a result no attempt is made to assess the income generation in the local economy and the savings of the local community. The banking institutions must make an attempt to mop up savings that could be generated in the rural economy which in turn could be recycled through investment for the development of the economy. Such a complete circulation process consisting of income generation, savings, investment and further generation of income has yet not been attempted for the rural economy, by the banking institutions, though it is a vital part of an integrated horizontal plan.

Building up of Infrastructure Facilities

Development of agriculture, industry, marketing, processing and financing of an area is not possible without the infrastructure of roads and electricity.

Road plan consisting of the national and state highway, inter-village communication and village roads must be prepared and implemented in a phased manner. In the absence of such an integrated planning it is seen that roads are taken and left half-way with stacks of metal lying unused. Another example is that even large villages surrounding a marketing centre remain unconnected by proper communication. Irrigation development is not possible without ayacut roads. Transport is rightly considered to be the crucial factor in the development of the economy. The green revolution in the Punjab is attributed not only to the productive effort but also to the existence of a good network of rural communication.

Rural electrification is crucial for agriculture development, industrial development and improvement of the style of rural life. While some areas have been fully covered through rural electrification many others are in much inferior position. Regional and local planning should bring out such regional disparities and correct them.

Identification and Developement of Growth Centres

The concept of hierarchy of centres has been discussed earlier. The nodal points in the rural economy consist of city and town marketing centres which many a times coincide with the taluka headquarters but would also include other municipal towns and large villages in the areas. A forward looking plan should be prepared for each of the centre so that they provide the focus of the development of the area around such centres.

Provision of Minimum Needs of Social Consumption

All the items dealt with so far, have aimed at the development of resources of the local economy. As these resources develop, they would automatically facilitate availability of goods and services and would provide gainful employment However, in addition to the individual consumption of goods and services there are certain items which are of the nature of social consumption and which have to be provided through general development plans. These items of social consumption include drinking water facilities, schools and health centres. These have vastly expanded in recent years and it is time to cover the areas which have been left out in the past.

Plan for Technological Development in Rural Areas

The scientists have realised that the research in science and technology should not be carried merely on an all India basis but it is high time that the research is undertaken at the local level.

All these eight components must form necessary part of the local development plan. But these are complementary components. Each component no doubt must be developed as an item in its own right, but each must also be integrated with the other components. For example, development of natural and man-power resources would require infrastructure facilities and various other services and hence the plan for the development of natural resouces and manpower resources must develop along with the plan for infrastructure facilities. In all aspects of integrated development, institutions like Panchayat and Co-operatives, have to play a crucial role.

Such horizontal district plans cannot be formulated without certain degree of expertise in the technology of planning. It was felt that it would be difficult for a busy administrator like the Deputy Commissioner/Collector under continuous pressure of day-to-day work to find adequate time necessary for formulation of such a plan.

Attention was, therefore, given to the strengthening of the District machinery of planning by the appointment of the District Planning Officers and training them suitably in the techniques of district planning.

The person appointed as a district planner must combine within himself both academic and administrative talent. This is not easy to obtain.

Though the concepts of an integrated plan for local areas as analysed, have not been unknown, we have yet to suceed in preparing an integrated development plan. We have to make continuous effort to get over the weakness in the planning mechanism, which have taken many forms. A lot of statistical Jata are generated but it is not always up to date and even when it is available it is not assimilated and linked up with design of development, because of the lack of capacity in the use of statistics in an intelligent and meaningful manner for development planning. There are District Statistical Officers at the District and Taluka level but they are engaged in the routine tasks of compilation of the data and sending it to their headquarters. They should be trained and motivated to use the data for local plan. The statistician must make himself useful to the administrator and the planner. But the planner and the administrator must have also the capacity to use the data. Apart from the officials like the Deputy Commissioner, the District Planning Officer and the District Statistical Officer, the other participants in the district planning machinery viz., Panchayats and Co-operative Institutions, have never taken interest in a rigorous process of local planning. Indeed, this indifference to local planning has to be found in the local community itself. The district headquarters have a number of educational institutions and competent people, students and teachers, natural scientists, social socientists and social workers, but unfortunately very few have taken interest in the development process and planning of their area. Thus the administrative machinery and the local society have not been as keen about the local horizontal planning or spatial planning as they ought to have been. They have to come together on the planning forum and combine their intellectual power and thinking faculties with their intimate knowledge of local area and community to formulate scientific development plans.

14

INTEGRATED PLANNING FOR URBAN SETTLEMENTS

Of late, there has been a clearer realisation in India that not only has the urbanisation gone apace, especially after the attainment of independence, but in the years to come, urbanisation is bound to be an inexorable process. The statistics reveal that while at the beginning of the century about 10 per cent of the country's population was urbanised, it has reached the level of 25 per cent by 1981. A very rapid and significant change in the rural-urban mix has taken place after independence and perhaps this process of urbanisation might go on at an accelerated pace during the years to come.

It is often stated that urbanisation is an inevitable concomitant of economic development. In support of this is cited the case of United Kingdom, which was the first country to become "the workshop of the world" – the first to start the process of modern economic development and which has now reached a stage where 75 per cent of its population lives in urban areas. Imagine what would happen, if this proportion is attained in this country's population mix.

In spite of this trend towards urbanisation, historically noted to accompany economic development, the city planners noticing their plans over taken by population growth often talk-perhaps in defence of their plans of "unintended growth" of population. But the population does not exist for the planners – the planners exist for the population, its growth and spatial distribution.

Why Indended Growth?

Mobility of population whether for earning livelihood or for better job opportunities is a sign of positive economic growth. And if the population of the country intends to migrate further to urban areas over the years, then all that remains for the bureaucrats and the planners to do is to take note of this tendency and to deal with it and not invent the concept of "unintended growth". We can not take an ostrich like attitude and say that we will not deal with this problems because it is a problem of unintended growth.

It is not only sufficient to take note of the growing tendency of urbanisation but also its character which differs significantly from the similar tendencies observed elsewhere in the developed countries. The main difference is that while, in the developed countries, it is the industrialization which preceded urbanisation, in India, it is not necessarily so and urbanization has preceded economic development. And this is because of the fact, that growing pressure of population on agricultural land has reached a point of saturation to such an extent, that vast masses of people living in India's 5,75,000 villages in the countryside are without any ostensible means of livelihood, without any means of life support whether in the form of land or other assets and in utter desperation, inexorably, relentlessly driven from india's villages towards a few metropolises.

Lack of Cultivable Land and Growth of Employment

In this context, we often talk of the "push" effect and the "pull" effect. Now what is operating in India is not so much the "pull" effect. And this "push" effect is bound to continue. A decade ago, the country's cultivable land had reached its saturation level to the extent of 167 million hactares. During the two agricultural census counts of 1970-71 and 1975-76, there was no increase whatsoever in the cultivable land. In one initial period of development for 10 to 15 years i.e. till 1967, there was "extensive cultivation" but now we have reached *cul de sac.* No more agricultural land is available in most of the States. Nor is there any development adequate in the field of subsidiary occupations and rural industrialisation. Hence there is bound to be an enormous increase in unemployed population in the countryside which is bound to rush in greater and greater streams to India's cities which are destined to be flooded with large influx of population. This is the historical tendency which is bound to operate with increasing force in the years to come. The question before us is how are we going to face with the problem.

Spill-over of Urban Poverty

The phenomenon taking place in the country is the relentless immigration of people without a wherewithal of living from rural India to India's towns and cities. While this tendency is going on, corresponding possibilities of employment opportunities and infrastructural facilities are not becoming available to the cities.

The character of migrating population to the cities has also to be noted here. It is the poorest without any basis who are coming to the cities. Prof. Dandekar and Rath brought out in their historic study on India's poverty that urban poverty is really the spill-over of rural poverty, in the shape of migration to the cities. And these migrants from rural areas are looked upon as "unwelcome guests". In Bombay, one rainy day, these "unwelcome guests" who brought about the "unintended growth" in population, were sought to be sent away to where they had come from, because they had no business to be in Bombay. This act showed that these administrators did not realise that the poor residents who had made their improvised dwellings on the pavements of Bombay streets come in Bombay precisely because the nation has nothing to offer to them at places where they had come from! So these planners acted as only city planners but not national planners, had blinkers and did not understand the problem at all. The subject, therefore, had to be considered in the context of totality of economic development in this country. We have urbanisation without corresponding economic development. We have urbanisation in the shape of the spill-over of rural unemployment and poverty, and therefore, our problems of urbanisation are far more acute than they were in the West.

Problems of Traffic and Transport World Wide Phenomenon

The character of cities in India and in fact, in most developing countries, is far worse than in the developed countries. The horrible shanties and slums and the traffic snarls which are endemic to the cities of Asia and Africa, are not to be found in the cities of the developed countries. The traffic snarls of Lagos the capital of

Nigeria are notorious. Similar are the snarls in city like Manila, where reaching the city from the airport is a very slow process. Experiences in both the cities remind me of traffic snarls in Calcutta where every time I travelled from the city centre to the airport specially in the afternoon hours, I wondered whether I would get out of the trap and reach the airport on time. The problems of urbanisation in our cities are really far more intractable than the problems in the cities of developed countries. Tokyo's population is more than 10 million, one-tenth of Japan lives in Tokyo. But one can't have these the experience of being caught of in a kind of traffic trap experienced on the roads of Calcutta and Lagos. Neither in New York nor in Pairs, nor in London nor in Tokyo, they have the kind of problems that we find in India's cities.

Although there are historic difference in the process of urbanisation in developing countries as distinguished from the developed countries, in tackling the problems of urbanisation. We should not hesitate to learn from the western cities or the Japanese cities. We should not say that our situation is different and, therefore, we have nothing to learn. If a city of the size of Tokyo could be managed without the problems of snarls and slums and intolerable burden on infrastructure including transport, then why not try and learn from that experience? The spectacles which are so common in our cities – people hanging all the time from the locals in Bombay or travelling on the top of the trains in the city of Ahmedabad and Delhi, or the chronic overcrowding of buses causing a great deal of hazard in Calcutta and also in Delhi, are indicative of an intolerable situation and show that we have reached the breaking point in urbanisation.

How to Deal with the Problem?

There are two ways of dealing with the problems of pressure on transportation and other infrastructural facilities in urban areas. The two approaches are (i) reducing the demand for, and (ii) increasing the supply of transport and other facilities. One can reduce the demand first by not allowing cities to grow beyond a point of accommodation i.e. they should not be allowed to grow beyond what may be called the "outer limit". The definition of such an outer limit should be a matter of national urban policy.

The nation has some kind of national urban policy in terms of promoting the development of small and medium towns and retarding the growth of metropolitan cities. The scheme for promoting the development of small and medium towns has been introduced in the Sixth Five Year Plan. But this is only an aspect of a national urban policy. Indeed what is involved is not just a national urban policy but a national economic policy, so that there is a deliberate dispersal of economic and administrative activities away from a few metropolitan centres. This policy does not seem to have emerged throughout the 30 years of planning in this country.

Complementarity of Spatial and Sectoral Development Plan

The Indian planners have been so much pre-occupied with the development *per se* or with sectoral development that the spatial aspects of development, seem to have been comparatively overlooked, if not utterly neglected. The time has come for us to recommend to the planners that complementary to the sectoral development plans in this country, we should have a spatial development plan which must delineate the design of development, in terms of the location of economic and administrative activities keeping in view the environmental aspects of overcrowding and over-congestion in urban centres. No isolated schemes of small or medium town development will make any impression, no urban policy *per se* will mean anything, without a total re-orientation in spatial terms of planning for development in this country. It is a matter of disappointment that in spite of hydra handed monsters which our metropolitan centres have become, we do not seem to have opened our mind to the situation to ask for and formulate development plan which will clearly bring out the spatial character of planning in this country. The imperative and most immediate need is for working out fully the spatial dimensions of planning and then to bring out a comprehensive spatial development plan as a document complementary to the sectoral development plan which has been brought out over the years by the Planning Commission.

Urban Policy – Macro-and Micro-Planning

Urbanisation policy or spatial policy is a matter of macro-planning and macro-management. It must be supplemented by micro-planning and macro-management for each urban settlement. To have an ideal approach, we should conceive of a micro-plan for a city which will reduce to the minimum, the pressure on transportation and other infrastructural facilities. Ideally speaking commutation should be reduced to a minimum. It is absurd that every one flocks to Bombay for daily employment from Virar 40 miles in the north or from Kalyan another 40 miles from the South and even from Poona people have started going regularly for employment. This kind of situation is a horror. Ideally speaking, we must have a situation where our cities are neighbourhood districts with employment and residence being close to each other. How nice it would be, if one gets up in the morning, spends some time with family and just 10 or 15 minutes before the appointed time, walks down to his place of work. This is an ideal because we think, the ideal is an impossibility. But ideals move the world and ideals alone could guide to right action. And, therefore, we must see why this cannot happen.

Integrated Spatial Structuring in Zonal Planning

In the spatial structuring of the city planning, we must have industrial zones where both the factories and the housing for the workers are together. We must have an administrative zone where both the offices and the workers in the offices stay in the same locality and we must have in each of the zones essential infrastruetural facilities, like education and entertainment. Now why cann't this be done ? It is true that the cities have already grown and we are not starting from scratch. But every city should have a deliberate policy of creating neighbourhood zones within the city. And if one really starts such a plan, even an imaginary one, and if all of us agree that such things should happen, then step by step, gradually we may not reach the ideal, but we will at least get away from the horrible reality. And this is really what I would like to suggest. This may be called an integrated approach or a systematic approach.

Once the idea of neighbourhood zones is accepted, the details could be worked out and things would start moving in the right direction. Going in right direction is extremely important in public affairs. Often we don't go in the right direction. In Delhi cinemas/theatres are dipersed and Delhi authorities can take credit for this considering what is happening in Bangalore where the Majestic circle and the Kampegauda road there are already so many cinema/theatres that one gets the impression, as if centralisation of cinema is a city policy. It is beyond anybody's comprehension why all licenses for cinemas have been concentrated on the Majestic circle and the Kampegauda road. Such mistakes take place in every field and these need to be prevented by adopting the neighbourhood planning approach. The present imbalances in city infrastructure could be countermanned by the kind of an idealistic development plan for the city suggested above. Part of this micro-plan is the development of transport facilities.

Transport and Planing the Neighbourhood for Human Enjoyment

Our transport system is variably a jumble of partly traditional modes of transport and partly modern mechanised mass transport system . "Centuries moving together", is a reality in most of the Indian cities. In the city of Calcutta even today, there are human rickshaws. The best mode of transport is, of course, walking. How nice it would be if our cities are so arranged that the commutation distance and time are almost zero. The head of the family can go on foot to the office or factory, the children to the schools and colleges and the house wife to the shop. But if distances cannot be covered on foot, then let us at least do every thing on a cycle. Ivan Illich strongly pleaded for changing the mechanised transport of the western cities into cycle transport in order to avoid pollution and traffic congestion. He has pointed that in fact, in the city of New York one can reach one's destination quicker on a cycle than in a car or in a taxi. This would be true in the case of many of our cities as well.

Jawahar Lal Nehru was very fond of saying that we have reached the cycle age. But if the commutation is beyond a certain limit, neither the human leg nor human rickshaw nor the cycle is of any use and then one has to think of mass-transport, like the bus or the local train or the intermediate means of transport called the street car or a tram which was ended in Bombay a few years ago as an obsolete mode of transport. But in Delhi, the authorities are thinking of bringing it back. One can think of new modes of transport but what about the existing transport? Is it working efficiently? This is the most important question to be asked to those in charge of the local Bus transport serving in our cities. In most cities except perhaps Bombay, bus transport is not working efficiently and the authorities concerned must give attention to see that it works efficiently. Bombay and Madras City Bus transport are rightly considered to be far more efficient than the Calcutta or the Delhi Bus transport. Can't Calcutta or Delhi bus transport systems be brought to Bombay Standards? Attention must be given to an efficient road transport before we think of new kinds of other transport possibilities though the circular railway or other kinds of local train services.

Integrated Transport Network

In consonance with an integrated outlook on urbanisation, there is a need for an integrated outlook on transport keeping in view the traditional transport, the mass transport and the intermediate transport. Intermediate transport is found particularly appropriate to developing countries such as the mechanised *rickshaws* in India and the Jeepnees in the capital city of Philippines-Metromanila. Jeepnees are war time jeeps converted into a convenient system of transportation. The jeepnees have a body which is very colourful with six horses on the engine bonnet at the front and colourful designs on both sides accommodating six persons on each side and three in front. In all 15 passengers are transported in each Jeepnee. Barring the fact that it makes a lot of noise and also occupies a lot of road space, it is a very ingenious device of transport which could be recommended for cities in this country because it is a passenger intensive mode of transport. We may, therefore, introduce these innovations of appropriate technology. The buses and the railways as mass-transport, the intermediate technology transport and the traditional modes of transport—constitute together a mix of transport network which has to be developed in an integrated fashion.

In such an integrated planning of the possibilities of transport systems of segregation, of traffic by different modes should be taken into account. These, to my mind, have not received the necessary attention in our country. In Copenhagen I was delighted to go walking along the narrow winding shopping street. It is a delight to do shopping there because there is no honking of the car or any other nuisance on the way. We don't know why we don't have such walking roads here. We should have some roads which are open only for the cyclists and not for the trucks. We should have others which are only for the pedestrians and only the main roads should be available for mechanised transport moving briskly. It does not move briskly here at all, because indiscipline is proverbial in India.

Transportation Education, Acculturation and Urbanisation

In Singapore, if the light green ends and if the traffic starts moving, there is no question of crossing the road because it will reduce the man to smithereens. But in India no matter, what the traffic signals are, pedestrians go on. Therefore, mechanised transport which ought to be quick is not quick, and inefficiency and indiscipline pervades every where. In fact, discipline must go along with urbanisation. But we have a peculiar urbanisation pattern in our country, where urbanisation goes with rural behaviour. Hence the question before the planners is that they must deal not only with the physical aspects of transport, but also with citizen education. We have done pretty little to educate the citizens in the imperatives of city transport. With our chronic indiscipline and unsocial behaviour which has already taken a turn from a difficult situation to a desperate situation, our transport which is already stretched to its limits, has become chaotic. Here again there are glaring contrasts in citizen behaviour. Bombay has queues, but in Delhi, the traffic behaviour is utterly rowdy and rural in behaviour and it is not characteristic of a city at all. There are no queues and no urbanity in Delhi. Urban behaviour must be urbane. A sustained educational campaign should be undertaken to change the behaviour of the citizens of urban areas which is consistent with the demands and requirements of both the urban economy and the urban civilization.

Also the cities must be totally free from through transport. All highways should bye-pass town and cities. The national road transport moving through towns and cities is an abomination and must cease to exist forthwith. Often financial constraints are mentioned as a pretext for not providing the bye-passes. Those who plead for economy, should realise that by holding up the national transport, the loss incurred by the economy is much more than the money spent on bye-passes. The towns and cities must be made totally free from the pressure of across the nation transport movement. The latter must take place speedily, briskly on roads without interruption of any sort.

Conclusion

To sum up, what required, first, is a macro national spatial plan deliberately aimed at the dispersal of economic and administrative activities away from the cities and towns, and second, supplementing this macro-plan by a micro-plan for India's cities and towns which will be an integrated plan of neighbourhood, of transportation and of citizens education. Formulation and implementation of this requires some kind of a watch group for each city and town which will be monitoring the implementation of the plan. The group should continuously see what is happening to the city development. Once a slum comes, it is difficult to remove, but its emergence could be prevented. And, therefore, what is required, is a continuous watching group. The watch group must have an efficient information system. There must be a continuous system of assimilation of information. Whilst the city problems are becoming fearful, and fraught with such serious consequences for the citizens of the country, everywhere there is dominance of partisan attitude and fragmented outlook. There is a multiplicity of organisation each looking at it's own problems but nobody is looking in an integrated manner and that is because the control brain is lacking. There is a need of a brain power for every city. A planning intelligence and information system must be developed for every city which should slowly check the disastrous tendencies manifested in cities and put development on the right tracks. If this happens, may be in another 20 years, Indian cities may be better places to live in than what they are today.

15

MAN POWER AND EMPLOYMENT PLANNING AT NATIONAL AND STATE LEVELS

Man power and employment planning has not received as much attention in our system of planning as is necessary. This is because our planning methodology is mainly oriented towards the financial size of the Plan and the allocation of financial resources to different sectors. Financial allocation of resources is linked with the physical targets of production though the link is sometimes tenuous and is adversely affected by price escalation and rising capital output ratio. Though employment generation is one of the objectives of planning and though there are specific schemes for employment generation, employment and man power planning appears to be more like an after thought than the central focus of Plan. In a country like India endowed with abundant man power resources not lacking in intelligence or skill, there seems to be a case for greater attention to employment and man power planning in the country. The human being is both the means and the end of planning and mobilisation of human resources and increasing their productivity may well hold the key to successful planning in our country.

The man power planning has three aspects, the macro aspects, the sectoral aspects and the area aspects. At macro level we are concerned with the demographic aspects of our planning—the increase in population, its composition specially with reference to the ratio of working population to total population, the occupational distribution, the spread of education and the sociological aspects. The goal would be to provide gainful employment opportunities to all the working population at the highest level of productivity. This goal can be accomplished in two ways, firstly by promoting the potential capability of man power through education, training and health and nutrition programmes and secondly by utilising the productive capabilities of human resources to optimum use in all sectors of economic development.

The sectoral planning would consist of specific task of man power development in the primary, secondary and tertiary sectors. In each sector there is scope for wage employment as well as self-employment and schemes and programmes have to be devised for full promotion of self-employment and wage employment. It is to be noted that wage employment can be only a small proportion of the total employment and therefore self-employment needs the maximum attention. In the rural sector apart from the development of agriculture and subsidiary occupations there are special schemes like integrated rural development programmes and various self-employment programmes specifically related to poverty alleviation. In the field of industry, modern industry seems to provide little scope for employment opportunities as compared with the small and cottage industries. Unfortunately the cottage industries are suffering a set back and therefore decentralised industrial development needs a great deal of attention.

Finally, the service sector seems to be growing comparatively at a faster phase. While the service sector is bound to grow with the on set of process of economic development, its disproportionate growth might well prove an unproductive burden of the economy.

The man power planning at a national level can be in the broadest term. But each State and indeed each district has its own special features regarding man power and employment planning. A State can be divided in separate regions like the hill area, the desert area, the drought prone area or the irrigated area or dry farm area. All these would need specific attention in terms of employment generation. At district level our planning exercises have not made much progress. District planning needs much greater attention and in district planning, man power planning should also find its place. The district man power utilisation councils have been set up and it would be their main task to attempt man power and employment planning in every district.

16

PROJECT MANAGEMENT*

In this age of productivity, if there is one subject which deserves special attention, it is that of Project Management. Every project represents investment of a chunk of scarce resources of a country for the production of goods and services. It is imperative that this investment takes place in an optimum manner. In other words, that project should be selected, which for a given input of resources would bring in maximum social return. Unfortunately, project management very often leaves very much to be desired with the result the projects are either wrongly conceived or located or their implementation delayed, resulting in cost escalation. The cost of such faulty project management has to be paid by the poor country which can hardly afford to do so. The key to raising national productivity is scientific and competent project management.

In the wake of planning for economic development in the developing countries and more especially with the entry of the World Bank and its associates and other financing agencies such as Asian Development Bank and the International Fund for Agricultural Development, the "project approach" to agricultural development has become extremely important, since all their aid to agriculture is almost exclusively in the form of project lending. No developing country can hope to receive international aid for economic development without developing the competence and capability of preparing sound and viable bankable projects. Taking a cue from the international lending agencies, those within the country such as the Finance Corporation and the development banks have also started

---

*Book Review—*Investment Projects in Agriculture* by McDonald P. Benjamin, Longman Group Limited, 1981, pp. xxiii + 297 £ 29.95 p.

insisting on DPRs from governmental and other agencies, asking for loanable funds for development projects. In response to these requirements, the governments have also encouraged participation of their employees in training courses focused on project management. The Economic Development Institute of the World Bank as well as national training institutions like the Indian Institute of Public Administration have organised over the years several courses on project management. Textbooks and manuals on project management have also come up, some of them under the auspices of the United Nations agencies.

However, economic projects cover a wide spectrum of development. Many of the project manuals are mainly focused on industrial projects. In view of the fact that a large part of international aid goes to support agricultural projects, there was a felt need for a specialised publication on investment in agricultural projects, apart from the fact that technology, organisation and management of agricultural projects materially differ from that of industrial projects. A lending agency like IFAD looks into social significance of agricultural projects e.g. whether the project takes care of the distributive aspects of economic development and whether the project redounds to the benefit of small and marginal farmers.

The author has been on deputation from the FAO to the IFAD and has been able to bring to bear his first hand experience in handling investment projects in agriculture on his treatment of the subject. As a result, the presentation is not only simple and lucid but bears the imprint of the reality of the situation in the developing countries – a task greatly facilitated by the rich case material that is included in the book.

The book is divided into four parts – the first part dealing with the project cycle, project types and rural development; the second, with principles of project formulation; the third, with project design and analysis and the fourth presenting three extensive case studies from three developing countries with different socio-economic situtations.

In the first part, the author deals with the main recognized steps in project cycle viz. project concept, identification, preparation, appraisal, negotiations and supervision. The agricultural projects include various sub-sectors such as crop developemnt, fisheries, forestry and live-stook development, institutional and support services such as agricultural credit, research extension, marketing and storage. The main components of an agricultural project are: farm development, irrigation, agro-industries, roads, electrification, housing, health and education facilities.

The author has proposed the following functional classification of agricultural projects:

Technological innovations, broadening the physical resouce base, improved status of disadvantaged groups, improved post-harvest handling and distribution and institution building.

While such a classification is all right conceptually, in reality several projects would be a combination of the different functions as is borne out by the case studies included in the book.

A project has also a three levels of intervention the planning level which is at the headquarters, the project management level and finally the farm level itself. In agricultural projects, the third level would be the most important.

In the identification of projects it is necessary to work out the basis for allocation of resouces between these various sectors. Once the sub-sector of project area is identified, it becomes necessary to delineate the main outlines of the project, including development potential of the project, project objectives, design, concept and the rationale, scale of the project, cost and benefits estimates, organisation and management structure, the constraints, physical and institutional features of the projects, and the framework of the Government policies.

If the identification stage establishes sufficient justification to proceed to the next stage of project preparation, then the need arises for the preparation of a feasibility study. This should include analysis of physical features, economic base, social aspects, infrastructure, institutional support, disbursement schedule and production, marketing and financial results.

The third stage is that of project appraisal by the lending agencies with a view to finding out whether major assumptions on project formulation are correct and realistic and the project has a satisfactory economic rate of return. At the stage of appraisal, the procedures relating to ecquiring of goods and services are also clearly spelt out. The end result of long negotiations is the drawing up of a set of loan documents, such as credit agreement, guarantee agreement, subsidiary loan agreement and other convenants. Several assurances and conditions of effectiveness are also mentioned in these documents.

While the execution of a project is the responsibility of the borrower, the lending institutions review the progress report required of the borrowers. Supervision also entails field visits.

In the second part of the book, the author has stated some principles of project design which should mainly help in the avoidance of major observed defects in project preparation. These principles are: firstly the project should have clearly specified objectives. This is not easy where economic or production considerations have to be balanced against social considerations. Secondly, there should be flexibility in project concept and design, facilitating continuous review and modifications as the project is implemented. Thirdly, there should be firm commitments of Government to the project. Fourthly, the project must provide sufficient package of incentives to generate the required response on the part of beneficiaries. Fifthly there should be in-built control system to monitor the project and to fill up the gap between the established goals and the actual performances. Only this would ensure that there would be no time and cost overruns. Sixthly, the decision to undertake a project should be based on evaluation of all the identifiable project costs and not just direct costs. Lastly, it is desirable that the project should have the quality of replicability.

In the third part dealing with project design and analysis, the author has discussed the technical basis, the institutional features, organisatonal and management features, financial and commercial aspects and economic and social aspects of the project. In agriculutral projects, the technical aspects include soil analysis, drainage, agricultural production practices, quality of seeds, pest control, fertilizer application, irrigation arrangements etc. Among the institutional features, the project has to take note of the work of the administrative system *vis-a-vis* public bodies such as public authorities, corporations, cooperatives, banking and credit institutions, and farmer organisations.

Organisational and management arrangements for the project are the most difficult to formulate. Often a choice has to be made between strengthening the existing organisation or building up a new institution. Whatever be the organisation, there should be clear-cut line of authority and responsibility and opportunity for beneficiary participation. Modern management techniques like management by objectives and management information system and proper coordination mechanism should constitute some of the essential features.

The project must be financially viable. In other words, it must give sufficient return for debt servicing. The project must have a financing plan. That project alternative must be selected where the benefit-cost ratio is the most favourable. Here a distinction must be made between economic rate of return and financial rate of return. The economic aspects refer to the quantitative expression of the project impact on the national economy. A project must maximise the contribution to the country's gross national product. For arriving at a value of the output of a product, shadow price might have to be preferred to correct the distortions occasioned by the market imperfections established in respect of items like labour and foreign exchange. The first is overvalued and the second is under valued. Risk should be taken note of by the application of senstivity test. The commercial aspects of a project include supply of inputs, marketing and distribution of the output. Amongst the social aspects are environmental considerations, that is, the impact of project on the ecology and effect of the project on the distribution as indicated by gini coefficients. In the ultimate analysis, social considerations relating to a single project form a logical part of a country's overall development strategy.

Three extensive case studies form the last and the fourth part of the project. The Nigerian case study relates to an integrated agricultural development project with components which include provision of physical infrastructure like roads and production components such as agricultural credit and seed multiplication and social components such as water for drinking. The project aims at more even food supply for Nigerian urban population and expanding commerical livestock industry. The Indonesian seed project aims at bringing fruits of genetic research undertaken by International Rice Research Institute in the Philippines to the masses of Indonesian rice growers. The project was a package of programmes comprising use of hybrid variety of seeds, intensive use of fertiliser, pest and disease control, improved irrigation practices and water management and improved cultivation techniques. Though the project could not be described as being financially attractive in its early years, the overall economic benefits were such as to warrant the undertaking of the project. The project aimed at increased rice production so necessary for Indonesia's rising population.

The third case study relates to agricultural credit in Jamaica. Jamaican agriculture remained stragnant for several years, especially the peasants subsistence sector as distinguished from the estate sector. The main element of the project was the establishment of agricultural development plans for five pilot areas. The programme related to beef, dairying, citrus, coconuts, and banana farming. The project envisaged a lending programme for all these components.

PART III

MANAGEMENT OF DEVELOPMENT

17

MANAGEMENT IN DEVELOPMENT : World Bank Prescriptions

Every year, the World Bank takes up a central theme for a comprehensive treatment in the second part of its World Development Report. Part II of the report of the World Bank for the year 1983 has been focused on "Management in Development". This shows that the World Bank, after years of preoccupation with the provision of resources for development has, at long last, realised that development has not just a matter of provision of resources but is rather one of achieving greater efficiency in the use of resources and this depends on a number of things which are included in the concept of good economic management. Efficient use of resources has emerged as a factor of critical importance in view of the fact that despite increased investment, the annual growth rate in developing countries has not increased because of the decline in growth per unit of investment between 1960 and 1970. Many factors are responsible for this decline in productivity like recession in world trade and ageing industry but it is the deficiency in economic management that needs to be singled out as a matter where improvements could be effected. Even, in order to maintain the growth rate, the developing countries will have to make proper use of resources.

Good management implies firstly the adoption of macro economic policies conducive to greater efficiency, and secondly improving the quality of public sector institutions responsible for execution of policies and for providing public services.

The most important aspect of macropolicy is related to the extent to which government should go on expanding its role and assuming increasing responsibilities for economic management. While administrative capacity is limited, and is the scarcest of the resources in the developing countries, governments are assuming increasing responsibilities for development.

The role of the state is expanding. The ratio of pubic revenue and expenditure to GDP has tended to grow in most countries. The public expenditure includes spending by Central, State and local authorities as well as semi-autonomous agencies and State-owned enterprises. It also includes subsidies and transfer payments owing to social security, medical care and unemployment benefit, as well as public consumption through public services. The State-owned enterprises have been established in the field of large-scale manufacturing and mining, public utilities like water, electricity and gas and finance. They are also involved in production and marketing of foodstuffs. They dominate the domestic credit market. As a consequence governments find themselves overstretched. The growing number of development projects and programmes has strained the managerial capacity of government in all development countries. The World Bank report suggests that the governments specially in developing countries should shed some of the burden of the administration through decentralisation and *greater use of market and prices.*

The expansion of public sector has stretched the managerial capacity of governments to a point where it has resulted in serious inefficiency. Pruning of what has become unmanageable will strengthen the effectiveness of the state in discharging its core responsibilities.

The World Bank has always been enamoured of the magic of the market. No wonder the report suggests that macro-economic policy should try to support *competitive markets* because they economise on scarce administrative resources by decentralising the task of handling information and decision-making. The World Bank Report, therefore, advocates less reliance on control and more on market incentive to achieve socio-economic objectives. To buttress its case for the use of the market mechanism, the World Bank Report has prominently cited the example of Socialist China. Even in China, it says in search of efficiency, the administrative reforms aim at greater decentralisation of productive and investment decisions to enterprises and farms. The other examples are the Republic of Korea and Brazil. The former liberalised imports and increased competitive pressure on industry. The way to establish competitive market is to dismantle the structure of administrative controls. The report approvingly cites the example of Brazil, which has set up the Ministry of Debureaucratization to cut down regulation and licenscing. On the other hand, to illustrate how controls come in the way of progress it has drawn attention to the procedure of industrial licensing in India which was so tortuous that it took 2 to 3 years for approval of a project.

The State as Regulator

Economic output would be maximised where resources are allocated by a method that takes full account of their relative scarcity and cost. Countries use a combination of market and intervention for the allocation of resources. Markets are not always perfect and do not handle public goods. Government interventions in the market, therefore, becomes necessary to alleviate market failures. But they, in turn, create bureaucratic failures like import licences giving rise to windfall gains, subsidized credit leading to capital intensive industry, minimum wages leading to reduced demand for labour, low consumer prices discouraging production, and regulations leading to large black markets.

Pricing for Efficiency

Government interventions in pursuit of some social or economic objectives lead to *price distortions* which contribute significantly to lower domestic saving and lower output per unit of investment leading to slower growth. Distortions exceed when the prices of goods and services as well as capital and labour do not correctly reflect their scarcity. Controls are introduced in response to scarcities of foreign exchange, capital or of certain goods but they continue even after their rationale has vanished. Trade restrictions contribute to over-valued exchange rates and discriminate against export. On the other hand, the system of protection gives windfall gains to those who obtain import licences and unequal distribution of income. The interest rate charged to borrowers and paid to savers even fall short of the inflation rate, leading to negative rate of interest. If the price of labour is increased by unrealistic wage rates and social security, capital intensive investment is encourged. Most countries fail to recover the full cost of infrastructural services leading to overuse of capital and energy intensive services. Inflation is the worst form of distortion. The year of 1970 was a decade of double digit inflation, leading to unproductive investment in real estate, durable consumer goods and foreign currency deposits.

Price distortions result in loss of efficiency. High price distortions lead to low domestic savings and low value added per unit of investment.

Thus ineffective exchange rate, faulty monetary and fiscal policy, excessive borrowing, inflation, abrupt policy changes, in-appropriate trade policies, poor investment analysis leading to low yielding investment, investment delays due to adopting an investment programme exceeding the financial and managerial capacity, underutilisation of capacity, shortage of materials and skilled staff, unrealistic infrastructure and market distortions, inadequate maintenance of assets – these are some of the important *aspects of mismanagement* of macro policy. Less reliance on control, and more on market incentive to achieve social and economic objectives would reduce the administrative burden.

Countrywise skill shortages, poor personnel management and weak administrative structures and procedures also are responsible for inefficiency.

The State-owned enterprises are established for a variety of reasons. In theory, the public enterprises could be as efficient as private enterprises. The crucial question is 'How they are managed'? If they are managed as public bureaucracy with more attention to procedures than results, and if they are habituated to subsidies, incentive for efficient management so as to minimise cost could be eroded.

National Economic Management

Every government has a fundamental responsibility to establish a sound macro-economic policy framework, in which economic agents can function efficiently and which can provide adequate incentive for long-term growth. The macro-economic policy framework consist of a series of interlocking policies that affect all aspects of economic behaviour including fiscal, monetary, exchange rate, wage and trade policies and determine in the rate of domestic inflation, capital accumulation, resources utilisation, maintenance of balance of payment equilibrium, and the pace of economic develoment. The Finance Ministry are responsible for macro-economic policies through budget and supervision of central banking but they tend to be preoccupied with short-term questions of financial management and give inadequate attention to long-term development. The planning agencies are expected to be responsible for formulating comprehensive long-term development strategy. However, planning agencies have generally failed to fulfil the high hope placed in them in the 1950s and 1960s and have been limited to formulating public investment programmes.

The task of macro-economic management is to adjust established policies to changing domestic and international economic circumstances. Where realistic exchange rates are adopted, trade regimes liberalized, and interest rate allowed to increase in response to market conditions and prices stablished, there are significant improvements in export performance, industrial growth, and faster growth in GDP and employment.

Though traditionally Finance Ministries have played a prominent role in economic management in recent years the planning agencies have been established in most developing countries. A recent World Bank survey shows that 80 per cent of the 80 countries surveyed, have resorted to multi-year development plans and have prepared 200 plan decuments. But planning agencies have not lived up to expectations. In India, there was a plan holiday. In Yugoslavia, two successful plans were abandoned in the early 60s. In Africa, planners were excluded from decision-making. Thus, developing countries have increasingly been disillusioned about the performance of the Central Planning Agencies. Available analytical techniques have not found to be adequate to cope up with the complexity of economic change and produce plans that are up to date, and comprehensive. Investment planning based on input/output models have fallen foul of changing demand patterns. Similarly, manpower forecasting has been highly inaccurate. Also planners have tended to favour ambitious targets and big public sector projects. This has seldom produced efficient use of resources.

The World Bank Report has underlined the need for rationalization of policy framework, through monetary, fiscal and exchange rate policies which would ensure macro-economic stability, correct price distortion, and provide incentives. Academicians and businessmen should be involved in policy discussion. The policies have to be flexible and based on collection and analysis of information. They should provide guidelines to subject-matter ministries. Central agencies should analyse intersectoral linkages. Coordination can be promoted by entrusting it to a central authority with oversight of planning, budgeting and policy-making. The linkages between planning, budget and policy-making need to be strengthened. Complete picture of public sector financial position should be obtained and should be reflected in the budget. Core investment programme should be identified and protected from across the board cuts imposed by Finance Ministry. Greater emphasis should be put on value for money spent through public expenditure. There has to be reliable monititoring of current developments. Data such as agricultural statistics or country's financial position should be improved. Planning entails processing of large quantities of data. Accounting system and programme monitoring should be rationalized to handle the data.

Managing State-owned Enterprises

If sound macro-economic policies constitute one aspect of good management, the other is operational efficiency through sound management of enterprises, projects and programmes.

The efficiency of State Owned Enterprises (SOEs) leaves much to be desired. Even though the SOEs are engaged in earning activities such as petroleum and mining, their aggregate performance is often poor showing low and declining profitability in countries such as Turkey, Maxico and Senegal. As a result the SOEs are unable to generate internal resources.

The efficiency of a State-owned enterprise could be measured by the maximisation of profit if it functions in a competitive market and the managers have the operational autonomy. But very often the State owned enterprises operate in non-competitive markets and the managerial autonomy is abridged by government intervention. However, though the State owned enterprises have to work under special constraints, their efficiency can be greatly enhanced by setting clear and attainable objectives, holding management accountable for results, reducing undue interference and designing a framework of incentives. The efficiency of the State owned enterprises has suffered from conflicting objectives, insufficient autonomy, inadequate measures for judging performance, lack of incentives and bureaucratic rather than commercial management style. SOEs need develop better financial management, and a more careful inventory control but above all there has to be proper relationship between the SOE's and government. SOE's are frequently expected to subserve the goals of government policy. They are often used to generate employment. Where non-commercial goals are expected of the SOE's, they must be made specific and their costs and benefits calculated. SOE managers must be asked to document the financial effects of having been required to meet non-economic goals so that they cannot be made an excuse for poor performance.

The autonomy of the SOEs needs to be interbalanced by Central control because unless governments monitor the performance of the SOE's, their macro-economic management will be undermined. The system of control should be so designed that while management is held accountable for results, it is given powers to achieve them. A satisfactory balance has to be reached between independence and control.

Assessment of SOE's requires a regular flow of reliable information. A system of management audit should be instituted which requires the enterprises to establish basic information system to facilitate control procedures. Another management tool is the action plan.

Exposing SOEs to market competition is one simple and effective way to promote their efficiency. Another approach is to split large public monopolies into smaller competing units. A third is organising public pressures through consumers' councils.

Appropriate managerial incentives should be provided including non-pecuniary rewards in the shape of recognition, promotion and national honours. There should be penalities for poor performance and reward for good work.

The skills of public enterprise manager need to be closer to those of the private sector counterpart than that of the government bureaucrats. Due to shortage of managerial manpower there is a high rate of turnover. This has demaging effect. Continuity accounts for good performance. Management selection boards and management training are essential for recruitment and retention of efficient managerial perosonnel. There has to be long-term development strategy for training of middle management and workers. There must be strong and stable technical and middle management team. There has to be training on the job. Training and incentive should form part of a single package.

Whereas a public sector enterprise does not perform properly, the remedy may be, as in Japan, that of privatisation. But this is not always easy to achieve for political or other reasons.

Project and Programme Management

The World Bank Report classifies programmes and projects into two categories – physical and people-oriented. As regard managing physical development, reliance can be placed on well-defined technology. But in respect of these targets it is necessary to avoid capital intensive construction. Also, realistic financial provision must be made for the construction of the projects.

While attention is paid to efficient project construction maintenance operations are often neglected. Maintenance can be improved by cutting down the red tape and ensuring prompt payment to construction workers in charge of maintenance or by entrusting to private companies or using local communities to maintain local roads. Where maintenance work is decentralised, it should be accompanied by complementary grant of resources and proper central monitoring system.

Management techniques appropriate for physical projects differ significantly from those relevant in people centred development projects such as small farmer agriculture, family planning, health and nutrition and housing. Less is known about how to bring about change in values and behaviour which are crucial to people centred development and whose success depends on stimulating people's voluntary participation, in particular, involving the poorest.

Managing People-Centred Relations

People centred programmes are, therefore, hard to manage. They involve changing human behaviour patterns. They require knowledge about local communities and social skills in dealing with them. The growing sociological awareness has now enabled the understanding of the relative lack of success in the implementation of people centred programmes, the device of pilot project is often adopted because it helps "learning by doing". It enables the production of local plans in conjection with local people and development of links between bureaucracy and people. There are different ways involving the local community. One is the use of part-time professionals recruited from the local communities. The other is developing people's institutions such as Water Users' Association for irrigation development.

Managing the Public Service

Higher management standards require not only well established institutions but also experienced and well trained people. In the public service there is a often a shortage of professional and technical staff exacerbated by brain-drain. While the labour force is growing there is a severe shortage of skilled people. In many developing countries there is overstaffing at a lower grade existing with severe shortage of senior professional and technical people. Between 1950 and 1980 considerable attention has been paid to build training institutions and training public officials in developing countries. In Malaysia the number of people attending courses at INTAN the central training institute, has increased from 1000 in 1960 to 9000 in 1980. For the Indian Central Government the corresponding expansion has been from 1500 to 7000 only. Private companies like UNILEVER spend five per cent of their pay rolls on training. By contrast, most developing countries spend much less. For example, only 0.5 per cent by the Indian Central Government in 1968. Only one civil servant in five in India is likely to have some inservice training during his entire career. Training should be problem oriented and structurally related to career development plan. There has to be a training policy. There should be better use of existing training facilities.

Personnel policies must aim at meeting the need of public services. They should aim at building career development systems. The responsibility in personnel matters should be located in a centralised personnel agency. There has to be efficient information system in the field of personnel management. Public servants should have a clear idea of the career policies. Frequent shuffling of civil servants should be avoided. Salaries of all public servants should be regularly adjusted for changes in the cost of living. The salaries of the junior staff in many governments have been raised more quickly than those of senior civil servants thus eroding their incentives. Promotion and pay increases must be related to individual performance. There should be an objective system of performance appraisal.

Administrative Reforms

The administrative reforms should aim at radical changes in a few critical areas rather than attempting comprehensive reforms. Selective radicalism will achieve more than launching into wholesale administrative reforms. The reforms should aim at creating the managerial skill and institutions which are required to cope up with rising expectations of the people, population growth, and technical changes. There has to be growth in government capability. Persistence is fundamental to bureaucratic reform. The World Bank Report refers to some successful examples of administrative reforms. Administrative management agency in Japan has kept the work staff under contorl. In Brazil the Ministry of Debureaucratization has simplified work and reduced paper work. Thailand had a systematic and effective programme of reform conscentrating on a limited range of objectives. The administrative reforms may be based on two broad prinicples. First, reducing managerial burdens on a over-extended bureaucracy. Second, making bureaucracy more responsive.

The burden on bureaucracy can be reduced by rationalising economic management, improved central coordination and decentralising government activities. Economic performance could be improved if government intervenes less in the market.

In improving coordination top level committees are set-up leading to centralisation. Ministers are overstretched coordinating everything. Excessive coordination will not always improve effectiveness. The need for coordination is reduced by decentralisation of functions to the lower levels of government, public enterprises, local communities or the private sector. Decentralization may be either: (a) decentralisation from headquarters to branches, (b) devolution to autonomous units of government; and (c) delegation to regular bureaucratic structures like the public corporations or farmers' cooperatives. The revival of local government depends on vigorous action to raise local revenue. Decentralisation can also be in the form of privatisation or involvement of local communities in the execution of projects. Even in socialist economy of Hungary decentralisation was attempted with the economic decentralisation in agriculture in 1957. By 1973, the new economic mechanism on decentralised basis achieved its objectives by making prices the main instrument for decentralised decision-making. The national plans were implemented through economic regulators rather than physical controls. Thus, economic decentralisation has been used as the means to promote economic efficiency. In socialist countries the main thrust of decentralisation has been to increase the autonomy of enterprise.

Rationalisation of the policy framework, improving coordination and decentralisation need to be supported by increasing the accountability of the bureaucracy. Bureaucracy must be made accountable to the users. Officials must be made accountable to their superiors. Bureaucracy must give "value for money".

Public bureaucracy would be more effective if they paid less attention to form and more to sustance, less to preparation of grandiose plans and more to analysis of action needed to achieve government goals. Administrative reforms should be achieved through persistent but selective efforts step by step rather, than through major reforms which will be neutralised by entrenched interest. Institutional and administrative reforms require vision, tenacity and strong leadership.

Thus, administrative reforms should concentrate on strategic institutions and functions, while simultaneously keeping up pressure for gradual systemwise improvements. Reforms need not only careful planning but sustained implementation.

This brings us to the one factor crucial for managament efficiency and administrative reform viz. political will. Increasing efficiency depends on political commitment. Where political leaders are recognised for their integrity, vision and concern for welfare, these qualities are reflected in the performance of service but if corruption is rife in politics, there is demoralisation and degeneration in bureaucracy.

The World Bank has rendered a signal service by drawing pointed attention of the developing countries to one crucial prerequisite for sustained development in the next decade viz. higher efficiency in public administration. The items in the agenda of action include sound macro-economic politics, and better management of public enterprises, physical projects, people oriented programmes and public services. This requires administrative reforms supported by strong political will.

18

MANAGEMENT OF ECONOMIC DEVELOPMENT: New Horizons

Successful economic development requires sound 'planning craft' which covers the entire range of techniques of planning starting from the macro-planning, and going onto resources mobilization, intersectoral balances, policy framework, grass-root planning, project planning and assessment of plan performance.

During four decades of planning the country has gone through eight Five Year Plans with an *inter regnum* of three annual plans between the Third Plan and the Fourth Plan.

It is necessary to work out and assess the *balance-sheet of planning*, its successes as well as failures.

Planning was introduced in India with a view to providing richer, fuller and better life for the masses of people in our country. The Plan sought to harness natural resources with the application of science and technology which together with the mobilisation of manpower resources was expected to create an increasing stream of goods and services, increasing gross national product and higher standard of living for the masses of people.

To some extent these objectives have been realised. The successive Five Year Plans have laid the foundation of the economic infrastructure in the country, modernised agriculture, built up basic industries and diversified the economy.

However, the shortcomings of our Planning are also quite apparent. Though successive Five Year Plans contemplated a growth rate of more than five per cent, in actual practice it has been 3 per cent to 3.5 per cent. With a steady growth of population of more than two per cent, the average increase in per capita income has been in the neighbourhood of only 1.5 per cent. The aim explicitly stated in the First Plan of doubling the per capital income in 25 years was not fulfilled. More specifically, almost 50 per cent of the population has remained below the poverty line.

Therefore, it becomes imperative on the part of those engaged in planning to find out the causes of shortcomings and work out improvements in the planning craft which should ensure more effective planning.

Planning has to be a long-term national commitment and it has to go on without interruption. It has to embody a national concensus not affected by the changing complexions of Government. Unfortunately, there have been interruptions in the planning process which may have adversely affected the rhythm of planning and plan performance.

Planning is not a matter of mere abstract economic models. It has to enter into the warf and woof of day to day administration. Unfortunately, administration is often buffeted by expediencies which upset the apple cart of smooth and steady progress of planning.

Though plans do embody hopes and aspirations of people, they have to be *based on facts*. Often ambitious planning extends far beyond the resources available; with the result that projects and programmes suffer from lack of resources and do not get completed on time and yield dividend. Often a smaller plan fully completed on time would yield more dividend than a larger plan that does not get completed on time because of the constraint of resources.

We have accepted the concept of balanced planning in our country. This assumes that there will be development in all sectors in a complementary manner. However, intersectoral and material balances are often upset by recurring shortages of one input or another. If we desire that planning does not remain a concept but become a reality, we have to ensure that the excesses and shortages do not become a recurring phenomenon.

In a large country like India, Planning has to be *multi-level planning*, i.e. planning at National, State and local levels. However, we have not yet developed a mechanism of truly integrated planning at all levels. The concept of planning from below attempted during the Second Plan did not succeed. We have only disaggregated national plans into State plans and State plans into the district plans and latter into block and the village plans. National schemes are completed in terms of features with universal all India application. Often this comes up against the disparities of development in different State and parts of States. Time has, therefore, now come to look at the unique situation in different States and parts of the States and devise programmes which will precisely meet with the requirements of these areas. The strategy of agricultural development appropriate for Punjab which has witnessed the 'Green Revolution' may not be suitable in under-developed State like Assam or parts of Madhya Pradesh, where agricultural development is still at a rudimentary stage. More attention need to be paid to spatial planning. Though in 1969 the Planning Commission gave detailed guidelines on district planning, the concept of district planning has not taken a practical shape in most of the districts. The very sectorial and vertical approach of administration at national and State levels comes in the way of horizontal planning in every district which is specific to its own requirements.

Even though it has been well accepted for quite some time now that for planning to succeed, we must have technically feasible and economically viable projects, we still find that sound projects are not always available, leading to schedule slippage and cost overruns. Project planning and its linkup with macro planning needs closer attention.

Plan programmes often fail to reach the objectives and do not have necessary impact because they are seen in isolation and necessary linkages are not provided. Often there are leakages and benefits do not reach whom they are intended to reach. Field agencies must concentrate more on reaching the real objectives of the programme than to get lost the targets of inputs and output.

There has to be a continuous *monitoring* of plan projects and programmes. Organisations and policies have to be under continuous examination to see that plans go in the right direction.

Successful Five Year Plans have seen the rising tempo of investment but we have seen the disturbing phenomenon of rising capital-output ratio, with the result that efficiency of investment is falling. Smaller investment with greater efficiency will yield larger dividends than larger investment with smaller efficiency. We have to concentrate on efficiency of investment.

Over the last three decades of planning, the processes and procedures have not changed much. We seem to be going on beaten tracks. There is need for change. We must impart a new impetus to planning. We must introduce improvement in the light of experience—not only in India but also abroad. Comprehensive planning in the USSR, indicative planning in France and concensus planning based on sophisticated forecasting as Japan have lot to teach us. We must draw lessons from abroad and adopt them in our own system of planning.

First of all, the economist's concept of the planning is in terms of a consistent model of ends and means of aims and instruments. The scientist looks at planning in terms of building symbiotic relationship between science, technology and development. The administrator and manager's concept of planning is that of assemblage of viable programmes and projects capable of being implemented successfully. The statistician's concept of planning is in terms of a satisfactory information system at all stages of planning. But transcending all these concepts of planning is the basic concept that concerns the politician, the statesman and the people at large, Namely, the plan as an instrument of a historical process of political, economic and social transformation through an integrated framework of ideological, technological and institutional change.

One basic idea concerning planning, is the "integrity" of planning. If planning has to have any meaning and validity, then each of the partners, the politician, the economist, the technologist, the administrator and the statistician must have basic integrity in planning. Planning is a matter of both political choice and economic arithmetic, but before economic arithmetic comes the political choice. The choice as between different goals of planning is essentially a political choice. Choice between faster or slower is growth rate, between rate of growth and pattern of distribution, rural growth and urban growth have all elements of political choice. Before planning is undertaken, the politician may decide between one pattern of planning as against another, but once the choice has been made, the politician must have the integrity to clearly take responsibility for his choice and must have the courage to go to the people and tell them what is possible and what is not possible and what the plan intends to do or does not intend to do. Making certain political choice for those who have to do the exercises of planning but saying something quite different to the people would cast doubt on the credibility of the plan itself.

The integrity of economists again lies in clearly telling the political authority the logic of a consistent economic model and its imperatives in terms of limitation of achievable goals in relation to resources or in terms of instruments of planning. Similarly, is the integrity of the administrator and the manager. While the administrator is bound to carry out as best as possible programmes and projects in pursuit of political choice of planning, he also like the economist, should fearlessly state what can be implemented and what cannot be. Planning which is incapable of being implemented, can only prove counter-productive in the long run. Finally, it is the statistician's onus to provide data base for planning as well as information system for monitoring. He must see that under no circumstances are data doctored or statistics manipulated because in that case statistics may be worse than the lies and nobody would believe in them and the plans based on them. Once this basic integrity is ensured on all sides, attention could be concentrated on making planning more effective.

In constructing the model, the economist is faced with multiple goals of planning like higher rate of growth, equitable distribution both classwise and regionwise and maintenance of the equilibrium of the economic system. For fulfilling these goals the economist must devise instruments which are adequate, robust and efficient but in the present economic situation in India the economist is faced with increasing difficulties in devising instruments of planning. Instruments like taxation, exchange manipulation, price and wage regulations have become blunt while on the other hand, the resource constraint is getting more and more acute despite the increase in the rate of savings of nearly 20 per cent of GNP. Faced with these restrictions on the resources and instruments of planning, the economist must lay greater emphasis on the efficiency of investment. In recent years, the capital-output ratio is getting more and more adverse. Causes for this should be identified and steps taken for increasing the efficiency of investment. In agriculture with the zero per cent growth in land availability, increasing production would be possible only if there is a greater investment in irrigation and other agricultural inputs. Agriculture, therefore, has become a demanding sector. It demands increasing investment but these investments do not yield adequate returns because they are not effective. For Example, because of the defective water conveyance system tailenders do not get water and because of waterlogging, it is estimated that 25 per cent of area under sugarcane is waterlogged. What is important is, therefore, not how much is invested but how well invested. One of the reasons for less adequate return from investment is the failure in the maintenance of assets and replacement. Replacement and maintenance have been neglected and therefore it has become necessary to prepare a "maintenance plan" as complementary to the "development plan". Also there has been in recent years heavy expenditure on non-development items which needs to be curbed.

Planning is faced with another difficulty, namely, demand for more welfare programmes. Forty-five years ago, Nehru said that the present generation was sentenced to hard labour. People, therefore, put up with capital investment which did not yield immediate return, but now their purchasing power has been eroded as a result of inflation and they cannot afford to buy essential consumer goods though at the same time their expectations have increased. Hence States are going in for welfare projects such as employment guarantee schemes, old age pension, subsidised distribution of rice, mid-day school meal and so on. These demands are bound to increase and are bound to cut into investments in heavy investment sectors like power or irrigation. It is necessary to find out how these welfare programmes can also contribute to the creation of material assets as well as productive efficiency of the people and thereby contribute to higher production.

Administrator has a crucial role to play in increasing efficiency of investment. He has to see that programmes and projects are carefully identified, scientifically formulated, resolutely implemented, closely supervised and monitored and properly evaluated. The statistician has to come to the help by providing adequate database for plan formulation and for constructing a management information and monitoring system which is both simple and comprehensive and workable at various levels and in different departments.

Development is not just a question of investment but also of technology. Significant development in technology is possible only on the basis of scientific advances. At the same time, breakthrough in scientific laboratories is capable of application in the field only on the basis of a range of intermediate steps which are required for the transfer of technology from the laboratory to the field. Adequate resources have, therefore, to be provided for providing an innovative chain. Building up symbiotic relationship between science, technology and development should be accepted as a long-term national responsibility, as in Japan.

19

MONITORING OF PLAN IMPLEMENTATION

Planning is not an end in itself. It is a means to an end, and the end is the achievement of pre-determined goals. These goals, to start with, are couched in aggregate terms such as increasing gross national product and per capita income, the distribution of the gross national product in a more equitable manner and the provision of full employment opportunities. However, these aggregate national goals have to be split sector-wise and sub-sector-wise to arrive at various physical targets in terms of quantities of foodgrains, coal or steel or the wagons of cargo and number of passengers moved by the railways. Related to these physical targets are financial allocations. However, mere higher financial allocations do not result in physical achievements. There has to be the necessary organisation and personnel who could carry out these programmes making best use of financial resources to achieve maximum results. Every plan scheme or project must, therefore, take into account the organisational machinery through which plans and programmes will be implemented. A plan which takes care of the efficiency in implementation would be able to accomplish much more than what it seeks to do; that too at the least possible cost.

Unfortunately, Indian planning has been deficient in this respect all these year. The contemplated results are not accomplished in terms of the increase in the national product. While we have been aiming at a steady growth rate of five per cent through all our Five Year Plans, in reality it has been around three per cent. Also because of cost escalation and inflation, the physical plan has been generally smaller than the financial plan. Because of less than optimum efficiency in the implementation of plan programmes the capital-output ratio has shown a tendency to rise. All this underlines the importance of paying continuous attention of setting up a strong and efficient machinery for implementation of plan schemes and their constant monitoring and evaluation with a view to ensuring satisfactory result. These aspects have been sadly neglected in the past and immediate steps need to be taken up to improve the monitoring of implementation. The Prime Minister has taken keen interest in this and has asked the Planning Commission to undertake monitoring of plan implementation. This is undoubtedly a step in the right direction but the lead taken in this respect should not mean action only at the national level. Similar, and even more intensive action needs to be taken at all other levels. Indeed as we go nearer the fields, monitoring has to be all the more intensive. There should be close and continuous supervision over the actual implementation of plan programmes in the field and their periodic monitoring and evaluation.

The monitoring of implementation, however, is not as easy as it looks. In the past, monitoring has simply meant checking of expenditure. This is not only unsatisfactory but even counter-productive. Often it results in the rush of expenditure in the closing months of the financial year. What is required is monitoring and evaluation with reference to the real objectives of a project and the real objectives are not in either financial terms or even physical terms. The manner in which the results are obtained is equally important. If the results are accomplished by wrong means, there may be a temporary gain but a set-back in the long-run. For example, if the programmes of family welfare are implemented through coercion, targets regarding tubectomy or vasectomy may be accomplished. But use of coercive methods may create such a strong revulsion against the programmes that they may suffer a long-term set back. What is required is the need to educate the targets group and elicit their voluntary participation and cooperation. This aspect is important in respect of most of our programmes.

Thus, while data and statistics are important, evaluation and monitoring are not entirely a quantitative process. There is also a qualitative process involved. A satisfactory system of monitoring and evaluation should take care of the qualitative, no less than the quantitative aspects of the plan implementation.

Monitoring and evaluation ought to take care of the "ultimate", "penultimate" as well as "instrumental" targets and goals of every plan programme. The "ultimate targets" are the final objectives of a project or scheme in terms of output or generation of employment opportunities. The "penultimate targets" are one stage before the realisation of the ultimate targets. Thus, if the ultimate target is in terms of quantities of foodgrains produced, the "penultimate targets" may have to be in terms of distribution of seeds, fertilizers and insecticides or utilisation of irrigation potential. The "instrumental targets" have to be in terms of the means through which the penultimate and ultimate targets are accomplished. Thus, they may be in terms of the centres for the distribution of inputs, the personnel incharge of such centres, construction of wells and field channels necessary to create the irrigation potential, the field organisation required for discharging this work, etc. One of the defects of our planning is that while "ultimate targets" are fixed, "penultimate" and "instrumental targets" are left vague. The increasing of area under high yielding varieties of seeds is a penultimate goal. The realisation of this penultimate goal would be meaningless unless the spread of high yielding varieties results in higher production of foodgrains or other commercial crops. At a recent meeting of the Agriculture Production Commissioners, it was noticed that this had not actually happened. This happened because high yielding varieties of seeds had to be accompanied by increased supply of fertilizers and irrigation water. High Yielding Varieties (HYV) programme has to be a part of a package; and where the package is missing, realisation of goals in only one item does not show results. In some States the increase in agricultural productivity or production was not commensurate with increase in area under high yielding varieties. Plan implementation requires coordination without which programmes may go on in a lop-sided fashion and results would not be accomplished. Monitoring and evaluation, therefore, has to take note of the realisation of the ultimate goals or the ultimate impact of planning and cannot stop short of them and be confined to some instrumental action.

Plan programmes can broadly be divided into two components. The first relates to the activities where investment is concentrated and the second where it is dispersed. Irrigation and hydro-electric projects and establishment of plants and erection of building fall in the first category while such schemes relating to agriculture as agricultural extension, cooperative development or crop production would fall in the second category. The success of planning in the first component substantially depends on the organised machinery of

Government but the success of the schemes falling in the latter component depends as much on people's initiative as on machinery of Government. Indeed, in respect of these schemes, the main role of the machinery of Government is to motivate and activise millions of farmers on whose efforts depends the accomplishment of goals.

Monitoring and evaluation of activities falling in the first category is comparatively much easier than of those falling in the second category. In spite of this, surprisingly enough, evaluators have paid more attention to the latter than to the former. This balance needs to be set right. There has been a lot of schedule slippage in respect of several irrigation and hydro-electric projects and establishment of public enterprises resulting in considerable losses. An evaluation of these projects would have brought out the deficiencies. One of them might be dispersal of resources over too large a number of projects leading to the delayed completion of several projects. In a hurry to bring in too many projects in the ambit of planning, no more than token provisions are made in respect of several projects which then go on hibernating for any number of years. This is hardly a way of making optimum use of plan resources.

Expansion of the public sector has been an impórtant feature of planning in our country. But it is sad to reflect that massive investment in public sector enterprises has not yielded the necessary dividend. It is necessary to undertake comprehensive evaluation of the public sector enterprises in order to set right the deficiencies of the past.

Evaluation has to go deeper than doing mere cost benefit analysis. it must bring out latent as well as patent deficiencies in organisations, institutions and personnel so that these could be set right. For evaluation of this sort, it might well be necessary to follow the case study method to supplement the methods of collection of data en mass and their analysis.

While evaluation may require a specialised machinery monitoring has to be an in-built feature of the normal machinery of administration. For every important scheme or enterprise, there should be a Review and Monitoring Committee in every department or organisation of Government. On this Review Committee, there should be all persons connected with that particular scheme or enterprise. The Review Committee ought to meet periodically at regular intervals. It should have a regular management information system which would feed the Review Committee regularly in terms of what have been called the instrumental, penultimate and ultimate targets. The Review Committee ought to pin-point shortfalls or deficiencies whenever they occur and immediately set about rectifying these deficiencies before any further damage is done. An alert machinery for review and monitoring can save much wastage of resources and enable plan progress to be made on the right lines.

20

ADMINISTERED PRICES : A Factor in High-cost of Production

In an inflationary economy, costs and prices tend to move in tandem in a rising spiral. Rising prices push up cost and rising costs push up prices. In India, the inflationary era began during the Second World War. But even thereafter, it has continued unabated throughout the past three decades. The occasional reversal in the direction of low cost and prices has been a weak and a short-lived phenomenon.

The inflation during Second World War was induced by deficits due to mounting war expenditure. After the World War, though pressure of war expenditure ceased, ever-increasing expenditure on development during the successive Five Year Plans kept up the pressure and deficits became a chronic feature of the Indian fiscal system. The defence expenditure also mounted in the wake of wars with neighbouring countries and this further added fuel to the fire of inflation.

Some people have argued that inflation is an inevitable concomitant of development. However, if development expenditure is adequately productive, it cannot be inflationary. The inflow of goods and services, out of successfully completed development projects, would, over a period of time, absorb and neutralise the inflationary effect of development expenditure. It is only when development expenditure is not sufficiently productive that it poses a threat of inflationary spiral.

Quite a large part of development expenditure is on investment in the public sector which, according to the recent budgetary pronouncement, accounts for half of the development investment in the economy.

However, if the public sector enterprises are not able to meet their costs, there are only two waysout. One is to meet the public enterprises deficits with the budgetary resources. But when pressure of development on the Exchequer itself is very great, budget cannot bear the burden of deficits in the public sector. Indeed, the budget would expect the public sector to contribute sizeable resources. In such a situation, the only way in which the public sector enterprises can raise resources to pay their way is to raise the prices of their products.

Prices of products of the public sector enterprises are not determined in the market. They are administered prices. They are determined by Governmental authorities who are in a monopoly position to determine the prices.

The recent economic survey has drawn attention to increases in a number of administered prices, such as, coal, electricity and steel. Since these are basic inputs for the economy, hikes in prices of these trigger off a cost-push price spiral.

In recent years, the Government has raised the prices of a wide variety of public sector products with the aim of raising more revenue partly to meet the deficits of the public sector enterprises and partly for meeting its own rising expenditure. In 1980, the extra-budgetary levies came to Rs. 800 crores, while in 1981 they exceeded Rs. 1,000 crores. Last year, pre-budget hike in prices of petroleum products came to Rs. 800 crores, while the increase in railway fare and freights was of the order of Rs. 500 crores or more.

The most recent example of the hike in prices of critical inputs is that of coal. On 8th January, 1984, the Government announced a hike of 25 per cent in the price of coal. The hike was justified by huge deficits in the public sector coal industry. However, fears have been expressed that this would lead to a cascading effect in terms of rising costs of major consumers who would pass on the burden of increase to down-stream users. Power and steel would bear the brunt of coal price hike. There may also be an increase in freight cost as the Railways pass on the increase in coal prices to the consumers. Viability of steel industry to bear the hike may be even less. The Steel Authority of India, as it is, has been incurring loss of as much as one crore of rupees each day. Because of increase in coal prices, the SAIL may have to fix higher prices in order to prevent further deterioration in their financial position. Similarly, the fertilizer industry would be hard put due to increase in coal prices, without a corresponding rise in their selling price. According to the Planning Commission estimates, the impact of the 25 per cent hike in coal prices would be as under: Power, Rs.70 crores; Steel, Rs.34 crores; Railways, Rs.14 crores; and Fertilizers, Rs.6 crores. This would have a multiplier effect on pushing costs of the downstream users over a wide range.

The phenomenon of cost-push inflation due to rise in administered prices is not confined to the public sector alone. Important industries in the private sector and agricultural commodity prices also have administered prices which keep on increasing. Thus, last year, cement prices were increased by Rs. 52 per tone. The cement price hike was the consequence of the increase in the railway freights in the previous budget. Another example of administered price hike in respect of industries in non-governmental sector was 25 per cent increase in the price of sugar which followed as a result of repeated increase in the administered price of cane.

The recommendation for increasing minimum prices of several agricultural commodities by the Agricultural Prices Commission have also contributed to the cost-push inflation. Economists have pointed out that, though production of industrial crops may be price-elastic, the production in the agricultural economy as a whole is price-inelastic. If this is true, increase in agricultural prices on the recommendations of the Agricultural Prices Commission may not neutralise by increase in agricultural production.

The basis of the technique of fixing administered prices is such that it tends to go on pushing prices upward. The formula adopted by both the Agricultural Prices Commission and the Bureau of Industrial Costs and Prices is to add a reasonable margin over and above the existing costs. This formula leaves little scope for the examination of justifiability or otherwise of the existing cost level and the possibilities of economy. For example, in the case of coal, the hike has been justified on the ground that it was required to restore the coal industry in healthy state, (in fact, the coal Department wanted rise to be of the order of Rs. 210 per tone instead of Rs.183 per tone) to enable coal industry to meet the financial burden to the tune of Rs. 225 crores imposed on the coal industry by the Third Coal Wage Agreement and for additional investment. However, the fact remains that the record of coal industry during the post-nationalisation period has left much to be desired. Massive doses of investment in coal industry did not result in commensurate increase in production. Productivity in coal mines in India is comparatively low even with that in most of developing countries. There is vast unutilised capacity as well as surplus labour. Despite this, manpower employed in coal fields has increased in Coal India from 5.68 lakhs in 1966-67 to 6.4 lakhs in December 1972. The single largest element of cost of production of coal was salary wages which was almost 61 per cent of the total cost. The average coal-miner has no motivation and absenteeism is rampant, resulting in a loss of six million tonnes of aggregate production.

The authorities incharge of administered prices must, therefore, concentrate of making investment more efficient. Enterprises which are persistently inefficient should not be propped up by raising prices of their products at frequent intervals which unleashes all round cost escalations and serves as grist to the inflationary mill. The phenomenon of rising capital output ratio reflects, in the ultimate analysis, the low productivity of our enterprises. Sustained drive for improving productivity and efficiency is what the nation requires for accelerating development without allowing it to be overtaken or jeopardised by cost-push inflation.

21

TOWARDS A LOW-COST ECONOMY

Control on inflation has been an important goal of economic policy. The inflationary phenomena in India have been of both demand-pull and cost-push types. The fires of inflation have been fuelled, on the one hand, by rising public expenditure and consequent deficit financing and, on the other, by the persistent trend of rising administered prices leading to a high-cost economy. Control over inflation demands resolute action on both the fronts. Success on one front would open out possibilities of success on the other while failure on one would aggravate problems on the other.

An administered increase in the prices of products of public sector enterprises has a cascading effect on the cost structure of the entire economy. Hence control over these prices has a critical bearing on dealing with the phenomenon of cost-push inflation. Products prices of losing public enterprises have to be raised to reduce the budgetary burden in absorbing these losses. Raising prices of monopoly enterprises is an easier course of action. The alternative of reducing the cost to prevent losses is difficult. But it is wholesome for the strength and stability of the economy.

The second alternative requires a critical look at the cost component of crucial public enterprises. They fall into two broad groups-infrastructure enterprises, such as power, railways, ports, telecommunications and the Food Corporation of India (FCI), and basic industries, namely, coal, mines, steel and fertilisers. The disaggregation of the cost structure of these enterprises would enable identification of those components where economies are possible and on which attention and effort could be concentrated in the battle of cost reduction.

Power

The seeds of high-power tariff are sown during the construction phase itself due to time and cost overruns of many of the power projects. Construction of power projects on time and within estimated costs can significantly bring down the unit cost of electricity.

During the operating phase, a high Plant Load Factor (PLF) and saving in oil consumption are the key factors that can reduce the cost of generation. Another factor causing high-cost operation is surplus manpower. When, on completion of the construction of a project, manpower is retained rather than retrenched or deployed at new projects, surplus manpower results.

Railways

Since the Railways are labour-intensive, with staff constituting 55 per cent of the working expenses, attention must be focused on measures for improving staff productivity in terms of traffic units, both goods and passengers, moved per employee. A second set of measures relate to improving fuel-efficiency, since fuel represents 22 per cent of the working expenses of the Railways.

With progressive electrification, substantial economies in the energy bill can be accomplished. Introduction of modern high-power electric and diesel locomotives incorporating, the latest technology can also achieve the same objective. A third set of measures relate to use of better management techniques such as value engineering, inventory management and computerisation of freight operations.

A fourth set of measures relate to rationalisation, closing of uneconomic branch lines and of locosheds as steam locos are replaced by diesel and electric traction.

Ports

Like the Railways, ports are also labour-intensive. Expenditure on salaries and wages constitute nearly 50 per cent of the total cost – though it varies according to the degree of mechanisation of different ports. The expenditure is related to manning scale and gang strength. These were fixed three or four decades ago under various awards of the industrial tribunals under the Industrial Disputes Acts, when cargo handling operations were essentially manual based on less advanced technique.

Modern mechanised techniques need reduction in manning scales. But this is not possible without modifications of existing awards and settlements which requires consent of labour. The position of high-cost operations due to existing manning scales is worsened by the high degree of absenteism and consequent overtime payments. Ports can make contribution to low cost economy if highly organised port labour is persuaded to accept reduction of manning scales consistent with modern techniques of cargo handling.

Telecommunications

Telecommunications, too is a labour-intensive area, with the staff constituting 58 per cent of the total working expenses. In 1985-86, the number of employees per 1000 telephones was as high as 114. It could progressively be brought down to 75. Introduction of electronic equipment can improve staff productivity in terms of staff telephone ratio.

Food Corporation of India (FCI)

The Corporation has rendered yeoman service in procurement, supply and consumer distribution of foodgrains. But it has also been criticised as a 'White Elephant' in terms of costs of its operations. These could be reduced by a concerted effort to introduce the following measures – reduction of storage and transit looses; efficient management of surplus stocks; optimisation of freights, dehiring of uneconomic godowns; and closing down of non-viable purchase centres.

Coal

There is a considerable scope for improvement of output per man shift (OMS) which is 0.92 tonnes in India as compared with 16.85 tonnes in the US and 17.46 tonnes in Australia. Surplus labour force in depleted coal mines can be redeployed. Fresh recruitment has to be kept under control. Absenteeism has to be curbed.

The traditional one-man-one-job approach ought to be replaced by an all-men-all-jobs one. A second means of cost reduction is the adoption of systems approach in mechanisation equipment selection, standardisation, operation and maintenance, computerised information system and training. A third approach to cost reduction has to be in the area of material management through streamlining purchase procedures. A fourth measure should be reduction in electric energy and fuel consumption.

Mines

Capacity untilisation, energy conservation and labour productivity are the three main physical efficiency parameters which need to be tackled. Use of lithinum carbonate and modernisation of smelter can bring about a substantial reduction in power consumption in the aluminium industry. Metallurgical plants need to undertake de-bottlenecking programme to reduce costs.

Oil

In the field of oil exploration and production, physical efficiency can be improved by taking various measures for improving cycle speed such as deployment of light rigs and use of state of art technology. In the case of refineries constant efforts are needed to increase crude throughput, capacity utilisation and fuel-efficiency.

Steel

Substantial reduction in cost of production can be achieved by improvement in energy consumption and capacity utilisation. If the capacity utilisation is increased from 79 per cent to 95 per cent and energy consumption reduced from 10.8 G cal/tonne of steel to 9 G cal/tonne the cost of production can be reduced by Rs. 640 per tonne. The large manpower employed on steel plant has resulted in high wage costs and lower labour productivity. Every reduction of workers can reduce cost of production.

Fertilisers

Two factors can contribute to cost reduction in fertilizer industry-namely capacity utilisation and consumption efficiencies. The two are correlated. Consumption efficiencies improve with higher capacity utilisation. Another important factor is the continuous running of plants. Stoppages and start-ups adversely affect consumption efficiencies. The fertilizer industry has been badly hit from time to time by power cuts and stoppage of water supply. Hence, where feasible, captive power plants and alternative sources of water supply should supply be installed.

A tailor made approach is thus required in each sector. Two factors common to most sectors are labour productivity and fuel consumption efficiency. Success in cost reduction in one sector would facilitate success in the other, eventually facilitating cost redaction throughout the economy.

22

ROLE OF THE GOVERNMENT SECTOR IN ECONOMIC DEVELOPMENT IN THE CONTEXT OF THE NEW WORLD ECONOMIC ORDER*

The structural change that we wish to introduce on a global scale is often termed as the ushering in of "the new world economic order". The old economic order was a heritage of the colonial past. It was the consequence of the dominance of the imperial countries over the countries of Asia and Africa. The imperial countries tended to look upon their colonies as the base of raw material which they bought at very low rates and transported to their own countries to feed their factories. They also looked upon colonies as a market for the finished products of their factories. Thus England emerged as the leading textile manufacturer using the cotton grown in India. Rubber from the plantations of Malaya was also similarly turned into a finished product and this applies to large number of other agricultural commodities such as, tea, sugarcane, jute etc., where the only role of the farmers in the colonial countries was to work on land and produce the raw material. They were thus 'drawers of water and hewer of wood', not for them any benefit from the "Value added" nor any other benefit from rendering services in the secondary and tertiary sectors like transport, banking or distribution. All these services were the monopoly of the firms registered in the imperial countries. There was nothing for the farmers of the developing countries than eking out a bare livelihood from low level agriculture.

---

*Based on address to 82nd World Marketing Congress.

It was, therefore, a typical world economic order where rich became richer and the poor became poorer. While the economies of the developed countries got increasingly diversified with ever increasing gross national product and higher standard of living for its people, the economy of the colonial countries sank into morass of poverty and stagnation. A particular feature of exchange between the raw material of the colonial countries and the finished products of the imperial countries tended to accentuate the disparities and that was the phenomenon of the deteriorating terms of trade against the raw material and in favour of the finished products.

In the 'fifties and 'sixties the developing countries emerged to freedom. They looked upon their political freedom as a means of economic freedom, of economic development which would create a richer, fuller and better life for the masses of its people. They were no longer content to let their people play the role of 'drawers of water and hewers of wood'. They wanted a rapid diversification of their economy and industrial development which will enable them to transform their raw material into finished products – an economic system in which the advantages of value added would accrue to their own people. They wanted to build up all the infrastructure of a modern economy with the help of application of science and technology.

Moreover, they did not want to confine their relationship only to the erstwhile imperial masters. They saw new possibilities in developing relationship with the countries of the second world – the socialist world-consisting of USSR and other eastern European countries. These countries had abandoned the path of capitalism and chalked out their own path of socialism and they sought to bring about economic development and social change through planning. Some of the developing countries felt that they should, with suitable modifications, adopt the approach of planning and develop some linkages between their own plans and the plans of the socialist countries. Since socialism itself proclaims to be an ideology without exploitation, it was expected the relationship between socialist countries and the developing countries would be free from the element of exploitation.

Thus the developing countries looked upon to the new economic order as the one in which the old exploitative relationship between the developed and developing countries would be a matter of the past and developing countries would have a chance to develop their economy by getting the benefit of the value added through activities in the secondary and tertiary sectors. In the new World Economic Order as envisaged by them, the change of goods between developed and developing countries would be non-exploitative and would be based on fair and equitable relationship and without one-sided deterioration in terms of trade against the products of the developing countries. The developing countries visualise a new orientation of the world institutions with IBRD and IMF which would help develop and maintain such a new World Economic Order.

The external structural changes implicit in this world economic order had to commence with the modifications in the internal structures of the economies of the developing countries. These changes could not be expected to take place if left to the normal operations of the market forces. It is no doubt true that the economic development of the developed countries in the past took place through the operation of the market forces but those who were at the helm of affairs of the developing countries felt that if left to market forces, economic development would not be rapid enough. The leaders of the Third World Countries were anxious to leap frog centuries in a few decades. Moreover, economic development required investment of an order which they felt may not be readily forthcoming in conditions obtaining in most of the developing countries. In the developing countries, the state came to be looked upon as the main initiator of change. The role of the State could not be confined to the traditional concept of law and order State or a Police State or a night watchman. The State would be responsible for the comprehensive effort for the mobilization of industrial and manpower resources with the help of science and technology in order to modernize agriculture, promote industrialisation, diversify the economy and provide infrastructure of development.

This does not mean an immediate taking over of the means of production by the State. Land which is the main means of agricultural production was to be left in the ownership of the millions of farming families. Similarly, small sector industry in the private sectors or even the larger enterprises could flourish provided they conformed to the overall priorities of national development. Indeed, the State has to set up institutions for the promotion and development of agricultural economy. The State also directly established and operated enterprises in fields where private sector was neither forthcoming, nor was considered to be an appropriate agency – Sectors such as that of basic industries such as steel, mines, coal, power, oil and natural gas, heavy locomotives and coaches, ship building, air craft building, electronics, machine tools, heavy engineering, heavy electrical etc., came to be looked upon as the commanding heights of the economy where the public sector would dominate.

Thus the role of the Government sector could be the following:

(i) To establish and operate public sector enterprises in the commanding heights of the economy;

(ii) To encourages and promote cottages, small scale and even large enterprises consistent with the goals of national development;

(iii) To set up financial and promotional institutions;

(iv) To provide a broad framework of planning and policy making; and

(v) To promote educational, technological and scientific institution for training necessary manpower.

The manner in which this role is played by Government in respect of these various aspects may differ from country to country and there will be much scope for exchange of experience in all these fields between the various developing countries. Here I would contend myself to make a few observations against the background of the Indian experience:

(i) Thanks to the initiative of the State, a number of public sector undertakings have been established in the shape of corporations or public companies. Some of the firms includes, Steel Authority of India Ltd., National Coal Development Corporation, Coal India Ltd., Oil and Natural Gas Commission, Bharat Heavy Electricals, Heavy Engineering Corporation, Ranchi, India Fertilizer Corporation etc. All these giant organisations have provided the foundation of industrial and economic development of the country. A new generation of public sector managers has come up and developed a greater deal of expertise. A good deal of understanding has developed regarding organisation and management of public sector enterprises.

(ii) The promotion of cottage industries and village handicrafts is both a matter of preserving the hereditary skills as also the provision of employment opportunities since capital intensive industry cannot provide necessary employment. Khadi and Village Industry Commission has been established to promote cottage industries. Similarly handicrafts and Handloom Boards and export corporation for handloom and handicraft an well as the district industry centres have all been established to promote small scale industry.

(iii) For the promotion of private enterprise of a larger category, financial institutions such as the Industrial Finance Corporation, and the Industrial Development Bank of India have also been established.

In the field of agriculture, Government has played a major role in modernising agriculture and increasing its production and productivity through agriculture research institutions, agriculture extension services, National Seeds Corporation, Agro Industries Corporation and a large number of credit institutions including the Reserve Bank of India, State Bank of India, nationalised banks and the cooperative credit institutions as well as regional rural banks.

Cooperative sector has been given a major role in agricultural development for the supply of agricultural inputs including seeds and fertilizers, agriculture credit, marketing and processing of agricultural commodities. The National Development Corporation has been set up to promote cooperative development.

(iv) The Planning Commission was established in 1951 to provide a broad and comprehensive framework of planning in which an appropriate role would be assigned to the private and public sectors. The role of planning is to bring about an optimum utilisation of natural and manpower resources through the application of science and technology with a view to reaching some pre-determined goals which include not only increasing the gross national product but also its equitable distribution. The Plan also aims at providing gainful employment opportunities to all as growth without justice could be self-defeating.

Public policies constitute the instrument of planning. They include control over inflation, conservation of foreign exchange, industrial regulation and suitable fiscal policies. Whether it should place reliance on fiscal controls or physical controls and how Government should regulate, is of course, a matter of discussion.

It is not enough to do broad national planning. Plans have to be disaggregated to State and local levels. Since planning is a congregation of projects, project planning also assumes importance and so does block and village level planning.

(v) Development cannot take place without the application of science and technology and technology has to be an appropriate technology. Developing countries have therefore set up their own research institutions including those in the field of agriculture research and in many other fields including National Physical Laboratory, National Institute for Food Technology, leather technology etc., as also the institution of high learning like Indian Institutes of Technology and Management, all of which have derived support from Government.

During the hay day of *laissez faire,* the ideal was that of less government in business and more business in government. In the situation of developing countries, this may not be an ideal. At the same time the development demands a collective effort between business people, managers, administrators, scientists, technologists and political leaders for a concerted effort to bring about rapid economic development and social change. The Government Sector has to join hands with the private and cooperative sector to accelerate national development on the right lines.

23

COST AND MANAGEMENT ACCOUNTANTS AND DEVELOPMENT

Planning, control and evaluation are the three stages in any enterprise or project. The Cost and Management Accountants are being increasingly involved in all these three stages. There was a time when role of the Cost and Management Accountants was conceived in somewhat narrow terms. As a result the Cost and Management Accountants conceived of planning, control and evaluation only in micro terms i.e. in relation to individual projects or companies. However, one can unmistakably notice a process of the broadening of the vision of the professional accountants. The broadening vision would require that the accountants discuss planning, control and evaluation in macro terms.

If we look upon our national economy as the balance sheet of "India Incorporated", then we can start applying the techniques employed by the Cost and Management Accountants in the case of individual companies to the analysis of the national economy as a whole.

There are some business economists and Cost and Management Accountants who have a predilection in favour of free enterprise and they consider planning as an abridgement of free enterprise. However, we have to take note of the fact that planning is not confined to socialist economies only. Countries such as France, Japan and South Korea have taken to planning even though they are liberal economies with a large private enterprise. They have found planning a useful method of accelerating the progress of the economy. Private enterprises in these countries have been active partners and participants in this process of planning, often called 'indicative planning'.

So far as India is concerned, we took a deliberate decision in favour of planning and we embarked upon a series of Five Year Plans in the year 1951. The need for planning was clearly stated in the very First Five Year Plan. Our plans were aimed at harnessing our natural and manpower resources, with the help of science and technology, for broadening the base of our economy and for producing an increasing stream of goods and services, to be placed at the disposal of masses so as to make their lives richer, fuller and better.

Our process of planning was conceived in comprehensive terms. It was not confined to public investment alone but covered the economy as a whole in all sectors – primary, secondary and tertiary as well as public, private and cooperative sectors. The public sector was expected to attain the commanding heights of the economy. It was established in the field of basic, heavy and strategic industries in which in any case the private sector was not expected to be forthcoming because of the long gestation period. At the same time wide field was left open to the private sector which, however, was expected to work within the framework of planning. It was also expected to subserve the Directive Principles stated in the Constitution which the planning was expected to promote. These principles stated that the working of the economic system should subserve public purpose and redound to the common good and there should not be undue concentration of the economic resources in few hands.

After more than four decades of planning, it has been felt that while planning in India has contributed to building up of the infrastructure, mobilisation of natural resources, diversification of the economy and steady growth of the gross national product, the growth has not been enough, the full potential of the economy is not realised, and further the fruits of production have not reached the poorest strata of the society. Almost 50 per cent of the population still continues to be below the poverty line.

These shortcomings have to be remedied by the planners and the policy-makers with the advice of the economists. But have not the Cost and Management Accountants also a role to play in this process of reappraisal of planning in our country?

There is one aspect with which the Cost and Management Accountants would perhaps be more directly concerned and that is related to the increasing capital-output ratio which has become a feature of our economic development during the last few years. As a consequence of the rising capital-output ratio, the country is not getting enough out of the resources invested. A poor country has to sacrifice a great deal to raise resources for investment. In the early years of planning, it was often stated that there are limits to our growth because of the limited savings which our poor economy could generate. It is a matter of pride as well as admiration that the ratio of saving in this country has gone up above 20 per cent of the national income. However, the rise in savings is not reflected in the increase in the rate of growth because of rising capital output ratio. Our savings are invested in projects which are now yielding less and less returns.

Our main strategy for rise in the rate of growth in the country should be to increase the productivity of resources that are invested. How can we reduce capital output ratio? This is the question to which the Cost and Management Accountants should also address themselves.

This question has to be raised in relation to investment every where in the public sector as well as in the private sector; in agricultural, industrial and infrastructural projects and in public utilities. This examination has also to be extended to non-plan investment and expenditure. Even in respect of non-plan expenditure, it is necessary to ask the same kinds of questions which Sir Derek Rayner asked in relation to the expenditure in the British Government namely—what exactly is the activity? What does its cost? What is its value? What is required is a thorough value for money analysis in all sectors and for all projects in our economy.

Unfortunately, we have not made even a beginning with a wide ranging enquiry on these lines. This is a vast field for the effort of Cost and Management Accountants. Traditional cost and management accountancy techniques may not be adequate to conduct the analysis on the lines suggested; the accountants may have to evoke new techniques and methods.

Traditionally, Accountants have been concerned with industrial projects in the private sector but when they widen their horizon to the whole process of planning in our country, they would have to be concerned with non-industrial projects such as those in the field of agriculture, public utilities, banking and insurance. They may have to deal with costs and returns which are not marketed. These are new areas for the Cost and Management Accountants in our country.

In practical terms the plan has to be an assemblage of projects and programmes. The capital-output ratio for the economy as a whole will come down if it comes downs for individual projects and programmes. Hence each project and programme needs a close scrutiny by the Cost and Management Accountants. In view of socio-economic goals attached to most projects and programmes, they too need to be quantified precisely. Otherwise they may serve as a cover to hide inefficiencies. Concepts like Social cost and benefits and shadow pricing need to be sharply defined and not left vague.

Going further, accountants have also to be concerned with poverty and quality of life of people. Can the Cost and Management Accountants evaluate various projects in terms of their contributions to the reduction of poverty in the country or in terms of reduction in unemployment and disguished unemployment? These are perhaps new concepts and new areas of activities for the Cost and Management Accountants but they must address themselves to the quantification of these concepts.

The effort of this sort is required not only at national level but at the levels of States and district. We have been thinking for the last few years in terms of decentralisation of the planning process. A panel of economists has recently advised the Prime Minister to promote planning at the level of division. The success of divisional and district planning also depends on the availability of the Cost and Management Accountancy services at the district level.

There are new challenges facing the Cost and Management Accountants in the country in the context of national planning.

24

LIBERALISATION, MARKETISATION, PRIVATISATION AND ECONOMY IN PUBLIC EXPENDITURE

When India became free, it made a choice in favour of a planned economy, a mixed economy and a controlled economy. Jawaharlal Nehru was greatly influenced by achievements of the Soviet Plans during his visit in 1927. He was the Chairman of the National Planning Committee appointed by the Congress President even before Independence. And after Independence, he lost no time in setting up the National Planning Commission in 1950. He thought that only planning can give proper direction to the national effort to mobilise natural and manpower resources with the help of science and technology to raise the level of living of the masses of people. He, however, was not in favour of totalitarian planning of Russia model. He favoured democratic planning. This had many implications. First, it meant participation of the people in the planning process. Second it meant, that there would be no comprehensive socialisation of all the means of production including land. There would be vast scope for the private sector not only in agriculture but also in industry and trade. The Industrial Policy Resolution spelt out the basis of the mixed economy by earmarking the scope for the public, private and cooperative sector. Finally, a system of controls was the inevitable adjunct of planning since controls were required to ensure that the private sector fulfilled the overall objectives of planning.

The planned economy, the mixed economy and the controlled economy had major administrative implications not all of which were clearly perceived. Even though these decisions appeared to have at that time a wide acceptance, it is not as though they went unchallenged. The then Finance Minister, Dr. John Mathai was opposed to the establishment of the Planning Commission. He felt that Planning Commission would come in conflict with the Finance Ministry. With his long association with private industrialists, Dr. Mathai also was not enthusiastic about the public sector or a regime of controls. As pointed out by Dr. Gopal in his biography of Nehru he feared that planning, public sector and controls will be used by Nehru as tools to reduce the importance of the industrial and commercial classes. Ultimately Mathai resigned on this issue.

That Mathai's fears and reservations were not entirely uncalled for has been borne out by our subsequent experience. In the hey-day of the Planning Commission, it was often accused of being a super cabinet or a super ministry. But in its days of decline, it was often described as the fifth wheel. In any case, the relationship between planning and rate of growth has not always been of cause and affect. For example, the critical accomplishment of the Green Revolution was during the period of plan holiday from 1966 to 1969. Nor has public sector enterprises run into losses and the return on massive investment in them is not considered adequate. The quality of products of public enterprises has left something to be desired and this is often attributed to the monopoly position of some public sector enterprises. Finally, the rationale of the entire structure of a controlled economy has been called into question. Talking about the regulatory process, Shri L.K. Jha in his Sardar Patel Memorial Lectures on "Towards More Efficient Economic Administration" observed, "The aim should be to do away, as far as possible, with a regime of controls applied on a case by case basis, each being examined by an army of administrators, and to replace them by more sophisticated instruments of influencing economic activities and performance. In order to canalise investments into priority sectors, greater use should be made of price policies, fiscal policies and the financial institutions". Shri Jha also found fault with numerous inter-departmental consultations without which no case is decided. The inter-ministerial committees do not take decisions quickly and files move both vertically and horizontally. Every file goes to the highest level, that is the level of the Minister who gets over-burdened and as a result of the Minister being over-burdened with day-to-day administration, enough thought cannot be given to formulation of policies and giving a sense of leadership. He emphasised that ministries should function as "think tanks" for formulating policies rather than executive agencies dealing with individual cases. He strongly made a case for greater measure of decentralisation and downward devolution of decision-making, with those at the top concerning themselves primarily with policy issues.

The World Bank Report on "Management of Development" also underlined the importance of greater scope to the market mechanism as a principal reform in the macro economic system. This would mean that much of the system of economic controls must be dismantled and market forces of demand and supply allowed to have their free saway in order to enforce economic discipline and efficiency. The prices of the public sector enterprises must be determined according to the market requirements and not administered. Regime of excessive control is bound to lead to excessive bureaucratisation which would stultify the economy. The deficiency is not in the operation of a particular economic control but rather in the control regime itself.

Earlier the Narasimhan Committee had proposed replacement of physical controls by fiscal controls.

The reforms suggested for the replacement of physical controls by sophisticated fiscal controls are in the direction of introducing "market mechanism" rather than "administrative mechanism" for influencing the decisions of private enterprise in directions desired by national plans and policies. Preference for market mechanism over the administrative mechanism implies the belief in the efficacy of the market as well as the need for the elimination of personal factors and biases and even corruption involved in the administrative mechanism for controlling and regulating the economy. Whether arising out of these recommendations or its own independent assessment, "in policy-forming circles in India, opinion is gaining weight that the regime of direct controls and quantity restrictions has proved a failure ... and dynamism could be injected into industry through a policy of liberalisation and open competition. ... Over some time gradual liberalisation has already taken place in terms of licensing procedures, control of capital issues, export and import controls etc." By reducing the scope for the clumsy operation of a maze of physical controls through administrative mechanism, the administrative capability is released for more effective discharge of the functions of policy-making, monitoring and review.

This trend towards liberalisation in India after more than three decades of the regime of physical control is in tune with the trends in other countries as well. For example, in China drastic economic reforms have been initiated under the leadership of Deng Xiaoping. The newly adopted programme of economic reforms initiated by the Communist Party of China include price reforms in regulation of enterprises and the distribution of fruits of production according to ability. The reforms began with the agro-economic sector in 1979 when the peasants were told that they could sell their surplus produce in free markets after meeting the State's quota. The peasants responded positively to this incentive leading to high yield of record harvest. Similar policies are now being pursued in the urban sector. Enterprises in the city are given more power to make decisions affecting the output and sales of their products. They can now adopt flexible and varied management methods to encourage greater productivity, including bonus to diligent workers and punishing the lazy. The State controls over all forms of enterprises in China had led to a crippling effect on the economic structure. Under the reform programme the State Council has decided to release half of China's sixty industrial products from the scope of planning. In the past, State-appointed managers were interested only in carrying out government orders regardless of their impact on the business. It was the government which decided where factories will get their raw material and in what quantity. All this now will be a thing of the past. But this drastic change requires transformation of the attitude of managers and other cadres. The enterprise will have to get used to the pricing system. Prices of goods will no longer be fixed by the State. They will be fixed by 'supply and demand' factors.

In non-Communist countries also similar changes are taking place. In England and Japan the reforms have taken the shape of privatisation. In Japan the state monopoly on salt and tobacco has been given up, and the Conservative government of Thatcher in England introduced denationalisation of telecommunication and the airlines.

To what extent can India go in the direction of liberalisation of economic controls, marketisation and privatisation? When the controls were adopted they were for a purpose. And the purpose was that in the process of economic development there should be no concentration of resources in the hands of a few monopolists and the fruits of development should be available in the widest possible manner. It is pointed out that in spite of the regime of controls, two big business houses have grown by leaps and bounds. Moreover, many of the monopoly houses have been able to steer clear of the regulatory system in the shape of Industrial Licensing System (ILS). Studies undertaken by the Corporate Studies Group in the Indian Institute of Public Administration have shown that many of these large companies have been able to undertake production without licence or far in excess of the licensed capacity. At the same time there are also cases of failure to utilise the licences obviously to pre-empt the licences going to other producers. Monopoly concerns have also stepped into the sector reserved for the small scale sector. These finding are a warning against an indiscriminate attempt to dismantle the regulatory structure.

Economist Krishna Bhardwaj has also expressed similar view. "We must remember that physical controls were strongly advocated in our economy precisely because it was believed that under oligopolist dominated market structure, market forces would not serve the attainment of the goals of planned development and that State would have to intervene directly and actively". The position is valid even today. It has also to be remembered that under selectively controlled and planned economy Japan forged ahead on all frontiers.

This caution does not mean that we should continue with an archaic system of economic controls. Some times large enterprises themselves are in favour of control because they are able to manipulate the control mechanism in their favour. Also, controls lead to monopolies and unearned incomes at the cost of the consumer. They often lead to black economy and corruption. However, criticism of the operation of the existing network of controls does not mean wholesale liberalisation. Rather we should assess the effectiveness of liberalisation moves undertaken from time to time, before advocating any general policy of markertisation and privatisation. This is an area where administrative reforms and economic reforms go hand-in-hand. Controls have a justification only when they fulfil a purpose. Where they do not serve such a purpose or where controls themselves turn out to be ineffective, there is a clear case for doing away with the controls and the cumbersome administrative mechanism that goes with them.

A concomitant of this drive to reduce the involvement of State in the economic activity is a drive for economy and reduction in the number of civil servants. Japan has by law fixed the maximum strength of the number of civil servants. It has also adopted scrap-and-build technique under which no new administrative bureau could be created for any new function without at the same time abolishing an old bureau. This has meant elimination of obsolete administrative structures and proliferation of agencies. In Britain, the Prime Minister Thatcher invited Sir Derick Rayner, Joint Director of Marks and Spencer to propose economies in government. He studied the whole range of government organisations. In this study he asked the question: What does the organization do? At what cost and what is the value derived from that service? This 'value-for-money' analysis has enabled substantial economies to be effected in government expenditure. As the election manifesto of the Conservative Party (1983) says – "Far reaching changes were carried through to secure greater economy, efficiency and better management in government. This has saved the taxpayer about 500 million pound sterling a year. . . The efficiency scrutiny launched by Lord Rayner and other money saving techniques have identified savings worth 400 million pound sterling a year to the taxpayer. We have abolished 500 *Quangos* (quasi non-governmental organisations) and done away with no less than 3000 different types of government forms". We in India have serious problem of scarcity of resources and consequent deficit financing and could with advantage adopt the techniques of Japan and Britain for effecting economy in expenditure.

25

THE RATIONALE OF THE NEW ECONOMIC POLICY

In the wake of the new policy of economic reform, a new wave of economic thinking is sweeping over the country. The wave is of marketisation, deregulation and privatisation. There is a sense of disenchantment about the concepts of planning, public sector and command economy which were the pillars of the model of the economy adopted after India became independent.

The *raison d'etre* of the new economic policy stems from the proposition that it would usher in a competitive economy which can ensure optimum allocation and utilisation of economic resources. In the competitive market economy, the resources utilisation is governed by the laws of demand and supply, and prices, costs, profits and losses. In a competitive market economy, profit is a measure of efficiency. If the individual enterprises are efficient, they would in a competitive economy, make profits. If they are inefficient, they would make losses and go to the wall. In the market economy, there are free entry and exit and unhindered recruitment and retrenchment of staff and labour.

Even theoretically, the stipulation of the optimum use of resources is contingent on the assumption which are never realised in practice. There is no perfect knowledge and no perfect mobility of factors of production—especially in a developing country such as ours. Monopoly duopoly, monopolistic competition and imperfect competition in one form or another prevail. Far from consumer demand governing production, it is the producer who governs the consumer choice through the pressure of advertisement—however misleading it may be.

There has also been another point of view which says that efficiency and progress are the result of monopoly rather than competition. It is monopoly which has enabled the producer to reap the advantages of the scale of operation. It is monopoly enterprises which introduce innovations as was pointed out by economist Joseph Schumpeter. Per contra, it is because of the introduction of innovations that there has always been a historic tendency towards the emergence of the monopoly. Competition cannot survive under conditions of increasing returns to scale and therefore the claims of a competitive economy are very weak in terms of efficiency. It is astonishing that all these tendencies which have repeatedly been noticed through the history of economic evolution should now be allowed to go into oblivion and should receive no consideration at all.

Apart from the theoretical and analytical considerations, common experience shows that the private sector is not always efficient. The so-called advantages of the competitive economy are seldom realised in practice. Consider the working of the taxis in cities. They are hardly responsive to the consumer. The passengers have to suffer silently the evils of the taxi system such as resort to circuitous route, overcharging ignoring the meter and down right refusal to ply over short distances. To protect the passenger from these exploits or worse the Air Port authorities had to introduce pre-paid taxi system. The business executives with a bias against the public sector have been elitistic passengers always finding fault with the service of Indian Airlines Corporation (IAC). Now that the IAC is in shambles, passengers are at the mercy of private airlines. The privations of the passengers under the dispensation of the private airlines have now become a daily experience. The desultory ground service is to be seen to be believed. I buy a ticket for a flight and within an hour I am told that the flight is cancelled! The passengers go through the security check only to be told that the flight is cancelled. The passengers even with a boarding pass are liable to be off-loaded! And now fares are drastically increased without notices. This is not to the benefit of a competitive economy, rather it is the worst form of exploitation.

Exploitation of the consumer is also seen in professional field like doctors and lawyers. Lawyers charge by the hour, hefty fees and doctors insist on all kinds of specialist tests which the patient cannot afford. Here is a recent write up on the advantages of privatisation (*Times of India*, December 5) "The recent decision to introduce the system of private contracts for providing food to patients in municipal hospitals is likely to hurt patients' interest and also fail to bring about the expected degree of savings for Bombay Municipal Corporation. Dr. Amar Jesani from the Foundation of Research in Community Health objects strongly to private contractors entering in hospital kitchens. The contractor will be driven by profit motive and will readily compromise quality. This is evident in the city's roads which give way after the first showers. The private contractor will not be sacked by the Civic authorities due to political pressure. How will it be different with the food contractor?". The reference to building contractors in the above quotation draws attention to another area where the blessings of competition are rarely seen. Most of the time, the house owner has to put up with a contractor who provides poor quality of work, at an expenditure way beyond estimated costs and completed much beyond scheduled time. By the time he enters into his own house his patience and resources are long exhausted. Similar is the experience with the garages repairing cars or the tailor or the jeweller who will rarely do timely work. The customer will never be free from fear that the goldsmith will not keep back a certain quantity of gold or the tailor certain quantity of cloth!

Self interest is the motive of private enterprise. Economists from the days of Adam Smith have argued that perfect competition would turn private pursuit of self interest into public service at least cost. The underlying assumption is that pursuit of self interest is the universal motivation to the exclusion of everything else.

Some economists have started arguing on the basis that even in the public service self-interest is the only motive. Public servants will work only to the extent to which they can fatten themselves through commission and corruption misusing the public offices which they hold. This is quite contrary to the theory of bureaucracy as envisaged by Max Weber and the concept of the ethic of public service. Max Weber envisaged bureaucracy as a rational institution, and bureaucrats as holders of public positions, paid according to prescribed scales, recruited according to prescribed qualifications, governed in their work by prescribed rules and regulations and inspired by a code of conduct of public service. It is not correct to dismiss all this as unrealistic and impose on public service and those who render it the norms of a private entrepreneur pursuing private profit. Public service, like some other professional services, is or should be governed by higher considerations as a matter of honour.

At one point soon after independence, when values of fight for freedom still governed our actions, profit was the dirty word and public service was considered honourable. Even private sector industries started talking of social responsibility of business. Now with corruption and inefficiency in public sector 'service' has become a dirty word and 'profit' the watchword of the new era of liberalisation. It is necessary that we do not lose our sense of values and standards in pursuit of competitive economy. We should give proper scope to the concept of public service as a matter of honour, social service as a motivation for action and social responsibility of business as a manifestation of Gandhiji's concept of business as a trust held on behalf of society. These concepts seem now to have become out of date but they need to be revised through conscious attempts.

We should also think of and allow for co-operative economy as an alternative to the competitive economy. Cooperative economy is based on self-help and mutual help rather than mere self-interest envisaged in a capitalist economy. By eliminating dichotomy between supplier of raw material and producer of finished product, buyer and seller, worker and employer, it eliminates the scope for exploitation so widely prevalent in a competitive economy.

If the wealth and welfare of the society as a whole is our goal, then we cannot have a system where each individual engages himself in naked pursuit of self-interest in an aggressive manner, with no holds barred and with little regard to the concept of social good. In our euphoria for economic reforms we should not ignore alternative sources of motivations, springs of action and alternative forms of economic organisation. The shocking bank scam is a warning against an economy based on mindless pursuit of profit as an exclusive goal.

26

ECONOMIC REFORMS : India and Latin American Countries

India is currently undergoing similar phase of development as the Latin American countries underwent during the last decade and there is a lot to be learnt from the success as well as mistakes in the structural adjustment programme attempted in countries such as Mexico, Argentine and Colombia.

New Historical Perspective

Though the structural adjustment is a comparatively short range economic phenomenon, it has to be seen in the historical perspective of the colonial rule.

Developed and Developing Countries: Erstwhile Colonising and Colonised Countries

The world today is divided into two categories of countries viz. the developed and the developing. In the parlance of the colonial era, they were described as imperial countries and the colonies. The countries of Asia, Africa and Latin America belong to the category of under-developed countries, though some of them, by now, have acquired the status of NIC, i.e. the newly industrialising countries. But all of them had experience of colonisation and bear the marks left by centuries of thraldom.

Difference in Timing and Character of Colonisation

No doubt, the character and historical timing of the advent of the colonial rule and liberation from it varied. If we compare the Latin American countries with the countries of the Indian sub-continent, we could readily note the different character and historical background of colonisation. While the countries of the Indian sub-continent had to wait until the second half of the 20th century before they liberated themselves from the shackles of colonisation, the Latin American countries were liberated in the first half of the nineteenth century.

The difference is not in the time dimension alone of colonisation. The nature of colonisation also differed. In the Latin American countries, colonisation was by way of large scale settlement of the white people in the Latin American countries after a virtual extermination of the local people viz. the red Indians as a consequence of savage wars and terrible epidemics. However, after some passage of time, the white immigrants settled down in the new land and with some racial mixture with the natives, saw themselves to be under the tutelage of the whites of their own race of the 'mother' countries. The colonial relationship, was therefore, between the people who had left their land and settled down in Latin America and those who were left behind in the colonizing countries. In the case of Brazil, the Portuguese Prince Dom Pedro became the ruler of the 'natives' of the colonised countries who included the whites, the originalised Indians as well as the Negroes originally brought in as slave labour. In contrast, in the Indian sub-continent, the white people came in as rulers, administrators and traders and after liberation left for their mother countries, leaving the colonised people to be masters of their own destiny. There people were of different stock with different culture and language. However, though native in colour and skin and other physical features, through education in English language and introduction to English literature they came under the influence of Western ideas and culture.

Similar Economic Character of Colonisation

Despite this difference, the economic character of colonisation was the same in both the countries. Basically the colonies were treated by the imperial countries as a source for raw material and market for finished products. The pattern of trade was based on the supply of raw materials produced by the colonised countries for industries of the colonising countries with the former providing a captive market for the latter. Thus, Brazil supplied coffee and sugar, Argentine supplied beef and wheat and Chile supplied copper and nitrate. All natural wealth of the colonised countries went only to promote high standard of living in the colonising countries. India supplied cotton for textile industry of Britain. Before Mahatma Gandhi went to Chaparan, the farmers there produced and supplied indigo for paints manufacturing in Europe.

This typical relationship of the colonial era was rightly described as one of dominance and dependence, the colonised countries became the economic subsidiaries of the colonising countries. It was entirely unequal and titled in favour of the latter. It promoted prosperity in the colonising countries.

This process of colonial economic explatation was described by Dadabhai Naoroji as a phenomenon of "economic drain" from the colonised to the colonising countries. Later Dr. Raul Prebisch the Latin American economist described this as a Centre-Periphery phenomenon - the colonising countries being at the centre and the colonised countries at the periphery of the economic system, with balance of economic advantage in favour of the Centre.

After Colonisation – The Road to Industrialisation

The first concern of the newly liberated countries after decolonisation was to correct this unequal relationship. How was this to be accomplished ? The colonised countries should no longer remain as "drawers of water and a hewers of wood". They should be able to stand on their own legs by transforming their raw material into finished products and enjoy the benefits of value added through the process of manufacturing. This alone can raise the level of living of people in the erstwhile colonies.

Infant Industry Argument

However, industrialisation and economic diversification in the colonised countries was not easy. How could the newly set up industries of the colonised countries face the competition of the established advanced industries in the erstwhile colonising countries which had all along gained, over centuries, from the exploitation of colonies? In fact, this phenomenon of uneconomic relationship was not unknown to economic history. It was faced by the countries such as Germany whose industrialisation followed that of British. The German economist Prof. Fredrich List had put forward the "infant industry argument" in support of protective tariff while England was pressing for free trade. The argument was that the infant industry of the newly industrialised countries must be given protection from open competition with the developed industries in Britain by raising requisite traiff barriers. This argument became a generally accepted argument in textbooks on Economics with a proviso that "infants cannot remain infants all the time." That is after they are firmly established, the protection should be removed. The argument of Prof. List became the basis of the policy of protectionist tariff and trade policies introduced in the several Latin American countries in the second half of the 19th century and by India in second half of the 20th century.

Industrial Stagnation

While the policy led to the industrial diversification in the erstwhile colonies and the newly independent countries, the fear that infants would remain infants came true. With the sheltered market that tariff provided, industries in these countries did not work in a competitive environment and catered only to the sheltered domestic market. In terms of prices and quality, they could not hold their own in the international market. Hence the countries developed an industrial structure characterised by low productivity and backward technology. This led to industrial and economic stagnation, lack of dynamism and low rate of growth.

Debt Trap

It was, therefore, necessary to break out of this vicious circle of stagnation. The answer to this was some kind of liberal open door policy known as policy of globalisation. If the newly industrialising countries gave free scope to import of capital goods and technology, their industry would be competitive and develop the ability to participate in world market. Import substitution must give way to export promotion. In pursuit of this policy, imports were liberally allowed, but the expected export promotion did not take place, and this led to heavy balance of payment dificits.

The problem of external deficit was compounded by internal budget deficits. The burden of subsidization and payment of interest on accumulated internal debt led to huge amount of deficit financing. Slowly internal and external debts resulted in an economic crisis.

In order to pay their way externally, the countries resorted to borrowing from multilateral and bilateral sources. Sometime even on commercial terms. As the external debt piled up a substantial part of export earnings had to be diverted towards payment of interest and amortization of debt. This was a typical situation of debt trap. Latin American countries in eighties and India in the beginning of nineties fell into such debt trap.

Finding themselves in the debt trap, some of the Latin American countries like Peru disowned all responsibilities for payment of debt. Some other countries had to resort to further debt, but the further loans could be extended by the lending agencies, only on certain conditionalities. They came to be known as Structural Adjustment Programmes (SAP) whose acceptance by the debt incurring countries was a precondition for fresh lending. This was something like an abridgement of the economic sovereignty of these countries. But this price had to be paid by the countries caught in the debt trap and unable to get out of it through their own effort.

Structural Adjustment Programme

The Structural Adjustment Programme by and large, had the same principal components namely viz. domestic fiscal discipline, abolition of subsidies, reform of the tax structure, devaluation of the currency, curb over monetary expansion as an anti-inflationary manner, deregulation, privatisation or divestiture of public sector enterprises, removal of tariff barriers and liberalisation of external trade regime. This programme was followed with varying degrees of success by several Latin American countries and is now being followed by India. To what extent have Latin American countries succeeded in their structural adjustment programme? To what extent can India benefit by their experience?

Mexico

The most important country which had some success in structural adjustment was Mexico. During the eighties Mexico suffered from an extremely grave economic crisis. It had hugefiscal deficit of 18 per cent of GNP and an enormous amount of capital flight resulting in unsustainability. For Mexico the eighties were a difficult decade. It was engulfed in a vicious cycle of high inflation and low output. Its oversized and outdated Governmental structure inhibited efficient economic performance. The State was involved in too many activities. It participated in every aspect of society. What was helpful in the early phases of industrial growth was an obstacle in the later phase for initiating dynamic economic growth. The State had become weaker as it grew in size. The first item on the agenda was, therefore, reform of the State. While the State should be strengthened in discharging its sovereign duties, the non-strategic area of activity had to be privatised. The Government divested of a total of 960 parastatal enterprises. Privatisate commercial banks were reestablished. The reform of the State was followed by drastic changes in the economic policy. Prices and wages were controlled and comprehensive anti-inflation programme was introduced. Fiscal discipline was enforced and budgetary deficit reduced. As a result of these measures, the annual inflation was brought down from 200 per cent to 20 per cent. Stable market supply was ensured. Thirdly, control over industries was removed. Deregulation promoted industrial competitiveness. With a competitive economy, Mexico could increase her exports. Foreign investment was allowed in all sectors. Social support was given to the poor. Fourthly, fiscal system was reformed to eliminate tax evasion. The economy was made open and foreign trade liberalised. The tariff reduced from 100 per cent to 20 per cent, the average standing at 10 per cent. The economy became more export oriented. Mexico became a partner in the largest trade zone in the world along with the USA and Canada. These reforms led to modernisation of the economy.

Colombia

The reforms in Colombia were on similar lines following the debt crisis of eighties. Basic changes were felt to be essential. The anachronistic concept of "Promoter State" had to be given up.

Genuine enterprises efficiently combined capital, labour and technology had to be nurtured. Non-Governmental organisations had to be called in to compliment the State. What was important was not the sphere of State activity, but its efficiency. Confrontation between owners and workers had to be given up as a pugnacious out of date idea. The fourth factor of production namely knowledge had to be given the highest importance. Both macro-economic equilibrium and macro-social equilibrium had to be established. The Colombia market had to be integrated with the entire world economy.

Colombia has effectively faced the debt crisis. It realized that excessive and disproportionate debt burden was the outcome of past economic policies which were not in keeping with changes taking place in rest of the world. Under the new policies the economy was opened up for private investment. Colombia was able to overcome the debt crisis without having to undergo a great deal of suffering and painful adjustments. The rate of inflation was brought down in 1991 by 26 per cent and the average growth of GDP has been 4 per cent in the last ten years. Foreign exchange reserves were built up to more than US $ 6.5 billion sufficient for a period of eight and half months. Exports are constantly growing and getting diversified. As a result of 20 years judicious Government, fiscal deficit is scarcely of the order of 0.5 per cent of the GDP. The average tariff of 34 per cent has been lowered to 12 per cent in 1992. Railway services have been privatised so also ports. The vigorous process of industrailization in Colombia has started creating new economic opportunities.

Argentine

As a result of disenchantment with economic models of revolutionaries of the 50s and the early 60s, Argentine introduced the new economic policy in the eighties to usher in an open system with greater scope for participation by different sections of the society. The economic reforms initiated by President Menom aim at giving up indiscriminate state interference in favour of a competitive model of the economy where resource allocation is not in the hands of government officials. The keynotes of the reforms are liberalisation, fiscal balance, full convertibility of the currency, privatisation, deregulations, competition, openness to foreign investment and ownership and reduction in tariff and customs duties to promote foreign trade.

India

The above account of the economic reforms attempted in the eighties shows how similar is the package of economic reforms in the Latin American countries initiated in the eighties as compared with that introduced in India in the early years of the nineties. The historical background is similar, the change in economic outlook and philosophy is similar and similar is the package of economic reforms. The similarity of economic reforms can be attributed to the advice of international agencies like the World Bank and the IMF.

We, in India, never thought we will develop the Latin American syndrome of huge external debt running into billions of dollars. We praised ourselves for responsible economic management and economic and political stability. All these assumptions rapidly vanished in the second half of the eighties and we had to come to terms with reality. From the seventies onwards realisation was dawning that our rate of growth of 3.5 per cent was not good enough especially when Japan followed by the four dragons – Hongkong, Taiwan, Singapore and South Korea were growing at a compound rate of 10 per cent and above. And later, other Asian countries such as Indonesia, Malaysia and Thailand showed similar economic dynamism leaving us sadly behind. We thought we were the pace setters of resurgent Asia but we were reduced to the status of a camp follower.

Nehru had initiated in 1951 a planned process of economic development combining equity with growth after a great deal of thought. It represented almost a concensus in the nation save for people like Dr. John Mathai who resigned when Nehru set up the Planning Commission and Professor Shenoy who was constant critic of the model of planned and controlled economy throughout his life time.

But change became essential in the face of economic stagnation. Populist policies like indiscriminate nationalisation, monopoly control and ceiling on urban landholding only worsened the situation. We had neither equality (or equity) nor progress.

To break through the stagnation Indira Gandhi, in her post-emergency regime, started introducing modest doses of liberalisation but they were not enough to break through the stagnation of an immobile, low productivity economy. Some people started advising Rajiv Gandhi who succeeded Indira Gandhi that we must give up import substitution in favour of export promotion. We should liberalise imports of capital and electronic goods to stimulate export financing these imports even by taking commercial loans. The burden of imports compounded by the inevitable oil imports with expected exports nowhere in sight drove the economy into bankruptcy. Before we knew where we were, we had accumulated external debt of $ 70 billion raising debt service ratio to 25 per cent till our foreign reserves were reduced to be just enough for a fortnight's imports. The subsequent steps of import compression hurt the economy and gold sales which hurt the national pride. Our international credibility reached an all time low.

It is in these circumstances that the new Finance Minister persuaded the international institution to rescue the economy with massive oxygen of stand by debts. The situation was saved. Meanwhile as a price of this help, India had to accept Latin American type SAP which is a total reversal of the Nehruvian model – from planning to market, from public sector to privatisation, from controlled economy to deregulation and from autarky to globalisation. This was proceeded by devaluation of 22 per cent with no visible benefit in the form of export boost. Fiscal discipline to reduce budgetary deficit from 8.5 per cent to 5 per cent brought inflation down. Thanks to several years of successive good monsoons, our granaries are full.

But we are by no means out of woods. Our rate of growth of economy and our productivity have to go up several fold. This is not just a matter of liberalisation but greater social and economic discipline which has been severly undermined by bank scams, and a questionable programme of disinvestment of public sector enterprises which has drawn flak from the CAG. The links between people in political power and people of doubtful integrity busy in economic crimes for making a fast buck have seriously shaken the confidence of the people which is the foundation of a sound, progressive economy.

There was nothing wrong in the basic concept of Nehruvian model – equity and self-reliance. In the name of economic reforms we could give up those concepts only at our peril giving opportunities to scoundrels to indulge in looting of banks for reckless speculation in the stock market.

Even while we are implementing the needed reforms of removing irrational and obstructive economic controls, lowering savage tariff barriers and reducing fiscal deficit by curbing unproductive governmental expenditure, we should find out how an atmosphere of social discipline can be created by raising productivity everwhere – in fields, factories and offices. We need a revival of the national spirit. We should also learn from the experience of the model of export led development followed by Japan, South Korea, Singapore, Hongkong, Taiwan based on high work ethic and social discipline. We need not have gone the Latin American way and forced to adapt the same package of economic reforms which they had to introduce in the eighties, if we had gone the former group of countries.

PART IV

POVERTY

27

FIVE PERSPECTIVES ON POVERTY*

Over the last decade or so, understanding the nature and causes of poverty in different parts of the world and working out measures for overcoming it has been the principal concern of the social scientists, national governments, and international agencies.

It was the simplistic belief of the optimistic 50's that poverty was the consequence of low income and if the national income could be boosted up, through greater investment, poverty would disappear automatically. However, experience of over two decades has led to the dethronement of the Gross National Product (GNP) from the high pedestal on which it was placed by the economists. The hope that rapid rise in the gross national product would quickly trickle down to the very poorest groups in development societies was belied. Nor was rising GNP necessarily accompanied by rapid improvements in the physical well being of the people. This led to the abandonment, or atleast modification, of the development strategies of the first two development decades in favour of an alternative strategy that would more efficiently and quickly satisfy the minimum human needs of the poor.

---

* This article is based on five recent publications on Poverty viz. (1) Morris David Morris and Michelle B. McAlpin, 1982, *Measuring the Condition of India's Poor: The Physical Quality of Life Index*, New Delhi. Promilla & Co. Publishers. 94 p., price Rs. 80. (2) Albert Tevoedjre (1977): *Poverty: Wealth of Mankind*, Pergamon Press Ltd., U.K. 182 p., price Rs. 90. (3) David C. Korten and Felipe B. Alfonso (Eds.) (1981): *Bureaucracy and the poor closing the gap*, Singapore, McGraw-Hill International Book Co., 258 p.. (4) J.S. Brara, 1983, *The Political Economy of Rural Development*, New Delhi; Allied Publishers Private Ltd., 274 p., price: Rs. 70. (5) George Gilder, (1982): *Wealth and Poverty*, Buchan & Enright, London, 292 p., price £ 8.50.

What are the concepts and ideas embodied in this new strategy? Some recent publications bring them out in a striking manner.

The poineering work of Morris David Morris and Michelle B. McAlpin, *Measuring the Conditions of India's Poor*, is intended to help the national government in developing such an alternative strategy on the basis of the concept of Physical Quality of Life Index (PQLI) which the authors have evolved.

The reasons why per capita GNP, the widely accepted measure for general economic performance is not adequate are recapitulated by the authors to justify the need for evolving the physical quality of life index. Per capital GNP does not show how output is distributed among the people and groups within countries. Moreover, it is not certain that output of society however distributed is clearly related to the quality of life, since GNP is not the satisfactory measure of total welfare. Many productive activities are included though they do not contribute to better life but are mere regrettable necessities and costs of modern economic life e.g. commuter transportation. That GNP is an inadequate measure of performance becomes more apparent in inter-country comparisons because of the problem of exchange rate. Using the official exchange rate method the World Bank Report India's real per capita income to be $ 140. But, according to the purchasing power parity formula, India's real per capita income in 1975 amounted to $ 490. Recently using this formula the IMF has ranked India as the sixth in respect of the GNP. It is common to define world's absolute poor as those who live below the poverty line of $ 75. India is supposed to have 359 million below the poverty line but if the purchasing power parity method were to be adopted, at least 180 million of the absolute poor will move above the poverty line. Finally, the poorest countries in the poorest groups within the country consume a larger proportion of goods and services that are not produced for and exchanged in the market and therefore escape the net of monetary measurement. It is necessary to take note of these aspects of economic and social life which do not enter into the national income measurements.

The authors have, therefore, undertaken the task of constructing the composite quality of life index that measures the welfare aspects but (1) does not assume that there is only pattern of development; (2) does not reflect the values of specific cultures; (3) reflects results and not inputs; (4) reflects distribution of social measures; (5) is simple to construct and easy to comprehend; and (6) lends itself to international comparison.

The index evolved by the author incorporates three aspects of welfare namely (1) life expectancy, (2) infant mortality, and (3) basic literacy.

The physical quality of life index has been scaled from 0 to 100. The authors have used the index to measure the performance of the world's poor countries in meeting the most basic needs of the people.

The correlation between per capita GNP and PQLI for 150 countries as worked out by the authors shows that GNP explains only slightly more than half the life quality results. Thus, per capita GNP cannot serve as a surrogate for PQLI. The following are some of the outstanding examples: The oil producing Middle-East countries, more particularly Saudi Arabia, Qatar, United Arab Emirates and Libya stand out with high per capita income but low PQLI. In the same category are countries like Gabon and Iran where per capita GNP is more than nine times greater than in India but PQLI is exactly the same. This shows that money is not everything and there is no automatic link between per capita GNP and human welfare. The latter depends upon appropriate social infrastructural and institutional arrangements which take considerable time to build.

In 1976, Tinbergen group report on "Reshaping the International Order" suggested relatively unambitious basic human needs targets that are equivalent of countries achieving the PQLI of 77 @ 25 years. The PQLI of 77 implies a literacy rate of atleast 75 per cent, infant mortality rate of 50 or less per thousand and the life expectancy of 67.4 years.

The data assembled by the authors shows that some countries with less income have been able to achieve high PQLI. Thus, the per capita income of Sri Lanka (1970-75 average) was only $179 but its PQLI was as high as 82. China Peoples' Republic had a per capita GNP of $ 300 but the PQLI of 69. The Kerala State in India with per capita GNP as low as $ 126 could boast of a PQLI as high as 70. Countries with different economic systems such as Cuba, South Korea and Sri Lanka were able to achieve PQLI above 80 at the income levels below $ 700.

Of the 43 countries with lowest PQLI, 10 were African. The African countries individually and collectively tended to rank higher on a per capita GNP scale than PQLI scale. On the other hand, the Latin American countries have PQLI well above that of the African figures. The income of all Africa excluding South Africa averaged

$314 while in South Asia it averaged only $ 131 during the 1970-75 period. Nevertheless, the South-Asia PQLI (41) was meaningfully higher than the average for all Africa excluding South Africa (32). The authors attribute this to the historically determined institutional differences. While African countries did not go beyond the tribal system, the South Asian countries had historically built village systems.

The authors consider that PQLI captures the total effect of social and economic policy as well as distribution of income. At the same time, it is a much simpler measure of distribution. Substantial PQLI must require the presence of a solid social infrastructure and cannot be generated merely by some quick technological innovations. The Sri Lanka data show that PQLI can grow at the respectable rate of 3 per cent while per capita income is growing at quite a slow rate of about 1.8 per cent. The Sri Lanka case raises the question as to the conditions under which high PQLI could result despite low per capita income and whether these conditions can be transferred and sustained in other countries. Indeed, rapidly rising PQLI may be one of the causes of rising per capita income as in the case of Taiwan.

The PQLI may differ as between the different sections of the people. The authors have shown that women register poor performance than men.

The authors have used the census data to compare the performance of the Indian States. It brings out the extremely large variation amongst the States – Uttar Pradesh has a PQLI equal to 25 while Kerala has a PQLI equal to 70. The female PQLI is only 55 per cent of the male PQLI in Uttar Pradesh while in Kerala females enjoyed a PQLI of 93 per cent of that for all males.

The data presented by the authors suggest that PQLI can serve as a useful tool for policy analysis in India. More effective measures need to be undertaken to provide certain basic benefits to the people. That does not mean that striving for high PQLI is everything and GNP can be neglected. Sustained growth in GNP is needed to provide the infrastructure on which rising and high PQLI depends. But the emphasis on PQLI would not only make possible the higher rate of economic growth but also ease the tension that such growth generates.

The second book by Albert Tevoedjre with the Foreword by Jan Tinbergen and Dom Helder Camara has the paradoxical title *Poverty: Wealth of Mankind*. It starts with the philosophical statement that simplicity of life style constitutes the very purpose of individual and social development and categorically asserts that the Third World Countries rather than blindly following the cult of opulence characteristic of the Western way of life and that of the elite groups in their countries who follow their former masters, should rather evolve their own simple life style. The another derives inspiration from Mahatma Gandhi who abhorred with all his heart, "this mad desire to increase our animal apetites and to go to the end of the world to satisfy them". For the author, poverty is not indigence and destitution; it means having what is essential and no more. There is much to be said for poverty so defined since nobody is more independent than a man who could live on little. The two Asian religions – Hinduism and Budhism - hold that ascetic life enables the believer to transcendental purification. Gandhi believed that true civilization consisted not in multiplying the needs but in restricting them voluntarily. Marx observed, "the more the material world gains in value, the more the human world loses in value". Shopenhauer observed, "We obtain neither rest nor lasting happiness as long as we give ourselves over to the urges of our desire".

The affluent society, if unchecked and uncontrolled, becomes sick from the wealth it creates and its manifestations are there – water pollution, urban congestion, the breaking down of social structures, drug addiction and violence and destruction of the equilibrium of the eco-system. The people of the affluent countries make a disproportionate demand on the world's resources. They need to have a controlled reduction in their level of living. As an example of the appropriate standard of living, the author cites the example of Peking. It is not a wretched or unpleasant city but the people do not go about in motor cars since the idea of the private car has no equivalent in Chinese life.

It is not fair to human civilization that thousands of people do not even own a filtering jar for drinking water, when some use mineral water imported from Europe to fill the radiators of their cars! None should have the right to the superfluous so long as many want bare necessities.

But the elite in the developing countries have fallen prey to the folly of mimicry. The affluent countries provide financial assistance which encourages the purchase of goods which people do not really need. The technical aid has led only to the brain drain from the Third World, denying the opportunities to the people of the Third

World to use their critical faculties. The peasants have been taught that to be developed, they must acquire goods which are brought in exchange for cash crops. As a result, the production of cash crops is rising much faster than that of basic careals. Similarly, industries have been set-up which only cater to the needs of the foreign market. Foreign debt of developing countries has increased so much that they have fallen into a debt trap.

The author, therefore, pleads for rethinking on the part of the Third World countries regarding the management of their economies. They should give priority to the organisation of social services which can improve the work capabilities by providing direct services and goods of use value on the basis of decentralized organisation. The plans ought to concentrate on providing work in an intelligent way to increase the production of essential goods and create jobs as practical means for satisfying the basic needs of the individual as well as the community by using local natural resources and increasing productivity through labour intensive methods. Suitable vocational training should be provided. Thus, development should be self-oriented, based on the own resources, greater capacities of the people and the regime of strict economy. Production should be increased and diversified but losses in harvesting, transport and food preservation should be reduced. The simple village technology should have a vital role to play. A developing community should make maxium use of cheap materials which are familiar to the largest possible number of people. It should not lose contact with nature but make use of it as fully as possible. Unfortunately, the traditional materials are being replaced by imported materials. Waste material can also be used as natural fertilizer. So also can the traditional methods of medicine be used. The inventiveness, the creativity of individuals ought to be encouraged at all levels. Wealth can be acquired by bringing back the sun, the wind, the earth. It could reactivate the ties between man and nature. A country which relies on its own natural and human resources is able to use its entire economic potential. The Third World countries should not follow the techniques and organisational methods of the industrialized countries but those suited to their own resources and culture. Research must be based on the practical know how of workers and craftsmen. They should not be victims of technological colonialisation which destroy the original abilities of the people.

The policy of self-reliant development must take into account the following four factors:

(i) knowledge of local condition;
(ii) local leadership;
(iii) organisation of the population; and
(iv) training local leaders.

Women's participation is vary important.

The third book *Bureaucracy and the Poor-closing the Gap* sums up the experience of three decades of development effort.

The decade of the 70's has produced widespread recognition that though many Third World countries achieved creditable advances in overall economic development their record in the alleviation of poverty and equality was unacceptable.

780 million people in developing countries have been by-passed even by those development programmes intended exclusively for their benefit and continue to live in absolute poverty. A group of management specialists after examining specific programmes experiences from Asia, Latin America and Africa have come to the conclusion that the conventional bureaucratic structures and procedures of development agencies are not suitable vehicles of anti-poverty programmes. It is necessary to develop fresh approaches to modify the bureaucratic structures and procedures and evolve more effective participatory styles of development action. The small farmers and the slum dwellers, the rural and the urban poor must participate in the development process. The poor should be taught to pool their resources, and to derive confidence and power from one another through co-operative and community organisations. They must set goals for themselves and plan and organise for their own development.

Unfortunately, work policies and programmes related to the poor are often implemented through a centralised bureaucracy more responsive to central direction than the local reality and its experience is far removed from the people and their needs, This approach must be replaced by decentralised levels of government responsive to the people. The goals of growth, equity, well-being and participation should be achieved simultaneously. What is required is the holistic strategy. When development is defined in holistic terms, it is not a non-political technocratic process of the 50's and 60's but highly charged political process in which power, commitment, and leadership are key variables. The agencies engaged in rural development. require social intervention capability, institutional leadership and system management. A massive educational effort is required for the local leaders as well as the administrative personnel. The Community Health Worker Scheme (CHWS) in India could not succeed without necessary change at the primary heath centre level and the level of the BDO through intensive training in community health and participative methodologies. Similarly, in the Philippines, communal irrigation system required participation of planned communities in their development. The engineers overlooked a number of critical farmers' concern. They overlooked that technical information should be conveyed in a manner understood by the farmers. Farmers must be involved as full partners in the development process. The Increasing Rice Production Programme in a massive way in Philippines brought out the importance of mobilising the entire agricultural production system. At the same time, managers concentrated on a few critical elements despite a maze of confusion involved in the entire process of development. The programme also brought out. that developing community capability is a specific skill of the development system managers.

The district level administrators are the implementors of projects. In India it has been seen that the district officers limit their roles to implementation of the projects, rather than achieving the impact. The focus of these administrators has to shift from completion of activities to improving the well being of the people. They should be more responsive to the community needs.

In Venezuela, programmes for the social development of the marginalized squatter communities clustering round major cities did not succeed because of lack of inter agency coordination, and absence of community participation because of the top down approach. Agencies worked against performance goals than in the relationship to the communities they served. Each module agency operated its own independent programme with little evident interest in contributing to larger coordinating effort to improve life in the Barrio communities.

The experience of planning in Dharampur Bloc in Gujarat did not succeed because of the rapid turnover of the staff and inflexible procedures. Government sponsored programmes were seldom responsive to the local needs. There was no mechanism or mandate at the local level to make adaptations. Programmes must be based on the analysis of the needs of the local communities. Since poverty is an outcome of a number of inter-related forces, attempts to alleviate it must be multi-dimensional. Planners and implementors should be jointly involved in the planning process.

In Tanzania, after the adoption of the Arusha Declaration in 1967 an attempt was made to establish self-reliant village communities. A basic principle was that development projects should be planned by those responsible for their implementation. It was found that the Ujama villages formed under central direction had less community participation than those formed on a purely voluntary basis. The expectations regarding community production were not fulfilled in the former type of villages and therefore the emphasis had shifted to co-individual production.

In India, the public distribution system according to the writer of the study failed to provide the needs of poor consumers. He has suggested that the centralised service delivery approaches should be replaced by participatory approaches based on understanding the needs and resources of the people. There should be direct involvement of the poor in decision-making.

The task of building community capacity has to be recognised. Development is a process in which people are both the purpose and the most critical resource.

In the fourth book *The Political Economy of Rural Development—Strategies for Poverty Alleviation,* the author has dealt with what he has called "new style development models propagated by international aid agencies which have shifted their traditional emphasis on the growth of GNP and "trickle-down benefits" to the poor towards direct attempts at benefiting the target groups, namely, the rural poor. Thus the World Bank is now supporting a number of small projects which redirect investments in favour of the small farmers and the weaker sections rather than large scale projects in field of industry and infrastructure. These projects seek to provide credit and agricultural inputs and thereby raise their productive capacity. The International Labour Organisation (ILO) has adopted the "basic need approach" which seeks to provide basic facilities such as education and health and participation in decision making for the poorer groups. The Food and Agricultural Organisation (FAO) has supported agrarian reforms to deal with the skewed distribution of land for agricultural production. Finally, the

Economic and Social Commission for Asia and Pacific (ESCAP) and the Asian Development Bank (ADB) have adopted the integrated rural development model which includes employment generating development works like minor irrigation and feeder roads for the utilization of the season surplus labour. In response to this new approach of the international agencies, a number of projects have been undertaken in developing countries such as the IRDP or the SFDA and rural employment projects in India. However, the author feels that in spite of the strong terminology and rhetoric used by the international agencies and national governments for tackling poverty problems— words like 'assault" and 'attack' on poverty – both of them have avoided actual involvement in structural changes. Such radical structural changes in terms of control over productive assets, in view of the author, are not possible without restructuring of power. Indeed, in the absence of such restructuring, the benefit of the projects flow to the richer sections, thanks to their links with the bureaucracy in charge of such projects. Infact, these projects taken up ostensibly in the name of the poor, result in subsidising the rich at the expense of the poor.

The fifth book *Wealth and Poverty* by George Gilder deals with the poverty in an affluent country like America. The cause of poverty according to Gilder is a consequence of divesting creative individuals of productive capacity. Real poverty is less a state of income than a state of mind.

Wealth is the consequence of productivity of the work-force and the efficiency of management. Where these are lacking, as in the oil rich Middle-East countries or Venezuela, there is a mirage of money but not real wealth. The motivation for work is the concern for the family reaching towards children and future. It is imagination and purpose which make wealth. Families of zero wealth built America. Their only suitable asset was the disciplined brain. The drama of the creation of wealth and progress is of mind and morale. On the other hand, poverty such as that of poor white and the black in America is the consequence of refusing to work hard. As a result of divorce the motivation disappears, and poverty emerges. The key to the intractable poverty of the hard core American poor is the dominance of single and separated men in poor communities. The author feels that the growing welfare programmes in America have been mainly responsible for reducing the incentive to work hard. Such has been the proliferation of benefits under the Welfare State that resourceful welfare family could get benefits from some 17 programmes. These welfare subsidies lead to workforce withdrawal, and family breakdown and create a sence of dependence in millions of families capable of self support. The welfare programmes have little beneficial effect but a dramatic negative effect on motivation and self-reliance. The consequence of welfare state is a collective danger of national sclerosis. The anti-poverty programmes reduce the impulse to fight poverty by working. The goal should be, therefore, to restrict the system of welfare state as much as possible by making it unattractive and even demeaning. The welfare state benefits exceed prevailing levels of wages and productivity. Poverty can be removed through work, family and faith. The welfare state mutes these impulses. The welfare state erodes work and family, and destroys faith.

Like welfare programmes, the programme for creation of employment by government also replace potential permanent jobs involving real work by artificial jobs that offer a deceptive demoralising work experience. By expansion of the realm of subsidized work, morale of the entire work-force is undermined. The author also feels that high taxation undermines the diligence and determination to do useful work and feels that if capital investment taxes are lowered the rich consume less and invest more and there is greater progress.

Gilder, therefore, stands for less government. The government can bring miracles of productivity by promoting educational excellence, removing barriers of trade, restricting public powers to create monopoly, and lifting the dumb hand of bureaucracy.

The insights of the first four books can form part of an integrated perspective on poverty from which the policy-makers of the developing countries can benefit in their quest for abolition of poverty. The developing countries should not blindly follow the path of development followed by the Western countries. Firstly, they should just think in term of measures for augmenting GNP but also for improving the quality of life through suitable institutional and infrastructural development. Secondly they should not be slaves of mindless consumerism but rather think in terms of providing essentials to all their citizens through a programme of self-reliant development based on the local resources and traditional skills of the people buttressed by diffusion of appropriate technology. Thirdly, the formulation and implementation of such development programmes should be on a decentralised basis giving full scope to popular participation. The bureaucracy in charge of these development programmes should be trained to work as development managers with skill to elicit popular participation. Fourthly, the structural changes in ownership of assets and power should precede or at least accompany development projects directed to the poor or else they would benefit only the well-to-do sections.

The philosophy and perspective of Gilder is very different and so is his concern—which is with poverty pockets in affluent countries. But however, discordent and even harsh his views may appear, they have a grain of truth which populist leaders of developing countries, in their over-enthusiasm for welfarism as a vote-gathering device could overlook only at the cost of the real progress of their countries desparately struggling to cross the barriers of poverty.

28

TRICKLE-DOWN THEORY AND THE ANTI-POVERTY PROGRAMME

The beginning of the seventies marked a departure from the approach to development adopted in India in the fifties and the sixties— or so was it claimed. It was pointed out that though some economic development growth was accomplished, the gains of economic development had not reached the poorer strata of the society. This, it was argued, was because the old approach was based on the "trickle down theory" of the Western economists which was not valid for the developing countries. The plans of economic development based on the theory had gone haywire. It was therefore, asserted that the old approach based on the 'trickle down theory' should be abandoned and there should instead be a "direct attack on poverty". From the Fifth Five Year Plan onwards it was, therefore, decided that the plan should give a place of priority to the anti-poverty programmes which would directly benefit those people in the society who are at the low end of poverty.

It is more or less a decade since the new approach was adopted; it has not yet resulted in any significant decline in the number of people below the poverty line. It therefore, becomes necessary to critically examine the whole rationale of the revised basis of planning lest we should be in for disappointment.

The exercise might well begin with an examination of the justification for the rejection of the so called 'trickle down theory' of the Western economists. It is not clear to which western economists the so-called 'trickle down theory' has to be attributed. No Western economist from the days of Adam Smith to Kaynes has put forward the so-called 'trickle down theory'. It finds no place either in the text-books of economics or the history of economic doctrines. What the economists have put forward is the model of the "circular flow in the economy" where those who produce some goods and service are also those who consume other goods and services. Producers earn their incomes corresponding to their contributions to the productive process as factors of production. These earnings provide them the purchasing power as consumers who purchase according to their own "scale of preference". The consumers preference, in turn, determines the pattern of production. Economic development which leads to increasing production leads to greater employment of the various factors of production and therefore more income and more consumption. Production, distribution and consumption are, therefore, linked with each other in the web of economic activity. It is this circular flow of the economy which gives us the basis for believing that if we want the consumption to increase then production must first increase. If the basis of production is widened, it would also increase the opportunity for gainful employment to even the poorer sections of the community and hence the conclusion that increasing production is the surest way of reduction, if not elimination, of poverty.

There are many links, direct and indirect, primary and secondary between production and generation of income and employment. The primary and direct link is the income and employment generated in the shape of those who are directly engaged in any productive activity. But there are indirect and secondary consequences of every productive activity. Thus, the generation of one productive activity stimulates, at the same time, the production of raw materials which constitute inputs of the productive activity; also the output of the productive activity provides intermediate products or raw materials to some other productive activity and so to the flows of income and employment generated in a particular productive activity must be added to those generated, on the input side and output side of that particular productive activity. To this direct and indirect generation of income and employment must be added the secondary generation described by the economists as the consequence of the multiplier effect. Thus, those who earn income generated by the direct and indirect productive activity provide the effective demand for a number of commodities which are on the scale of preference of the consumers and this in turn through the multiplier effect on the entire gamut of production leads to the accretion of an additional income and employment.

If the 'trickle down theory' is nothing more than the account of the indirect and secondary consequences of the productive activity, it can hardly be faulted. The trickle down theory in the sense of the circular flow of the economy is as much valid for a developing economy as it is for a developed economy.

The validity of the theory has been demonstrated in some pockets in India. Thus, the Green Revolution in the Punjab has notwithstanding increase in mechanisation generated so much demand for human labour that it has led to the organised immigration of the poor from the rural areas as far as Eastern Uttar Pradesh and Bihar. Level of agricultural wages has gone up and the farmers are required to pay guest workers not only higher wages but other facilities and amenities. A similar upsurge of productive activity can create gainful employment opportunities in other parts of the country. States such as Madhya Pradesh, U.P. (Eastern part), or Assam have vast untapped potentialities for the Green Revolution. The quality of the population may differ from State to State but organised effort can help in spreading the Green Revolution to several other parts of the country.

It is no part of the assumption of the circular flow of the economy that the productive process would necessarily lead to an equitable distribution of income. In fact, economists from John Stuart Mill onwards have always made a distinction between production and distribution. It has been distribution of the fruits of production which might be inequitable and may have to be corrected by measures for redistribution of income. These measures advocated, from time to time, have included a progressive taxation systems, consumer subsidies for the poor, social insurance, control over monopolies, and compensatory employment promotion through public investment. All these have now become accepted features of reformed capitalism sometimes described as the welfare state.

The developing countries can certainly adopt the same measures in their own exercise to see that the fruits of production are equitably distributed. In fact, in India, from the beginning of the First Five-year plan, there have always been the twin basic objectives of planning, namely, that of increased production as well as that of equitable distribution. It is the Mahalanobis Report which, for the first time, drew attention to the fact that the distribution has not been equitable and that the gains of production of economic development have not accrued to the poorer strata of the community. But this conclusion, by no means, proves that the amelioration of poverty is possible without a faster rate of economic growth. What is does point out is the need to undertake additional measures to redirect the benefits of economic development to the poorer sections of the community.

One of the basic methods of redirection of resources was that of land reforms which was started with a revolutionary zeal in the early years of our Independence but its implementation was sabotaged in one way or another, especially in the old zamindari areas of Bihar, Bengal and Uttar Pradesh. If these measures had been property implemented it might not have been necessary to discover the percolation theory almost as an alibi. The task of land reforms still remains unfinished in many States.

During the last decade three sets of measures have been indentified for bringing about the desired redirection. First was the redirection of productive resources; the second was public investment for minimum social consumption; and the third was the creation of employment opportunities through public investment outside the normal productive system.

The first set of measures included nationalisation of banking and earmarking of the banking resources including resources of the cooperative banks in favour of small and marginal farmers, artisans and even landless labourers who could be encouraged to undertake supplementary economic activity in the shape of dairy, poultry, fishery etc.

The second set of measures related to public investment for minimum consumption, may be considered to be no more than a revised version of the earlier community development programme which did include a component of building up the basic infrastructure of drinking water wells, approach roads and school buildings etc. in the rural areas.

However neither redirection of the productive resources through cooperative and banking channels nor public investment for minimum social consumption could be of much benefit to those families in rural areas who are indentified as constituting the core of rural poverty. They are those without any assets— the landless. For them, Dandekar and Rath in their study on poverty recommended a massive programme of construction works. The approach was embodied in successive schemes such as the Crash Scheme for Rural Employment, Food for Work Programme, and now National Rural

Employment Scheme.

The current Scheme at redirecting the productive system in favour of the poor is that of Integrated Rural Development. Under this scheme, 600 of the poorest families are expected to be indentified in every block every year. Thus, 3000 poorest rural families are expected to be indentified and assisted under the programme making a total number of 15 million of the poorest rural families in 5000 development blocks all over the country. Each of these families would be assisted by provision of some asset through loans and subsidies. The subsidy to the extent of 25 per cent or 33 per cent is expected to make the asset a viable and productive asset for the poor. A shortcoming of the scheme, however, is that loan and subsidy for the acquisition of an asset to a rural family working on its own is hardly an adequate effort to make that family self-reliant. A cow or a buffalo may die and the entire asset may be wiped off, or else the milk may not be sold in market for an adequate price. What is required, therefore, is not an isolated transfer of an asset but the building up of a whole productive system which can support and see through difficulty every poor family till it becomes self-reliant. In other words, the assistance must not be to an individual as an isolated entity but as member of an organised productive activity where all linked activities are fully taken care of. Thus, it is no use helping an individual poor family with a couple of buffaloes or cows unless he is member of a co-operative diary which arranges to collect milk, sell it at a remunerative price and pass on the payment to the farmer regularly and unless there are arrangements for veterinary aid and the supply of the animal feed etc. The same applies to every productive activity whether sheep rearing, fisheries or horticulture. Isolated schemes are bound to fail for two to three reasons. First, the absence of the provision of inter-linked activities and supporting services. Second, absence of competent management which organises, communicates, and otherwise enables the participation of the individual poor families in an organised effort. Technology and capital would be of no avail without proper organisation and management.

The same approach is applicable even for the organisation of the works programme. It is often alleged that the benefit of the employment programme goes to the contractor rather than to the poor workers but if the poor are organised in the shape of a labour construction cooperative managed by the poor themselves then the entire payment for the construction could accrue to the poor themselves. Well managed labour construction cooperatives can undertake work not only under the National Rural Employment Scheme but many other construction activities under major irrigation or power projects where a lot of unskilled work without elaborate machinery can be carried out by human labour.

What is, therefore, required is not the rejection of the percolation theory or the spreading of an idea that the amelioration of the poor is possible without economic development. The right approach is to promote economic development in such a manner that the poor can find gainful employment opportunities in productive development effort in which the poor participate not only as workers but also as organisers and managers. It would mainly be the work of the administration at the field level to support and stimulate such a productive effort. This should constitute indeed the core of rural development activity in favour of the poor.

It has been argued that the poor would not benefit unless they are organised into militant trade union activity in rural areas. A militant trade unionism without a constructive effort to build up productive activity of the sort mentioned above would, however, come to nowhere. It would only lead to acrimonious conflict which a country like India can ill afford to generate. A poor country can hardly afford to pay the price of an internal conflict. The whole country itself may go down in the process.

The panacea for the poor in India is neither militant trade unionism nor populist welfarism but a determined and organised productive effort which would create gainful employment opportunities for the poor in large numbers in rural area. There is enormous potential for intensifying and diversifying productive activity in the field of agricultural and auxiliary occupations as well as agribusiness and agro-processing. What is required is organisation and management for tapping the potential with the active participation of the poor.

PART V

DEVELOPMENT AND ENVIRONMENT

29

POLICY FOR DEVELOPMENT AND ENVIRONMENT IN INDIA

When India emerged as an independent country in 1947 her main preoccupation was with rapid economic development to raise the levels of living of the masses of people. It was with this end in view, that in 1951 the country embarked on a series of Five-Year Plans.

Development at that time was conceived in terms of increase in the Gross National Product (GNP), and it was assumed that investment was the key to economic development. If adequate resources are mobilised and are invested in development projects, it was felt that development will automatically follow. It was, of course, recognised that development projects would require mobilisation of natural and manpower resources of the country with the help of science and technology for expanding and diversifying the production system in all sectors of the economy. Thus development would involve building up of infrastructure, modernisation of agriculture and industrialisation.

Creation of gainful employment opportunities was also mentioned as a goal, but it was assumed that with the expansion and diversification of the economic system this will automatically follow. Nor were the distributional aspects of development entirely overlooked. It was one of the stated objectives of planning that fruits of development would be available in an equitable manner to all sections of the society.

However, both employment and equitable distribution were strictly subsidiary to the goal of development, and more and even more investment was considered to be the key-note of planning for development in India. This then was the essence of policy for development.

However, as we started gaining experience of planning, it was found that these assumption which were at the back of the basic policy of planning for development were not fully justified. The assumption that industrialisation would create opportunities for non-farm employment was not borne out and even today more than 70 per cent of the labour force in the country continues to be engaged in agriculture as at the beginning of planning. The lopsided structure of the economy, with overwhelming dependence on agriculture, continues. Industry has proved capital intensive and the capital-output ratio has gone on increasing while unemployment goes on mounting with the back-log added to the new unemployed.

Nor were the assumptions regarding equitable distribution of the fruits of planning justified. It has been observed that the fruits of planning have gone in the hands of only a small section of the society. It was even stated that rich have become richer and the poor poorer. The 'trickle down' theory had not worked and therefore measures had to be taken to make a direct assault on poverty.

Hence greater emphasis on what came to be known as 'anti-poverty programmes for the small and marginal farmers, the landless and the rural artisans'. The new development policy was two-fold: First, to reconstruct the production system so as to confer benefits on the poorer section and second, to provide work opportuntiy for employment to the people who are without any assets and who are outside the central stream of the production system. Attempts were also made to develop skill formation among the unemployed rural youth so as to make them self-reliant. Whether these new programmes are adequate enough to cope with the problem of poverty, particularly in rural areas, yet remains to be seen.

But, in the meanwhile, yet another new dimension to development has been added. It has been recognised that development is not just a matter of increasing the Gross National Product or even average income. It is rather one of improving the quality of life. And this depends on conditions of health and nutrition, the expectation of life, spread of literacy, etc. The quality of life can be enhanced through minimum social consumption programmes of which one of the most important is the provision of drinking water supply to all the rural communities.

While all these development programmes were going on and the infrastructure of the economy in the shape of basic and heavy industry and irrigation and power projects was being built up, and attempts were made for development to keep pace with the inexhorable pressure of population growth, there was little time to take note of the environmental problems.

The need for dealing with environmental problems was considered to be typically that of the developed and affluent western countries. In these countries, industrialisation based on cheap petroleum supply and attendant urbanisation had gone apace at such speed and density of petrol driven cars had assumed such proportions that it had created serious problems of pollution. Lakes and rivers and even oceans were defiled by massive effluent from giant industries. Several species of fish in lakes and rivers had become extinct. The air was so polluted that fresh air was not available to the citizens, and the policemen in Tokyo had to use masks. What was even more disturbing was the realization that the non-renewable resources which were the base of industrialization were getting exhausted at such a rapid rate that they would not be available in the matter of few decades resulting in a mortal threat to the very survival of the industrial civilization. The sudden increase in prices of petroleum products by the oil-rich countries gave a shock to the industrial and affluent countries of the world. Thus concern for environment became matter of central importance, and that is how many policy-makers and thinkers in the west started considering that survival of the life supporting system would perhaps be the most important aspect of any policy for development.

That is how a world-wide consideration was given to the issue of environment at the UN Conference on Human Environment held in Stockholm in the year 1972. In that conference the Indian representative stated that while in the western countries environment might be the most important problem, the problem in the undeveloped countries was essentially one of poverty. For these countries poverty is the worst pollution.

Twelve years have lapsed since that conference, and the policy and opinion in this country has undergone a considerable change. Now it is recognised very clearly that though development for removal of poverty is still the most important goal and though, as compared with the affluent countries, the use of natural resources per capita in India is insignificant, the country can no longer give subsidiary importance to the problems of environment. It has come to be seen that environmental problems in this country have been so serious that they would threaten the continued process of development. In the name of development there has been indiscriminate deforestation which has led to the silting of major reservoirs like Bhakra-Nangal, described by Pandit Nehru as the 'temples of free India'. Deforestation and erosion of soil also has created serious problems of flooding. It has even affected the incidence of rain. Rich forest areas are turning barren, soil erosion has become extensive. This has been the "input-effect" on environment as a result of development. The outcome effect has also been equally serious. Major cities in India have started suffering from serious pollution. Effluent of fertiliser industry in Goa threatened the survival of the fish. Fuel scarcity has also increased the presure on forests to meet the fuel requirements of the growing population. In short, development in India, even though at an early stage, has also started threatening the life supporting system in the country.

It, therefore, became obvious that together with increasing Gross National Product (GNP), creation of gainful employment opportunities, equitable distribution, and improvement in quality of life, attention must also be focused on environment. Development must take place not by exploiting nature but in cooperation with nature, some of the environmental activists like Sunder Lal Bahuguna launched popular movements in favour of environment. The Prime Minister herself felt very keenly about this and appointed a Committee for Recommending Legislative Measures and Administrative Machinery for Ensuring Environmental Protection under the chairmanship of the then Minister of Planning, Shri Narayan Datt Tiwari. One of the basic recommendations of this Report was the 'Establishment of the Department of Environment' which has now come into existence and has become the focal point of action for environmental protection in the country.

As the Tiwari Committee Report pointed out that it is no use having merely legislation on the statute book, it has to be effectively enforced. The Tiwari Committee has drawn attention to the fact that implementation of several pieces of legislation for the protection of environment has left much to be desired. Amongst these legislations they have mentioned 'Water Prevention and Control of Pollution Act, 1974'; 'The Insecticides Act, 1968', both of which have served extremely limited purpose. They have also suggested unification of the Forest Act for the whole country.

They have emphasised the importance of environmental impact analysis to ensure that at the time of approval of development projects, compliance with environmental protection is ensured. They have also made several other recommendations for protection of grazing lands, catchment areas, and the creation of 'Biosphere Reserves'. Finally, they have recommended that the Government of India may adopt a 'National Environment Policy'.

30

ISSUES IN ENVIRONMENTAL DEGRADATION AND PRESERVATION

In the wake of continuous pressure of population on natural resources and increasing demands made on them by planned economic development, a process of environmental degradation has set in the country over the past several years but it is only in the recent years that the conscience of the nation has been slowly awakened if not aroused to the extent of environmental degradation which has taken place before our very eyes in the past few years. Some striking examples bring out the havoc wrought already. We have known from the text-books of geography that Cherapunji in Assam had the highest rainfall in the world. Today thanks to the toll taken of the forest wealth in this area, what was one of the wettest places in the world is now under the threat of being reckoned as a drought affected area! Kulu-Manali was considered to be, for long, the one hill station which had retained its natural environment. Some years ago no less a person than the President of India gave public expression to his anguish that the hills in these areas have started becoming barren. Enormous increase in the production of apples in Himachal has undoubtedly been a great productive achievement of the last few years. But such has been the demand on wood for packaging apples that the Apple Revolution has been accompanied by a wanton and indiscriminate destruction of the forest wealth for providing wood for apple cases. Bangalore was known as the green city where no air-conditioning was required. Today thanks to the cutting of trees, the summer in Bangalore has become unbearable'.

These are the examples of the degradation which has taken place before our very eyes but in the past also such degradations have resulted in the occurrence of drought. In the 16th century, the district of Raichur used to have 40" to 50" of rain and was covered with thick forest. Over the years the district became barren and the rain-fall came down to 5 to 15 inches. Because of years of soil erosion and degradation, large areas of land have gone out of cultivation in Bijapur District in Karnataka.

It is time that both at the macro and micro levels we start getting conscious of the environmental degradation taking place in our country and recognise the need for urgent measures to be taken to prevent such degradation.

Quite apparently, development and environment may appear to stand in contradiction to each other. In India, Development implies a continuously higher standard of living for an increasing population. The last population Census came as a shock to us and showed that the population increase in India was taking place at a faster rate than anticipated and if the population goes on increasing at the present rate, it will well exceed a hundred crore by the end of the century. The subsistence of the population of this size even at lower levels of living is bound to mean a heavy demand on the limited resources of the country. The Agricultural Censuses conducted in the years 1971 and 1975 show that while the total cultivated area has remained the same at 167 million hectares, the number of agricultural holdings has increased from 71 million to 81 million. This implies that the same surface of land, cultivated in holdings of ever diminishing size, has to yield to more agricultural production which has to go up from 130 million tonnes of foodgrains at present to some 190 million tonnes by the end of the century and from the present 10 to 12 million tonnes of pulses and oilseeds to about 20 million tonnes in not too distant a future.

Unless the soil resources are adequately conserved, the original and indestructible properties of soil would no longer remain at the same level over the years and may deteriorate unless the soil is reinforced through organic and chemical fertilisers. Here comes the importance of bio-gas development. The number of bio-gas plants in the country has to be not in thousands or lakhs but in million. More important, soil conservation measures have to become universal. *Jhum* cultivation along the slope of the hills should not be permitted because it leads to soil erosion. Land should be consolidated and bunded. Large scale soil conservation programmes should be taken up on a collective basis.

Next to soil are the water resources. In some areas like the hard rock areas in the south, such has been the density of wells and the exploitation of these wells through pump sets, that the sub-soil water resources have started getting exhausted. The sub-soil water resources survey should be universally undertaken and over-exploitation through wells has to be prevented, if necessary, through legal measures.

However, there is still a great scope for the digging of wells in the Indo-Gangetic areas where there is vast sub-soil water potential which can be harnesed for increased agricultural productivity and production.

While in some areas there has been over-exploitation of sub-soil water resources, there has been a prodigal and extravagant use of the surface water resources. As a result, under many major irrigation areas, problems of waterlogging and soil formation have emerged. Thus, far from agricultural soils producing more food and other agricultural commodities as a result of irrigation they have to be retrieved through special measures such as application of gypsum or extensive drainage system. If only the farmers had appreciated and adopted disciplined water management, these adverse effects on large structures of soil under irrigation projects would not have taken place. Apart from water management, there has also to be proper localisation of crops on scientific lines. Thus in black soil areas, heavy water crops like sugar-cane or paddy are not to be grown.

Apart from soil and water, forests are an important and significant part of the nature's life supporting system. They have been so considered throughout ancient history and are invested with a sense of divinity. The poet-saint Tukaram considered the flora and fauna as his dearest friends. The forest area in the country is today much less than the minimum prescribed for a country namely 33 per cent and the so called forest areas are forest only on the records of the Forest Department, in actual fact, may forest areas have been tragically thinned out. Apart from the forest in the custody of Forest Department, in earlier days there used to be village forests for the use of the villagers. These have almost completely disappeared through exploitation over the years. Hills had once a rich canopy of thick forests; they have now become completely barren. A tremendous programme of afforestation has to be taken both at the level of forest in the custody of the Forest Department as well as the village forests. The Programme of Social forestry has been introduced for the latter purpose. In addition, the individual can cultivate forests on their land. The concept of private forests has not yet become common in our country. The programme of afforestation has not become universally successful in our country. In this respect, achievements in Gujarat can provide some inspiration to the other States.

The problem of environmental degradation has now taken such an acute form and has so many manifestations, that what is required is nothing less than a national movement to create a widespread awareness among the people of the enormity of the problem and the total national commitment that is required, for its solution. Not only government agencies but the people have to be involved in the process of environmental preservation. The Indian Constitution has been amended to incorporate a national duty regarding environment. The Constitution enjoins on every citizen the duty to protect and improve the natural environment including forests, tanks, rivers and wild life. Hitherto this national obligation of every citizen seems to have remained only on paper. This duty has to be brought home to every citizen. Often, it is the tribal or the poor hill man who has been treated as the culprit whereas the real culprits are the forest contractors or the industrialists who manufacture paper or synthetic yarn or other products who in collaboration with the corrupt forest officials are responsible for wanton and indiscriminate exploitation of our forest resources. Here the principle of noblesse oblige needs to be enforced. The enforcement of the fundamental duty regarding the protection of natural resources should begin with the richest and the most powerful elements in our society.

To act as a watch dog of natural environment, we must have in every district a natural environment protection committee whose responsibility would be to prevent exploitation of the environmental system. At the same time, prevention is not enough. A positive programme of resource development is needed and such a programme for every district must be an integral part of the national planning in our country. Let us hope that the national plans and popular effort would combine to prevent the environmental degradation and help restore the ecological balance in our country. Development does not mean exploitation of nature, rather it is co-operative endeavour between man and nature. Development which is based on exploitation of nature can indeed be self-defeating. It would be like killing the goose that lays the golden egg.

31

HUMAN ECOLOGY : A New Perspective for Development

The term 'ecology' has a double meaning. It means first the branch of Biology dealing with the relations between organisms and their environment. It secondly means the branch of Sociology concerned with the spacing and inter-dependence of people and institutions. Both relate to aspects which have been generally overlooked or neglected in the process of development.

The Trodden Path of Development

The developing countries have been concerned with development during the last 35 years of the second half of the twentieth century. The UN declared the Sixties as the 'first development decade', the Seventies as the 'second development decade' and the eighties as the third development decade'. Development meant, at least in the earlier years, replication in the developing countries of the same process of development as it took place in the Western countries (now called the 'Northern Countries') during 18th, 19th and the first half of the 20th century. Development in the developing countries was to be a carbon copy of the earlier process of development in the developed countries. Development meant westernization. It meant modernization. Development meant economic development. Economic development meant increase in the Gross National Product. It meant increase in the flow of goods and services by an ever expanding system of production. Expanding the production base depended on investment and increasing capital accumulation. More specifically it meant expanding industrialisation with the use of machinery and the application of science and technology.

Urbanization followed in the wake of industrialisation. The industrialised cities were built around factories with increasing scale of production. The factories were based on the use of non-human energy derived from coal and electricity. While machines were moved by non-human energy, workers were required to operate the machines. Workers had to do the mechanical operations hour-after-hour no matter how monotonous they were. The work may be monotonous, but it had to be performed with discipline and precision. The question of work satisfaction was hardly relevant.

The workers initially were immigrants into the cities from the countryside. With mechanization of agriculture, men became redundant and had to find employment opportunities in the factories in the cities.

Thus a new industrial civilization came into being. It was dominated by industrial capitalism. The factories were owned by the capitalists who had accumulated capital to instal machinery and hire labour. The workers had to accept long hours of work in factories at low wages because they had nothing but their labour to sell to keep their soul and body together. Long hours of work for men, women, and even children in the earlier years of industrialization might have been harsh, but that was a price to be paid for the achievements of the industrial capitalism which was described by Karl Marx as more impressive than the Egyptian pyramids, the Roman aquaducts and the Goethic cathedrals. Very often, the workers lived in slums and were exploited by the truck-shops of the factories. Soon, however, the workers organised themselves into trade unions and demanded higher wages, reduced hours of work and better work environment. As industrialization progressed, the working class was able to improve its standard of living. There was almost continuous improvement in the standard of living; till today in many developed countries the blue-collared workers have proximated their style of living to that of the white-collared workers. Apparently, industrial capitalism in the West created more wealth though it might have been at the cost of exploitation of the colonial countries in one form or another.

However, wealth and welfare have often not gone together even in the Western countries; and economists and social thinkers have pointed out that the quality of life has not necessarily improved. For example John Kenneth Galbraith in his book *The Affluent Society* has pointed out that while there is 'private opulence,' it goes with 'public squalor'. Much earlier Pigou pointed out in his book *Economics of Welfare* that the market mechanism does not take "social costs" into account. Air and water are polluted. Rare species are extinguished. There is growing crime and violence in the metropolitan cities. Life has become impersonal. Neighbours do not know each other. "Rapid value changes in living styles have created serious problems for mankind. It has worked havoc with traditional mores and value patterns and assumption concerning the meaning of human existence. Materialistic values based on the belief that scientific progress would automatically lead to man's happiness and fulfilment have proved sadly disillusioning. The world is in a period of unrest and tension. Vast social changes seem to be the order of the day. There are hardly any places in the world today where people still follow the way of their fathers and fore-fathers". There is tension even in the family life. One-parent families have started becoming a rule rather than an exception. The rate of divorce and suicide in the affluent societies is high. The moral spiritual values are scarified at the altar of hedonism. There is a revulsion against materialism and many persons in the West have turned to esoteric religious movements, like the Hare Krishana Cult, Transcendental Meditation and Rajnishism. But the greatest threat to Western civilization based on mindless pursuit of materialism and the mass consumption society came from the sudden realization that the natural resources of the earth are finite and if they are exhausted the very survival of the human civilization might well be at stake. The 'oil-shock' of 1973 was the beginning of this realization.

An Alternative Model for the Developing Countries

If the developing countries were to follow the footsteps of the developed countries and try to imitate the mass consumption society of the West, a question that would arise is whether the progress of human civilization would be sustainable at all? New thinking, therefore, has started regarding the very objectives and process of development in developing countries. As a consequence new dimensions of development have started receiving attention. In many countries with sparkling economic growth, the social and political base crumbled bringing down the facade of economic development itself. Several authors, therefore, have made a plea that the developing countries far from following the footsteps of the developed countries, must evolve alternative approaches to development. These are often expressed in the following terms.

Technology

The developing countries may not follow the capital intensive technology of the West. It is inconsistent with the factor endowments of some of the developing countries which have abundant manpower resources. Capital intensive industialisation would only leave masses of people unemployed. The choice should rather be in favour of "appropriate technology" and raising the level of existing technology of cottage industries and handicrafts which have rich tradition in many developing countries. This path will not only ensure survival of cottage industries and handicrafts but also prevent over-crowding and slums which are attendant to the factory system of industrialization. Decentralised industry will minimise social costs, retain the traditional industrial culture, save the scarce resources of capital and provide meaningful and gainful employment opportunities to large numbers. What is required is labour augmenting rather than labour displacement technology. Also, the technology may not be energy intensive having regard to severe limitations on the availability of energy resources. This meant labour and animal power and renewable energy sources like wind and tide should be more relevant to the productive and development process in the developing countries. Social forestry which augments fuel resources also deserves priority. In styles of housing and infrastructure also appropriate technology should be adopted. Capital-intensive and energy-intensive technology can provide an extremely vulnerable base to human civilization. Mahatma Gandhi and in recent times Schumacher have, therefore, pleaded for a pattern of development based on the use of human resources and process of production which would no destroy the personality of man.

The new dimensions of development of which the developing countries are becoming aware are the following: First development cannot just be increasing Gross National Product (GNP). It is the composition of the Gross National Product that is important. If the Gross National Product consists of luxury goods rather than essential wage goods it is not progress by any means for the masses. Secondly, as important as the composition of the Gross National Product and related to it is the distribution of the Gross National Product. If the fruits of production are concentrated in a few hands and if the masses of people are not able to partake in the fruits of development because of inequalities accompanying the process of development, then that process of development is not worth having. It is better to have a slower rate of growth but with more equitable distribution of the fruits of development. Thirdly, if composition of the Gross National Product and its equitable distribution are significant then the goal of development is to raise people above the poverty line. Where should poverty line be drawn? Fourthly, this meant for measuring development we should have new indices of social development such as minimum standards of nutrition, housing, health, expectation of life span, and education. Fifthly, as the process of development went apace in the developing countries, even in the early stages the limits to development became apparent in the shape of denudation of forests and hills, disappearance of grazing lands and pollution of drinking water and air. The people of the developing countries started becoming conscious of the fact that development and conservation of natural resources should go together, otherwise the very life supporting system would crumble. Development must be in harmony with nature and not based on its exploitation. Sixthly, the human aspects of development have to be taken care of. Development, above all, means total human development, and if this is lost sight of, economic development may prove fragile. That is why economic development must be accompanied with social and political development. Social development has to be measured in terms of greater social cohesion and political development in terms of strengthening of the participatory grass root institutions.

Industrialization and Urbanization

The process of urbanization in the developing countries has been somewhat different than that in the Western countries. There urbanization followed industrialization which created the necessary employment opportunities. In many developing countries it is the "push effect" that is more severe. There is such an increase in the pressure of population on land that it could not sustain any further increase in population. The surplus population was per force required to migrate to the cities – a spill over of rural poverty. But in the absence of suitable employment opportunities in the cities, because of inadequate industrial development, these immigrants from the country-side thronged into so-called unorganised sector. The people of this unorganised sector live in slums or sleep on pavements and are often exploited. Many of them are used as instruments of violence and crime in the cities. The new immigrants in the slums are exploited for sumuggling and other illegal operations. It, therefore, has to be the conscious goal of public policy to ensure that the pattern of development is not such as to lead to the growth of such cities. The aim should rather be to develop small and medium towns dotted all over the country. These small towns would act as central places to the surrounding countryside. They would provide them with central institutions in the field of health, education and economy such as market centres. A deliberate attempt towards dispersed development based on cottage, village and small industries would be desirable pattern of development. These spatial aspects of development should be taken into account in the planning process.

The dispersed pattern of development using appropriate technology should be people-centred process of development than production-centred development of the past. The people-centred development would give importance to participatory institutions of the people and to grass-root organizations such as co-operatives and rural local self-government institutions. It would give rise to vigorous activist movements based on local social action. They will take much of the work of centralised bureaucracy. Centralised bureaucracy often acts in an impersonal manner and does not take into account the felt needs of the people. It adopts a uniform approach whereas what is required is adaptation to local situations. The decentralised development is based on community participation and social development. It will retain local culture and joint families which can provide the social insurance which poor countries otherwise cannot provide.

This, then, is the outline of an alternative approach to development which is consistent with human ecology which prevents atomization of the individual in societies, prevents the destruction of the joint family, retains traditional skills and institutions, and provides strength to the human being rather than dwarfing and debilitating him.

32

DEVELOPMENT AND ENVIRONMENT

While development has been the watch word of the fifties and sixties, environment has been the watch word of the eighties and nineties. Seventies provided the watershed. It was in 1972, that the first International Conference on Human Environment was held at Stockholm, Sweden. It was the first collective expression of the environmental awareness and concern of the global community. Fifteen years after the Conference, the Report of the World Commission on Environment and Development known as the Brundtland Commission named after the Prime Minister of Norway entitled "Our Common Future" has brought within the purview of the governments and people around the world the concept of "sustainable development".

Preoccupation with Development after the Second World War

After Second World War, the developed countries of the world who were the participants in it embarked on an era of unprecedented development and prosperity. The technology and the productive capacity developed during the world war was pressed into service to create a cornucopia of abundance of material goods and services to fulfil other ever increasing needs of man. The atomic age, the space age, the satellite age, the age of supersonic transport and the revolution of computer and communication all of these described by the Futurologist Alvin Toffler as the "third wave" have ushered in the super industrial society. Thanks to these technological advances the U.S.A. became a high mass consumption society. Even Britain which lost its world wide empire prospered and Prime Minister Macmillan could state in the sixties, "we never had it so good". Japan and Germany rose out of the ashes of Second World War like phoenix birds and became two of the most technologically advanced and materially prosperous countries of the world.

The Emergence of the Developing Countries

While the developed countries thus entered into an error of unprecedented prosperity, the countries of Asia and Africa hritherto under colonial domination amerged to freedom. These countries aimed abolishing their age old poverty and creating for their people a richer, fuller and better life. Freedom for them was a means for development. Hence the under-developed countries came to be known as the "developing countries of the world". Following the foot steps of the western countries, they wanted to use capital and technology for achieving higher growth rates. Growthmanship became the be-all and end-all of national existence.

Goal of Development

After two or three decades of hectic development, wisdom has started dawning on humanity that mindless pursuit of material prosperity is not the way to happiness. Wealth does not necessarily lead to welfare. Higher GNP is not always synonymous with better "quality of life". Moreover, development for short-term gains can have dangerous consequences in terms of destroying, depleting or degrading environment. This can threaten the "life supporting system" of nature on which the entire facade of development is based. Nature is no doubt the proverbial goose that lays the golden egg for man, but man's greed to collect all the nature's golden eggs can destroy the goose itself.

Human System – Part of Eco-system

It is the sharpening awareness of the impending environmental disaster, as a consequence of development, that made men understand that human system is part of eco-system. The community of man is embedded in the natural environment, and there has to be the ecological balance for man's survival. This is called the new socio-biological approach to development. This approach is not new to philosophical traditions and outlook of our ancient civilisation from Vedic times to Mahatma Gandhi. We here in this country were aware that flora and fauna, plants, birds, animals and micro-organisms are the kiths and kins of man and we all have to live together. As early as 1927, Mahatma Gandhi had warned against indiscriminate industrialisation which destroys nature. But this warning of his was lost in the midst of worship of the mammon and frenzied development.

Sustainable Development

More than 60 years after the Mahatma uttered his warning, we have now come to the concept of "sustainable development", that is development, while raising the level of living of people should not impair the current stock of natural wealth. Nature is bountiful, but not unlimited. It has enough to fulfil human needs but it cannot satisfy human greed—as Mahatma Gandhi observed. It provides resources for food, fibre and fuel for man and fodder for cattle. It also provides wood for timber. But many of the natural resources on which man depends are finite and non-renewable. If we go on exploiting them, many of the resources would be irretrievably lost for the future. What then will be in store for the future generations? Has the present generation the right to deprive the future generations of the opportunity to live a worthwhile life? That is why it is rightly said that we do not inherit the earth from the previous generation but have borrowed it from the future generations.

If we accept the concept of sustainable development, we must accept that approach to development which does not destroy, deplete or degrade natural resources, but which conserves, augments and upgrades them.

India's Rich Natural Endowments

Nature has endowed India with a rich ecology, mountain ranges like the Himalayas and the Western Ghats, rivers such as the Ganga, Yamuna, Godaveri and Kaveri, forests, pastures, vegetations, a rich variety of flora and fauna and the blessings of good air, water and soil, a variety of minerals, long sea coasts, numerous islands and marine wealth. India is the place of convergence or confluence of three major bio-spheric realms viz. Paleorctic, Ethiopian and Indomalayan. It has a variety of land forms and diverse geological and climate attributes.

Pressure of Population

Rapid growth of population and revolution of rising expectations sweeping through the population has put tremendous pressure on our natural resources and has taken the heavy toll of them during the last four decades. India's increasing human population which today is of the order of 840 millions and life stock population of 750 millions, are making heavy demands on India's natural resources. By the turn of the century, India will need 250 million tonnes of foodgrains, 250 million tonnes of fodder, 300 million tonnes of fuel and 60 million cubic metric metres of timber.

Development Planning and Environmental Security

While harnessing natural resources with the help of modern technology for meeting these needs, we have to take great care that our development plans are consistent with environmental security and stability.

Let me consider this approach of sustainable development outlined above in relation to our natural resources

Forests

Millions of year of evolution had resulted in an incredible diversity of tropical forests in India covering hundreds of millions of plant and animal species. Identified flora constitute but a small proportion of the total number of species believed to be existing in India.

Humidity of forests and coolness of forest bed, facilitate absorption of nutrients in the soil, and in the living system, so that nothing in leached away. Survival of humanity and propagation of vegetation are all inter-linked with each other. Insects, birds and animals play a significant role in pollination and seed dispersal.

While wild stock are needed to render hybrids free from pests and diseases several modern medicines of great significance own their origin to forests.

Deforestation

Deforestation is resulting in depletion of our genetic resources at an alarming rate. Extinction of species should be considered to be a threat to civilisation next only to thermo nuclear war. It is feared that one fourth of the species are likely to get extinct unless we stop the process of deforestation.

India's geographical area is of the order of 307 mill. sq. km. For environmental stability, one-third of the geographical area should be under forests cover. India's Forest Policy 1952, laid down that two-thirds of the hills and one-third of the plains should be under forests. The National Forest Policy, 1988 also laid emphasis on ecological balance and security. Yet today only 64 million ha out of 329 million ha that is only 19.47 per cent are stated to be under forests. At the time of Independence, the percentage was 22. However, on a more accurate assessment through remote sensing techniques, we have come to realise that in actual fact less than 10 per cent of the total land has satisfactory forests cover. There has been a quantum loss of forest area in India. 1.5 m.ha of forest land in India is disappearing every year. Forty-three per cent of the area attributed to forests is severely degraded. The Himalayas and the Western Ghats eco-systems have greatly deteriorated.

Floods

Deforestation in the upper regions of the hills and mountains has caused several devastating floods. It is estimated that the flood prone area in India has gone up from 20 m.ha. in 1971 to 40 m. ha in 1980. Annual floods today are fourteen times what they were in 1950.

Destabilisation of Hydrological Cycle

Deforestation for meeting domestic and industrial needs and heavy grazing by life stock has set in motion the chain reaction which has led to destabilisation of the hydrological cycle. Delayed run-off of rain water is necessary for percolation of water in the aquafers and conservation of underground water resources. On the other hand, deforestation leads to instant surface run off and reduces percolation.

Desertification

Destabilisation of hydrological cycle following deforestation leads to desertification and draught prone areas, even in a water rich State like Kerala. This should be warning to Goa. Steps will have to be taken to halt the process of deforestation in India. In Sweden where forest industry is major sector of the economy, forests are harvested in a big way but afforestation more than makes up for deforestation. We should learn from the rich experience of a country like Sweden in this matter.

Plan for Afforestation

We should follow a variety of approaches for development and retention of forest. These would include the following:

(1) Regeneration of degraded forests;
(2) Bringing denuded areas and wastes under forests;
(3) Afforestation of ravine land;
(4) Social forestry and community plantation;
(5) Farm forestry;
(6) Agro-forestry—which means symbiotic process of tree growing, crop production and live stock grazing; and
(7) Trees on farm boundaries.

All these programmes would require active involvement of the people.

In addition to these, there is the National Wild Life Action Plan introduced in the year 1982 for conserving biological diversity. Under this programme wild life sanctuaries, national parks and bio-spheric reserves are established.

Land-Soil

Land in India is exposed to degradation process leading to partial and permanent loss of productivity of soil.

Out of the 329 m.ha of total land area in India as much as 175 m.ha is affected by erosion, waterlogging, salinity or alkalinity.

As mentioned above, deforestation and loss of vegetation has been one of the principal reasons for erosion of land. Besides erosion due to floods, there is wind erosion. It is estimated that the top soil erosion in India has increased from 6000 million m in 1972 to 12000 m in 1985.

Waste Land

Continuous erosion of soil leads to increase in the waste land. According to the National Waste Land Board 30 per cent of the total land area has become a waste land i.e. about 130 m.ha. It is necessary to undertake a major programme for the reclamation of waste land. Biotechnology can be of great help in the attempt to reclaim waste land.

Drought Prone Areas

Special attention is also needed for the soil conservation in drought prone areas. These include contour ploughing, terracing, strip cropping, mulching, crop rotation, water ponds, check dams and water harvesting to conserve soil and water.

Bio-Mass

Both in waste lands and dry lands use of compost of bio-mass can lead to increase of production. Blue and green algae could also help in fixing nitrogen in soil. The organic fertilisers are free from the side effects of chemical fertilisers which often pollute the water bodies and destroy soil micro-organisms.

Grazing Lands

Attention needs to be provided to the grazing lands. Grazing has to be within safe limits. Surplus cattle leads to over grazing and causes fodder shortage. It is necessary to keep animals in stalls not allowing indiscriminate grazing.

Conservation of Water Resources

Water-shed Planning

India has adequate rainfall which is of the order of 370 million ha.

However, out of these only 8 m.ha are available in groundwater as sources of drinking and irrigation.

The water-shed management approach can greatly augment the ground water resources of the country. The Raleganshindi village in Maharashtra is an outstanding example of soil and water conservation based on the water-shed planning approach.

Conservation of water resources goes hand in hand with soil conservation. For both, the proper approach is that of water-shed planning and management. This approach is particularly important in drought prone areas which constitute 19 per cent of the total cultivable area.

Irrigation

Development of irrigation is another way of conservation of water. India has made great progress in this. Area under surface has increased from 22 m. ha to 66 m.ha and by the end of the century is expected to be of the order of 112 m.ha.

But while irrigation is expected to increase agricultural intensity and production, it has led to the unfortunate result of waterlogging and increased soil salinity, making fertile land unfit for cultivation. It is necessary to undertake drainage, canal lining, regulated use of water and proper crop planning to prevent the adverse effects of irrigation.

Major v/s Minor Dam

Major dams threaten the ecology and the life system. The tribals are the ones who are particularly affected. Narmada Dam and Tehri Dam are outstanding examples of the effect of big dams on the life of the people and environment. It may be much better to have a series of small dams than one major dam.

Industry and Environment

Mining and Industry actively has degraded 18 m. ha of land in India

Besides, toxic effects of various ingredients used in industry, discharges from factories such as effluents, gases, and solid wastes have created health hazards and polluted the environment.

Multinationals

Multinational firms get ready market in developing countries for products and processes which are banned in developed countries.

Union Carbide factory in Bhopal has been a glaring example of a multinational concern using dangerous ingredients. The leakage of lethal gas in Bhopal caused the greatest havoc in human history, and yet, their crime against humanity seems to have gone with impunity.

Mining

Mining causes water, air, soil and noise pollution and through ground vibration it disturbs the life of people. A number of measures are required to prevent these consequences of mining.

Urbanisation

Rapid urbanisation with attendant increase in motorised transport has created conditions of heavy pollution in India's cities and towns. Availability of public transport and encouragement to bicycle transport can to an extent relieve choking traffic congestion in the cities.

Balanced Approach to Development

From the above analysis, it is clear, that national plan should seek approach which would balance forestry and agricultural development on one side and industrialisation and urbanisation on the other side. In the name of modernity, it is not correct to discount agriculture in comparison with industry. While agriculture is based largely on renewable resources, industry is based on non-renewable resources.

Environmental Impact Assessment

For every project it is necessary to consider not only the benefit-cost ration as in the past, but also the Environmental Impact Assessment (EIA). It has now been introduced in our approach to project formulation and assessment, but more often than not, environment impact assessment is given a short shrift in the haste for getting a development project cleared.

Appropriate Technology

We have already referred to a number of technologies that are needed for forest, water and soil conservation and containing the impact of industrialization and urbanisation on environment.

Non-Conventional Sources of Energy

All development is based on energy. Conventional sources of energy viz. fossil fuels such as coal, gas, oil are non-renewable. It is, therefore, necessary to develop technology for generating non-conventional sources for energy generation.

Solar Energy

Of these solar energy is the most important particularly in India where plenty of sunshine is available almost throughout the year. Already solar energy is used directly for drying crops and fruits. It can be further used for residential cooking and heating. Moreover, with photovoltaic cells technology, sunlight can be converted into electrical energy. Such energy can be profitably used for pumping water for domestic and agricultural purposes.

Wind Power

The second non-conventional source of energy is wind power which is of great potential, specially for rural development. It is estimated that the wind power can generate 20000 m.w. of energy.

Tidal Waves

Yet another modern source of energy is the energy of tidal waves. This has been used in USSR, France and Canada, where rich and sophisticated techniques have been used using power from the tidal waves. With our vast sea coasts we can develop tidal energy in a big way.

Nuclear Energy

Nuclear energy has vast potential to support energy needs for generations to come. However, it has the risk of environmental pollution by radio active wastes. Chernobyl disaster in USSR is still fresh in our memory. In India there are 12 nuclear reactors and power generation stations which have one third of the power generation capacity in the country. It is, however, necessary to ensure safety and prevent the possible hazard of nuclear fall out.

Pedal Power

Pedal Power of animals is an important source of energy in the country. There are 84 m. work animals. Their energy can be put for better use by a modernised bullock cart with greater care and concern for the animals.

Recycling Waste

Another appropriate technology needed by our country is that of recycling the waste products. Solid waste like paper, plastics, rags, glass, etc, generated in urban and rural areas can be used for producing articles like stationery items. Such reuse can save resources and energy. It takes 50 per cent energy to recover a metal aluminium from a waste than from bauxite.

Sewage water containing human excreta can be used for agriculture, pisciculture, horticulture and energy generation.

Saw dust and husk can be used as fuel by using biomass dust stove. This can be good substitute for fire wood which provides 80 per cent energy in rural areas. Smokeless *chulhas* can also save energy by increasing fuel efficiency and improve environment.

Role of Educational Institutions in Promoting Environmental Awareness and Sustainable Development

Educational institutions can contribute a great deal in promoting an understanding of the eco-system about which many of our people even some of the policy-makers are ignorant. They can also make an assessment of the natural wealth. Thirdly, they can develop approaches for sustainable development. Finally, they can promote people's participation in projects for environmental preservation.

PART VI

WORLD ECONOMIC ORDER

33

OUTLINES OF THE NEW ECONOMIC WORLD ORDER FOR THE DEVELOPED AND THE DEVELOPING COUNTRIES

The economic world today is divided into two parts – developed countries and developing countries, the advanced countries and the backward countries, the rich countries and the poor countries or the "North" and the "South", as they are often described. The developing countries or the under-developed countries are those whose per capita Gross National Product is below the world mean of $200. These are the poorest countries which range from Nepal to Afghanistan whose per capita income is even less than $40. To these also be added other low income countries ranging from the Philippines to Argentina. All these countries lie in Asia, Africa, Middle East and Latin America. Many of them lie between the Tropics of Cancer and Capricorn. They include all the three countries of the Indian sub-continent – India with per capita income of $72 and Pakistan with per capita income of $56. These are the countries at the low end of the World economic ladder. At the top are countries such as the United States, Canada, New Zealand, Switzerland, Australia, Sweden, France, Belgium, West Germany and the United Kingdom with per capita income exceeding $1,000.

This sharp division in the world economic order is a product of history. The countries at the bottom of the economic ladder were the erstwhile colonial countries of the 19th and the first half of the 20th Century whereas countries at the top of the economic ladder were the erstwhile imperial countries. A peculiar pattern of a distorted economic order emerged out of the unequal economic relationship between the imperial and the colonial countries. The imperial countries were also the industrialised countries. England was the first country to undergo the process of industrialisation. The British industrial revolution took place during 1760 and 1820 and Britain emerged as the workshop of the world. Soon the other European countries followed as also the new world of America which soon surpassed the industrial achievement of the mother country. Science and technology were the engines of the industrial and economic development. The colonial countries, however, were unable to join this grand banquet of economic development. They were left out in the cold. Their economies continued to be backward and traditional. They were the drawers of water and hewers of wood. They continued to be a raw-material base for industrialisation of the developed countries of the West. Though India produced cotton, it was only shipped to Manchester for the highly developed textile industry. So was also the case with other forms of natural wealth of the colonial countries—be it rubber, tin or iron ore. These were exported to developed countries as the stock-in-trade of the industries in the West.

This partnership was highly prejudicial and adverse to the economic fortunes of the colonial countries. The bargaining power was entirely in favour of the imperial countries which were both politically and economically dominant. The prices of the raw materials were both depressed and fluctuating. Thus, there was a regular economic drain from the backward countries to the developed countries. While the standard of living in the West continuously climbed up, the backward countries eaked out a primitive standard of living, a hand to mouth existence, which was frequently worsened by famine and pestilence.

The colonial countries emerged to freedom after Second World War beginning with the Philippines in 1946 and India in 1947. The Asian countries in the fifties and African countries in the sixties were able to burst as under the shackles of slavery. These newly emerging countries considered their new-found political independence as an instrument of economic independence and of economic betterment of the lives of the masses of people. They, therefore, set about trying to develop their natural resources and build up their economic organisations to realise their dream of a satisfactory standard of living. They wanted to provide their citizens with food, clothing and shelter, with health and educational facilities, with roads and electricity. They tried to provide gainful employment opportunities through economic development so as, to effectively deal with the problem of unemployment and under-employment of their man-power. They sought to raise the standards of nutrition and provide for their citizens an expectation of a larger span of life.

Soon after the World War, the new set up of international institutions came into existence. They were symbolic of the one world of which the people of the under-developed countries, no less than those of the developed countries became the citizens. The United Nations and its subsidiary agencies and more specifically the International Monetary Fund (IMF) and International Bank for Reconstruction and Development were charged with the responsibility for the promotion of the new world economic order.

Behind this international effort was a philosophy that world peace is indivisible, that this is not possible in a situation where some wealthy countries of the world enjoy economic abundance whereas the people of the poor and the erstwhile colonial countries of the world have abominable conditions of living, unworthy of the dignity of man.

However, in spite of this growing realisation and the effort of the past 30 years the world economic order is far from satisfactory and the dichotomy between the developed and the developing countries of the world is not yet put to an end. What is worse, in the poor and the under-developed countries themselves there is a sharp dichotomy between the developed urban sector and the under-developed rural hinterland. The phenomenon of rich becoming richer and the poor becoming poorer seems to take place in the world as a whole as well as within the borders of the individual countries belonging to the under-developed world. The poorest segments of the population of the developing countries have received relatively little benefit of the increasing Gross National Product of these countries. Nearly 800 million individuals, 40 per cent of a total of two billion, people of the under-developed countries survive on incomes estimated in US purchasing power at 30 cents per day. They are the victims of absolute poverty a condition of life so degraded by disease, illiteracy, mal-nutrition and squalor, as to deny its victims the basic human necessities.

A new economic order, therefore, has to be one in which the people of the under-developed countries are able to get the minimum wherewithal of living. It should be an economic order in which the extremes of privileges and deprivation would no longer exist and the gap of gigantic proportions between the rich nations and the poor nations is bridged.

There are only two means to achieve this end: Firstly, the under-developed countries themselves must try to stand on their own legs and through individual and collective self-reliance must undertake a planned development of their natural resources, the utilisation of their man power, diversification of their occupational structure, increase productivity of agriculture through application of science and mixed farming and through industrialisation in fields in which they are specially endowed by virtue of their natural resources. Secondly, the richer and developed countries must support and supplement this programme of development of the developing countries through bilateral and multi-lateral aid and assistance.

The advanced countries of the world can support economic development in the developing countries through transfer of resources, through transfer of knowhow and through change in policies enabling the under-developed countries to get their due share in the world trade.

So far as the economic aid is concerned, it should be related both to the ability of the advanced countries to extend the aid and the need of the under developed countries to receive such aid. For long it has been proposed that every advanced country must provide one per cent of their GNP for assistance to the under-developed countries. However, the official development assistance available so far has been far below this limit. Even though United States has been the most affluent country of the world, the flow of official development assistance has been nearly at the bottom of the list of the developed countries. The current flow of official development assistance has been acutely inadequate. It has been far below what the developing nations need and what the affluent nations can readily afford. It has been only half of the modest target prescribed by the internationally accepted United Nations Strategy for the second development decade. That target called for reaching ODA levels of 0.7 per cent of the GNP by 1975. In fact, by 1975 it did not exceed .35 per cent. The achievement of the target of .7 per cent neither requires the people of the developed nations to reduce their already high standard of living nor to neglect their domestic priority. It asks them only to dedicate a tiny fraction of the increasing income that will be accruing to them in the decade of the seventies. It is estimated that during the decade the annual GNP of these affluent nations will grow in constant price from 2 trillion dollars in 1970 to approximately 3.5 trillion dollars in 1980 – an increase in output which is virtually beyond the human capacity to comprehend. In order to develop the under-developed countries and thereby reach the target of 0.7 per cent, the developed countries would need to divert to that end less than two per cent of the amount by which they themselves will grow richer during the period. If from the beginning of humanity the world objective is for the strong to help the weak then surely the developed countries must consider this claim on them by the developing countries as they are inescapable obligation.

Unfortunately, the aid forthcoming from the affluent countries was so small that the World Bank faced the danger of complete termination of IDA's activities. However, with the completion of the negotiations for the 5th replenishment of the IDA and the consensus on general increase in the Bank's capital and the provision of the increase in the capital structure of the International Finance Corporation which lends to private sector in developed countries, the outlook of ODA has become optimistic. Over the five years ending in June 1983, the President of the World Bank, Mr. Robert MacNamara, has expected the Bank group to provide between 30 to 32 billion dollars in net finance. The World Bank is planning for commitments in the fiscal year ending in June, 1978 to 8.7 billion dollars as compared to 7.3 billion dollars in the past year and 9.8 billion dollars in the following years. The World Bank Group hopes to begin the decade in 1980 at a level of operation in excess of 10 billion dollars a year. This will significantly accelerate the phased development in the poorest nations.

This development assistance must be neither tied to specific projects nor to specific countries. It should help increase the productivity of agriculture and industry more specially of the small farmers who constitute the majority of the productive agents in the developing countries.

The aid must be supplemented by expanded trade. Unfortunately, the policies of the developed countries have not been very helpful. Tariffs and import quotas adverse to the exporting countries were erected in the past and the same tradition seems to continue. The removal of such tariff discrimination and quotas would promote expansion of the exports of the under-developed countries. The principal trade regulating institution, viz. General Agreement on Tariff and Trade adopted policies which reflect the political dominance of the Western world. ODA must lay down policies which would provide stimulus to the export earnings of the under-developed countries.

No external assistance, however, would be of any avail unless the under-developed countries themselves make determined and dedicated effort for economic development, which internally is also directed to helping the poorer sections of their society. Their internal policies must promote the industrial skills of their people and raise the productivity of the millions of the small farmers. This would require massive investment in infrastructure, liberal credit, supply of agricultural inputs, agricultural research, dissemination of scientific knowhow, removal of exploitative land tenure system, etc., as ingredients of an integrated plan of economic development.

The developing countries can also do a lot by way of mutual aid, as a part of the system of collective self-reliance. Some of the under-developed countries have a large share of the scarce resources of the world. The more significant example of this are the OPEC countries. These countries can invest their petro dollars in the development of the under-developed countries. The latter can provide food of which the OPEC countries are in short supply. The under-developed countries can also pool their stocks of raw materials such as tea, coffee and rubber and collectively bargain for a better price. They can have division of labour in agricultural and industrial production and develop viable projects in the fields in which they are comparatively well endowed, with all the under-developed countries put together constituting a common market.

The creation of world economic order where no nation is so affluent as to indulge in reckless waste of scarce resources and at the same time no nation is so poor as to be deprived of the minimum wherewithals of living is well within the reach of humanity, if only it is governed by a spirit of self-help and mutual help. One can only hope that with the combined effort of all the new world economic order can come into being by the beginning of the new century. The appointment of a high level commission under the leadership of Willy Brandt by the World Bank is a step in the right direction.

34

ENDURING BASIS OF NIEO: Going Beyond NAM and Brandt Commission

NAM has given a fresh fillip to the concept of the New International Economic Order (NIEO). It has called for the immediate convening of the international conference on money and finance for development with universal participation for a comprehensive restructuring of the international monetary and financial system. Amongst several concrete proposals and recommendations made in this context are the following: multi-lateral framework for restructuring the debt burdens of developing countries; establishment of debt services facility by the IMF; raising the quotas of the IMF to 125 billion SDR's; replenishment of the IMF by gold sales and using it for subsidised lending to developing countries; review of IMF conditionality; compensatory financing facility to cover cereal imports; augmenting the capital resources of the World Bank; setting up of a producer council of developing countries; increasing World Bank landing for energy projects; and augmenting financial flows to developing countries for industrialisation on favourable terms.

NAM membership consists mostly of the developing countries and reconstruction of the international financial institutions on the lines indicated above is obviously in their favour but since the burden of reconstruction on these lines would fall on the developed countries, they do not seem to be very enthusiastic about the concept of the NIEO. What has added to the reluctance of the developed countries to positively respond to these initiatives, are the economic difficulties which they themselves are faced with and unless they are also taken into account in the process of the evolution of the NIEO, the position would be one of confrontation rather than cooperation between the North and the South, in evolving NIEO.

For years now, the developed countries have been suffering from the peculiar phenomenon of stagflation and high degree of unemployment. The phenomenon of stagflation has proved intractable. The old Keynesian remedy of compensatory fiscal policy no longer seems to work. It adds fuel to fire of inflation rather than stimulating the economy and increasing aggregate production and employment. The failure of the Keynesian prescription led to the rise of monetarism in recent years accepted by the authorities both in the U.S.A. and U.K as the proper approach of building up a sound economy. However, while, to an extent, monetarism has helped in containing inflation it has not been effective in stimulating the growth of the economy or providing full employment. Unemployment continues in the developing countries at a very high rate and stagflation has proved to be a baffling phonomenon. Laffer's Suply Economics also does not seem to work. A new Keynes is now required to properly diagnose the current situation and suggest effective remedies. So long as the developed countries are in the grip of stagflation they are unlikely to be enthusiastic about the proposals of the developing countries in relation to NIEO. In their concept of such an order, adequate solution to persisting stagflation must inevitably find a place. In other words, NIEO should mean both development of the developing countries and full employment in the developed countries.

The basic limitations in the development of the developed as well as developing countries is the energy crisis. It is this which sent shock waves in the early seventies and gave a blow to the optimistic outlook of the developed countries. However, the painful readjustments since 1973 have led to a new situation where temporarily a situation of oil glut has emerged which has threatened the unity of the petroleum countries and recently led to the downward adjustment of the petroleum prices by the OPEC countries individually and severally.

But the dwindling hydro-carbon resources is only a leading example of a general phenomenon which, in the long-run, has emerged as the basic limitation on development, namely, the phenomenon of the extinction of some of the finite resources of the universe in the foreseeable future. These latter include not only hydro-carbon but coal and other minerals. Ushering in of the new international economic order requires not just some readjustment of the monetary and financial institutions but basic changes in the economic system itself and indeed even more basic changes in the economic philosophy of the humanity. The entire human race has to come to terms with the fact of finite character of natural resources and the inescapable necessity of establishing a new balance between man and his environment.

The very first concept in this connection which is relevant is that of an "appropriate standard of living". Extravagent standards of living developed in some of the affluent Western countries had led to a scandalous claim on the life supporting system of nature in the form of finite resources of the universe. The bonanza of living indulged in by some of the most affluent people of world should be considered to be impermissible in the new international economic order as it is totally inconsistent with the abominably low levels of living of the masses of people in most of the developing countries which should be considered unworthy of human dignity. Indeed, the concept of an "appropriate standard of living" or rather a range of standards of living should be considered to be the central focus round which the concept of NIEO should be built. The clear-cut goal of that order would be that while there would be no excesses for a few, there would be sufficiency for all, and this would be concern, not of one nation but of the entire humanity. Even those who are compelled to curtail their excesses as a result of the acceptance of this concept would not stand to lose but rather gain because by now it has been well established that happiness does not necessarily grow with the indefinite acquisition of material goods and that beyond a point pursuit of unlimited wants is the source of unhappiness rather than real happiness for human beings. This is not a philosophy of poverty but a recognition of the concept of "quality of life", of the primacy of human values over the mindless pursuit of material values. The liberation of the affluent countries from their preoccupation with their excesses of material consumption and all the attendant expenditure of time, energy, money and natural resources on dispensable possessions would also liberate them from evils like high pressure life, new waves of crime, and fragmentation of the institution of family, which unbalanced hedonism generates. The people of the affluent countries must realise that "less is more" in terms of real happiness.

Once this concept of deliberate and conscious adoption of limits to material acquisition is accepted, it would have an enormous effect on the entire course of humanity. It will put a halt at long last to the "demonstration effect" of consumerism not only within the affluent countries but also in developing and "new rich" countries. The "demonstration effect" has resulted in internal imbalances between the elite and masses in those countries. If the evil influence of the "demonstration effect" is curbed, the future of the humanity would be guided on the right track away from the suicidal pursuit of sinister materialism. Liberation from the mindless pursuit of materialism would be a major source of the release of resources for building up the NIEO.

Another equally important source of the release of human resources for the proper goals of humanity is complete disarmament. The Brandt Commission's Report (Common Crisis: North-South Cooperation for World recovery) has drawn attention to the disastrous effect of the armament race in terms of diversion of resources of the order $650 billion during the year 1982 from the pursuit of the legitimate goals of humanity. Very recently, the Stockholm Institute also has drawn attention to this. The nefarious "demonstration effect" operates in the field of the armament also. Here also is the operation of the "vicious circle" as well as "the virtuous circle". If the vicious circle of armament is broken and the virtuous circle of disarmament takes command of the situation, humanity will be saved of terror of the cataclysmic armament race and the formidable burden which it imposes on the world economic order.

Once the endowments of nature and man are relieved of the burden of materialism and armament building, they would be available for a single minded pursuit of the noble and worthy goal of the NIEO namely, providing the entire humanity with wherewithals of a decent human life. This indeed is the basic economic philosophy of NIEO, deriving inspiration from Gandhian thought which goes much beyond the perceptions of the NAM and the Brandt Commission.

Once natural resources are released from the commitment to excessive materialism and the arsenal of war, humanity could address itself to the proper task of the harnessing them in an optimum manner for the fulfilment of the more essential needs of humanity. The basic consideration governing the optimum use of natural resources for this purpose is the finite nature of many of the natural resources. The development would take place in cooperation with nature and not by exploiting nature. Preservation of life supporting system and regard for environment would be the basic consideration in the choice of development processes. In this context, the concept of "appropriate technology" could be very relevant. That technology should be considered relevant which economises on the finite resources of nature and which provides full employment to under-utilized human resources. These concepts have already been putforth by Schumacher in his book *Small is Beautiful*.

The world strategy for the productive use of resources for the fulfilment of essential human needs would be based on a balance between production of raw materials in the primary sector, namely, agriculture, their processing in the secondary manufacturing sector and their handling in the tertiary sector. Too often, there has been an imbalance which has manifested in itself in the fluctuation of agricultural prices and deterioration of the terms of trade against the agricultural commodities. Stabilisation of prices of agriculture and mineral commodities would go a long way in the steady economic progress of the developing countries which are the base for the supply of raw materials. Production of commodities would then be a truly cooperative endeavour of the international community rather than based on "beggar-my-neighbour policy" of the past.

During the twenties the policy pursued by the European countries led to a competitive devaluation of currency and imposition of protective tariff which ultimately proved to be the undoing of the West. Today by imposing tariff barriers even against the developing countries, the developed countries have given a new lease of life and a new version to the discredited "beggar-my-neighbour" policy of the past.

The concepts which have been stated above, namely, concept of an appropriate standard of living, (eschewing material excesses), the concept of peace (eschewing armament race), the concept of appropriate technology (eschewing mindless exploitation of the finite resources of the life supporting system) and the concept of cooperation and balanced relationship in the production of agricultural commodities *vis-a-vis* production in the secondary and tertiary sectors are basic to the evolution of NIEO. These are not the concepts which can be properly developed in a conference confined to money and finance. They should go to the basic roots of economics and human life. They require going back to some of the basic philosophies of Mahatama Gandhi which he preached to his people in his time. To usher in NIEO, a new world Planning Commission is needed which could transform these basic ideas into an international economic reality.

35

INDIAN MANPOWER : Link Between India and the Third World

More than three decades ago, India and some other countries of Asia attained Independence. This was followed by several African and Asian countries emerging to freedom in the sixties and seventies.

The picture of the Third World, as it stands today, is some what different from what it was thirty years ago. Not all the countries of the Third World have fulfilled their promises or translated their dreams into reality. In many cases, such governments have not necessarily been good governments and in many other cases the pace of economic development and social change has not been rapid as it should have been. The general expectation that the Third World countries would rapidly realise all their potentials and the disparities between the developed countries who were erstwhile colonial powers and the developing countries who were the erstwhile dependences would diminish has, unfortunately not borne out.

India's progress has not been up to its expectation. At the same time, it has not entirely been disappointing. India has held together as a political entity and as a functioning democracy an achievement which few countries of Asia and Africa have to their credit. India has been able to feed her population without resorting to large-scale imports. It has developed diversified economy and its educated manpower is a growing asset.

No country can achieve more in the field of foreign affairs than what its own internal strength can provide and the question is to what extent India would be able to use its strong points to influence the Third World countries.

We do not seem to have yet learnt to derive full mileage from our skilled and educated manpower. India is in a position to influence the Third World countries through the medium of its manpower, with diverse skills in administration, management and technology at various levels. In distant Kingdom of Tonga, the Secretary in-charge of Industry is an officer of the Central Secretariat Service who has been instrumental in introducing the idea of industrial estate. At Abu Dhabi airport the author recently found that the entire catering arrangement were incharge of a group of Indians who have migrated from Kerala. Some years ago, the author found that it was an Indian who was looking after the aircraft of President Julius Nerrere in Tanzania. A team of Indian railway officer set the Nigerian railways on the rails. Hundreds of Indian engineers and doctors are serving in several countries of Africa like Nigeria, Libya, Tanzania and now the several Middle-East countries.

There is an ever increasing demand because the Third World countries have found that the expatriates from the colonial countries are not available at the rate at which the Indian manpower is available. Nor are they as hard working as the Indians. The presence of such skilled manpower in the Third World countries as well as Indian who migrated in the past to develop sugarcane plantation in Mauritius, Fiji and West Indies or rubber plantation in Malaysia or build Railways and retail trade in East Africa should be a great asset in strengthening the bonds of friendship between India and the Third World countries. Not much has been done to use this possibility. The contacts between the skilled manpower in these countries and our Embassies do not appear to be as frequent and intimate as they should be. The presence of Indian manpower in various fields of administration and economy can open large opportunities for the export of Indian made machines and goods. A proper nexus therefore, needs to be established between the export of manpower and the export of Indian goods and services.

Closely related to manpower are the institutions for the training of manpower. In the past personnel of the Third World countries have gone for training in several fields to training institution in western countries. However, the training courses in these institutions in the West are not always found to be suitable. For example, a worker in the field of cooperation can gain much more by training in the cooperative training institution in India rather than undergoing a course at Laughborough in U.K. where the conditions which the cooperatives function and the nature of their functioning are indeed different. In the vast field of development administration India can afford many training opportunities. These need not be provided free of cost. But if their presence is brought to the notice of the developing countries, they could make fuller use of the training opportunities at the Indian centres of training. Recently, an International organisation wanted India to organise courses in project management for project managers in several countries of Asia and Africa.

There seems to be lack of linkages between the various components through which India influence the Third World countries. Foreign policy is not just a matter of diplomatic activity. It has to be a total interface between India and the rest of the countries of the Third World. The persons who man the Indian Embassy abroad ought to know a great deal of the various institutions functioning within the country.

As the various aspects of relationship between India and the Third World come to be fully developed, it should be possible for India to revive the ancient cultural linkages which seem to have been lost. It is necessary to revive the cultural linkages which could impart a sense of emotional identity to the Third World solidarity.

Index